MUTED MODERNISTS

MADAWI AL-RASHEED

Muted Modernists

The Struggle Over Divine Politics in Saudi Arabia

HURST & COMPANY, LONDON

First published in the United Kingdom in 2015 by
C. Hurst & Co. (Publishers) Ltd.,
41 Great Russell Street, London, WC1B 3PL
© Madawi Al-Rasheed, 2015
All rights reserved.
Printed in the United Kingdom

The right of Madawi Al-Rasheed to be identified as the author of this publication is asserted by her in accordance with the Copyright, Designs and Patents Act, 1988.

A Cataloguing-in-Publication data record for this book is available from the British Library.

ISBN: 9781849045865

This book is printed using paper from registered sustainable and managed sources

www.hurstpublishers.com

In memory of my father Talal and my mother Aidah

CONTENTS

Acknowledgements ix
List of Illustrations xiii
Glossary xv

Introduction: Divine Politics in a Profane World 1
1. Petitions and Protest on the Eve of the Arab Uprisings 31
2. Civil Society in an Authoritarian State 55
3. On Revolution 75
4. Between Force and Choice: Debating Sharia in a Salafi Context 95
5. Deconstructing the Religious Roots of Authoritarianism 115
6. Democracy against the Islamisation of Repression 137
Conclusion: Islamist Modernism beyond Radical and Moderate Divides 157

Notes 165
Bibliography 183
Index 193

ACKNOWLEDGEMENTS

Research for this book was supported by Open Society Fellowship, which is funded and administered by the Open Society Foundations. The opinions expressed herein are the author's own and do not necessarily express the opinions of the Open Society Foundations.

One of the major drawbacks of writing a book on Saudi modernists who are either in prison, banned from travel, or expecting harsh punishment for thinking and writing, is my inability to thank all those who contributed in one way or another to this intellectual journey. In 2012 Amnesty International reported that former judge Suleiman al-Rushoudi (see chapter 2) 'was convicted on charges including possessing banned articles by Professor Madawi Al-Rasheed, an academic at UK university' (Amnesty International, 'Reform activists in Saudi Arabia must receive fair appeal hearings', 25 January 2012). The long list of charges against other prisoners included storing an Arabic article I wrote and one of my books on their computers. These incidents brought to my attention how paranoid the Saudi regime can be about a particular discourse deemed subversive.

I embarked on writing this book knowing that I cannot thank all those people who helped, explained, and tolerated my intrusions. They agreed to be contacted, and we met outside Saudi Arabia. We met in cafes, often on the periphery of big Arab capitals with their glamorous shopping centres. I was full of admiration for my contacts, who were exceptional intellectuals and youth activists, seeking to fulfil their dream of living a decent and dignified life without repression. They exemplified courage, politeness, and insight. After our encounters I worried about them when they returned to Saudi Arabia, fearing interrogation and possibly arrest. They took risks when they agreed to be interviewed, and were generous with their time. They informed me about

ACKNOWLEDGEMENTS

their projects, made available to me a plethora of literature and websites, and explained ambiguous ideas. They also taught me how to benefit from several means of electronic communication that I did not know or that I desired to know. They trusted me and invited me to join chat sites run by young Saudis seeking political change by peaceful means. They were by far ahead of me when it came to accessing sites censored by the Saudi authorities and using social network communication technology. They drew my attention to invaluable data that circulated on the internet. As a result of corresponding with them, and later meeting them, my ability to navigate social media improved. They not only taught me how they were working to overcome authoritarian rule, but also how to make technology serve to circumvent restriction and surveillance. They adopted my research project and helped it to materialise. This book would not have seen the light without their trust and support. I am grateful to all those who will remain unknown soldiers.

In addition to my real contacts, virtual supporters whom I will never have the opportunity to meet were also numerous. They had funny pseudonyms to escape the censor and punishment. They constantly kept me informed about relevant events and drew my attention to images, documents, and other relevant data. I thank them all for their support, sense of humour at difficult times, and courage.

I owe a great debt of gratitude to my colleagues in London. The Middle East Centre at the London School of Economics and Political Science provided a comfortable and stimulating environment to write this book. Special thanks should go to ex-director of the centre, Professor Fawaz Gerges, Professor Toby Dodge, and Dr John Chalcraft. The centre's staff Robert Lowe, Sara Masri, Sandra Sfeir, and Ribale Sleiman-Haidar were helpful and supportive. I am greatly appreciative of their encouragement and the luxurious office they provided me with.

The arguments in this book are tremendously enhanced by conversations I had with my colleague Carool Kersten, whose expertise in South East Asian Islam offered a most cherished comparative perspective. His critical gaze allowed me to place my arguments in a wider context. The meticulous research skills and punctuality of Reza Pankhurst added great details and chronology to my focus. I am most grateful for his help. Finally, the dedication and attention of my copy-editor Mary Starkey are always an added advantage, much appreciated. Mary is a pleasure to work with during the last months of producing a manuscript. My publisher Michael Dwyer and his team deserve special thanks for their professionalism, punctuality, and attention to detail.

ACKNOWLEDGEMENTS

Finally, I regret that my mother and father did not live to see this book. Writing it while they were both ill was a struggle, made easier by my mother's incredible ability to love and support and my father's intellectual sharpness and alertness even when he was frail. He was my first teacher, and his rich and eclectic library was and will remain an intellectual source of enlightenment.

LIST OF ILLUSTRATIONS

1.1: Protest in Buraiydah
1.2: *Irhal* (leave) protest in Qasim against interior minister Muhammad ibn Naif
2.1: Abdullah al-Hamid and Muhammad al-Qahtani surrounded by supporters outside court
2.2: Abdullah al-Hamid and Abdullah al-Maliki on the pavement where al-Hamid used to tweet before entering the court
3.1: Salman al-Awdah
4.1: Abdullah al-Maliki
5.1: Muhammad al-Abd al-Karim
6.1: Muhmamad al-Ahmari

GLOSSARY

ahl al-hal wa al-aqd — (lit. 'people who tie and bind': religious scholars and other people of importance who are permitted to participate in *shura*)

al-amr bi al-maruf wa al-nahi an al-munkar — see *hisba*

baya — (oath of allegiance)

bida — ([religious] innovations)

dawa — lit. 'call': mission

dawla (state) — *dawlat al-huquq wa al-muassasat* (a state of rights and institutions); *al-dawla al-madaniyya/dawla madaniyya* (a civil state)

fatwa — (non-binding legal opinion)

fiqh — (jurisprudence): *fiqh al-taa* (the jurisprudence of obedience to rulers); *fiqh taharur* (liberation theology/jurisprudence)

fitna — (chaos, discord)

hakimiyya — (sovereignty of God)

hisba — (commanding right and prohibiting wrong)

hukuma — (government): *hukm al-ghalaba* (government by conquest and force); *al-hukum al-rashid* (righteous government); *hukm shuri* (government by consultation)

ijma — (consensus): *ijma al-umma* (consensus of the *umma*)

ijtihad — (independent reasoning): *ijtihad bashari* (personal reasoning)

xv

GLOSSARY

istibdad	(tyrannical rule, repression)
jihad (struggle)	*jihad al-kalima* (struggle by word); *jihad madani* (peaceful struggle such as civil disobedience, demonstrations, and strikes); *jihad silmi* (peaceful jihad)
mufakir (intellectual)	*mufakir islami* (Islamic thinkers)
al-mujtama al-madani	(civil society)
muthaqaf	(an intellectual)
nasiha	(advice [in the context of advising the ruler, Saudi Wahhabi scholars insist that it is given in private])
nitham asasi	(foundation statement)
al-sahwa al-islamiyya	(Islamic awakening)
tanwir	(enlightenment, a rethinking of traditional concepts)
tawhid	(unity (of God), monotheism)
thawra (revolution)	*thawrat hunayn* ('Day of Rage')
ulama	(sing. *alim*: religious scholars)
umma	(the Muslim community)
wali al-amr	(pl. *wulat al-amr*: ruler)

INTRODUCTION

DIVINE POLITICS IN A PROFANE WORLD

Saudi Islamists are not known as vanguards of democracy and advocates of civil and human rights. Their image is closely associated with Jihadi suicide bombers and preachers of controversial opinions on women and minorities. They regularly feature in reports on radical movements in many places in the Arab and Muslim world. They make news as radicals, terrorists, religious bigots, sectarian fanatics, and socially conservative and misogynist preachers. This dark image became well established from 1979, when a violent fringe group seized the Mecca Mosque to obtain a platform for accusations of corruption against the Saudi regime and to highlight its closeness to Western powers. Subsequently, the participation of many Saudis in the Afghan Jihad in the 1980s and the 11 September 2001 attacks on New York, in which fifteen of the hijackers were Saudis, did little to alter the association of Saudi Islamism with violence and radicalism. Most recently, they have taken the lead in sectarian conflicts in both Syria and Iraq, supporting and participating in a global Jihadi movement to establish an ideal Islamic state, purged of unorthodox Muslims, and promising to eliminate the enemies of Islam.

There is, however, more to Saudi Islamism than what is represented by this stereotypical image. This book aims to highlight a certain intellectual mutation that has been fermenting amongst a minority of Saudi Islamists, referred to here as modernists. This modernism corresponds to what Muhammad Qasim Zaman defines as an attempt to 'rethink Islamic norms, reinterpret foundational Islamic texts, and reform particular Muslim institutions in ways that aim to align them more closely with both the spirit of Islam and current needs and sensibilities of society'.[1] While many observers will frown upon associating Islamism with modernism, the Islamists in this book venture into the rethinking of foundational texts in their attempt to combine Islam with current political needs. In scholarly work in general and on Muslim societies in particular, modernity and modernism have been problematised and cannot be considered as totally defined analytical concepts. However, without returning to this old debate, suffice here to say that the approach of those Islamists seeks to revisit Islamic foundational texts and institutions to find solutions to problems and challenges of the modern age in which Muslims live.

This book focuses on the Islamism of a minority that has carved a space for itself in the public sphere and distinguished its outlook by peacefully calling for democracy and a civil state. It consists of a small number of *ulama*, intellectuals, and activists who present their society with an alternative third way, between the radical Jihadi Salafi movement and the acquiescent official Salafi trend. This third way relies on reinterpretations of Islamic political theology, especially that which provides justifications for repressive government. As such, they have challenged their own Salafi intellectual heritage from within in order to break the rigid polarisation between those who blindly support the status quo and those who aspire to overthrow it by force. They call for a rational assessment of Islamic history and an endorsement of contemporary modern projects and strategies to reform the state and allow people greater political representation. They are highly critical of the violent path of some Islamists, which they attribute to the rigid political context of Saudi Arabia where peaceful political action remains prohibited, political participation non-existent, and civil society banned. They are also critical of other Islamists who prioritise reforming personal conduct, purifying creed, and Islamising society at the expense of calling for justice, freedom, and political rights. They attribute the rise of radical violent Islamism to the persistent conditions of oppression and exclusion, in addition to the closure of the religious and political spheres to debate and diversity. The hegemony of Wahhabiyya is considered conducive to further radicalisation and dogma. The solution, in their opinion, lies in opening the religious sphere and loosening the political controls in order to allow citizens to debate and participate in the making of a new Saudi Arabia. The new Saudi Arabia they envisage is not a project that aspires to recreate an ideal, imagined, or generic historical Islamic state, associated with previous caliphs, nor the eighteenth-century polity that emerged after the alliance between the founder of Wahhabiyya, Muhammad ibn Abd al-Wahhab, and the Al-Saud ruling dynasty.[2] Their reinterpretation of the Islamic texts aims to create a modern state based on representation, accountability, and freedom. They all agree on *al-dawla al-madaniyya* (a civil state) and reject theocracy.

INTRODUCTION

This modernist project has proved to be a challenge in the Saudi context, as several personalities associated with it have been imprisoned, banned from travel, or marginalised. As a group, the modernists do not occupy high-ranking jobs in the large Saudi religious, educational, and media institutions. Instead, the regime increases the pressure on them by means of marginalising them, criminalising their activities, and banning their books and pamphlets. No doubt a modernist intellectual trend that promises to deconstruct the religious roots of authoritarian rule is challenging, subversive, and dangerous in the Saudi context. Increased repression of dissident modernists during the Arab uprisings succeeded in putting several of them behind bars after lengthy trials, but their discourse continues to flourish and gather momentum, thanks to the proliferation of social media in Saudi Arabia. These modernist Islamists will remain relevant to future generations as they have truly succeeded in providing an alternative reformist discourse that goes beyond violence or acquiescence. Because of their peaceful strategies and prolific ideas, the modernists may not be easily dismissed. This book analyses the discourse and mobilisation strategies of a range of *ulama* and intellectuals who are stretching the limits of reinterpretation of foundational Islamic texts in order to promote new thinking about politics and society.

The Arab uprisings of 2011 offered Saudis an unprecedented opportunity to observe the power of peaceful mass mobilisation. As members of a society denied the right to organise itself to pursue political goals, many activists and intellectuals became enchanted by the Arab masses who occupied public squares and demanded the end of authoritarian rule. The quest for political change has long been overdue in Saudi Arabia itself, but has been stifled by successive waves of repression. Many modernists in Saudi Arabia were hopeful that a new era would allow them greater political freedoms, civil society organisations, and real respect for civil and political rights. Their hopes were shattered as they witnessed their own government put its weight and resources behind forces that were determined to reverse the wave of democratisation that started in Tunisia and Egypt.[3] By 2014 it was clear that the Saudi regime had devoted substantial funds and diplomatic efforts to thwart the 'Arab Spring' for fear of its domino effect. A mixture of strategies ensured the derailing of the uprisings and the reversal of their desired outcomes. Yet many Saudi modernists watched the unfolding of events in neighbouring countries with great hope that eventually the waves of change would reach their own homeland. A small minority amongst them increased their activism, demanding greater opportunities for political participation and freedom. Some activists, both old and new, mobilised on the ground while others articulated the quest for change in books and articles. With increased repression of the expression of dissident opinions, it was no surprise that many dissident modernists were targeted and put behind bars. Many amongst them were put on trial in courts specialising in terrorism, despite the fact that all of them had engaged in peaceful mobilisation, denouncing violence and offering an alternative path towards reform. Human rights lawyers such as Walid Abu al-Kheir and veteran judges such as Suleiman al-Rushoudi and many others faced ambiguous charges in courts, followed by very long prison sentences. Those who limited themselves to intellectual debates, focusing on writing and research, remain under surveillance, but activists who sought to mobilise people were less fortunate, with lengthy prison sentences imposed on professionals, young human rights defenders, and anybody who dared to voice critical opinions.

The Arab uprisings also raised big questions about the role of Islamists in bringing about mass protest. As in other Arab countries, Saudi Islamism represented the most prolific, diverse, and organised religio-political trend. Many observers agreed that Islamism was not the main force behind the Arab protest, but it was the first winner after the overthrow of old Arab regimes in, for example, Egypt and Tunisia. Unlike that in other Arab countries, Saudi Islamism has been operating within a context of a state that claims to rule according to sharia and that its constitution is the Quran. The close association between the Saudi regime and the Salafi–Wahhabi movement made the political context of Saudi Islamism different from that in other Arab countries. Both the regime and its Islamists are embedded in what I call in this book divine politics. Divine politics is not 'pure' religious politics as opposed to secular politics, but is in fact a blurring of boundaries between the religious and political realms. Divine politics is at the intersection of the religious and the secular rather than simply a quest to return to a religiously enchanted world. In this book I do not endorse the idea of divine politics as opposed to and different from secular politics. Because divine politics has to deal with a profane world, it is bound to be at the intersection of the religious and the secular profane world of reality, negotiation, and compromise. Divine politics retains an enchanted religious language, but it is constituted and enacted in situations that are profane. At its heart is participation in this world, which means that the sacred can never remain separate from the profane as imagined by an early generation of sociologists, notably Émile Durkheim. Rather than imagining that Islamists strive to impose sacred norms on the profane world, we can see that it is this profane world that shapes the way they reach the sacred, interpret it, and reinterpret it at different historical moments.

INTRODUCTION

Saudi modernists call for new, alternative interpretations of this divine politics, and so their intellectual debates have become subversive and challenging for the regime. The regime and its Salafi loyalists and dissident Islamists invoke divine politics as a mechanism to assert compliance with God-given laws and practices, thus blurring the boundaries between the sacred realm and the profane world of politics. The regime asserts that its legitimacy rests on its compliance with sharia; but dissident Islamists, especially Jihadis, accuse it of deviating from Islam. Consequently, the battle between the two sides is focused on a contested divine politics with each side claiming that the other had deviated from its principles.

A new modernist divine politics calls for the freeing of the religious field from both religious and political control. Modernists go as far as calling for a civil state that does not patronise and instrumentalise religion to justify inertia and repression. They seek a divine politics that frees religion from state control by relying on vigorous reinterpretations of Islamic texts and history. The modernists do not call for greater restrictions on personal conduct or more vigorous application of sharia. Instead, they highlight the spirit of Islam as one that frees individuals and societies from political repression, protects human life, and guarantees the sovereignty of the people.

This book is an attempt to capture the intellectual and political positions of a small group of religious intellectuals and scholars who challenge our understanding of divine politics and classifications of Islamists as actors embedded in an uncompromising quest to merge religion and politics. The modernists consist of Islamists who are engaged in revisionist interpretations of classical Salafi texts, deconstructing the religious roots of repression, and offering nuanced arguments in favour of political reform. This is articulated as a quest for democracy, political representation, civil society, and respect for human rights. The modernists considered in this book do not call for the abandonment of Islam altogether, but they seek to recover its sources and spirit in order to consolidate a position that allows the Saudi state to move beyond legitimacy claims based on applying sharia and upholding tradition. A modern state is not necessarily an un-Islamic or secular project, but is in their opinion an outcome of engaging with tradition in novel ways that make processes such as democracy, the establishment of civil society, and political representation anchored in a reconstruction of religious heritage.

The religious intellectuals who are engaged in this project are locally known by various names, but Tanwiris (promoters of enlightenment) is the most common.[4] It is worth noting that when Salafis use this label to describe their opponents, it carries a pejorative connotation, implying blasphemy, rejection of authenticity, and Westernisation. This is so because the modernists have deviated from traditional Saudi Salafis with their entrenched rejection of democracy, man-made constitutions, elections, pluralism, and human rights. The modernists call for democracy as the only solution, and overlook Salafi reservations over the term. Defence of democracy has come from traditionally trained *ulama* such as the veteran Salman al-Awdah and intellectuals such as Muhammad al-Ahmari. Both called for democracy, and justified its adoption by Muslims despite Salafi claims that it leads to the abandonment of Islam. These modernists are disappointed with the *shura* (consultation) that is allegedly practised in Saudi Arabia.

The modernists discussed in this book are known as Islamic thinkers (*mufakir islami*), committed to Islam and its teachings, but they offer alternative interpretations of the tradition in order to break the hegemony of Salafi dogma, especially that which abhors politics, insists on total obedience to rulers, and outlaws political activism. The thinkers discussed in this book include famous religious scholars such as Salman al-Awdah and others who have been trained in religious studies without becoming religious scholars. I deliberately include a traditionally trained religious scholar such as al-Awdah among these Islamist thinkers in order to demonstrate the porous boundaries between *ulama*, intellectuals, activists, and Islamists. All the thinkers discussed are a product of the Saudi religious education system. But they have stretched the boundaries of religious interpretation to go beyond a classical reading and endorsement of the sources they learned and studied. Some of them maintain the role of intellectuals whose words and utterances are expressed in books, lectures, articles, and short statements posted on Twitter and Facebook, while others do not hesitate to turn their thoughts into blueprints for action and mobilisation. They are all concerned with anchoring divine politics in this world, a project that requires above all compromises, interpretations, and reinterpretations. They show great willingness to learn from the history and contemporary experiences of other nations, thus ignoring Salafi obsession with authenticity and purity. They are all enchanted by the Arab uprisings and wish that the winds of change would reach their own country. However, as intellectuals or religious scholars, not all of them are in a position to openly call for mobilisation, especially after the Saudi regime criminalised all peaceful protest and imprisoned several activists since 2011. Despite repression, many intellectuals remain committed to raising awareness and deconstructing the religious roots of authoritarianism. Others among the

INTRODUCTION

modernist thinkers, for example Abdullah al-Hamid, mobilised followers to defend human rights and called for the freeing of political prisoners from Saudi prisons. He theorised jihad as a peaceful struggle akin to protest, civil disobedience, and demonstrations. He then applied what he preached and formed a civil society organisation concerned with political and human rights. He and his colleagues denounced the repressive practices of the regime, especially during the sporadic protests that have gripped Saudi Arabia since 2011. They translated their reinterpretations of Islamic thought into real action, forming an organisation that promotes a new type of peaceful jihad, and an end to repression.

The Tanwiris discussed in this book blur the boundaries between the classically trained religious scholars (*ulama*), intellectuals, Islamists, and activists. Such boundaries do not make sense in the context of Saudi Arabia, where religious education is pervasive and not confined among those specialising in religious studies. Both al-Awdah and al-Ahmari had grounding in religious studies, but the first moved to become a member of the *ulama* while the other specialised in history. When it comes to the primary sources discussed in this book, we find little difference between the styles of the two authors as they both write as *mufakir islami*, eager to enter the public sphere with accessible ideas.

Moreover, in Saudi Arabia it is common for a religious thinker to become an activist as soon as he issues a statement, delivers a sermon, or abandons his office to join women protesters who assemble to call for the release of their relatives from Saudi prisons. A religious scholar such as al-Awdah, who preaches in the study circle about Ramadan rituals, moves out of his role as preacher and becomes a political dissident the moment he tweets a statement denouncing repression and the unlawful detention of human rights activists. The repressive context of Saudi Arabia makes it difficult to draw the line between activists, on the one hand, and intellectuals and religious scholars, on the other. It is better to consider them simply as political actors who resort to various means in their struggle towards more representative government and justice. Therefore, this book traces the intellectual journeys of different actors (*ulama*, Islamic intellectuals, and activists) who resort to multiple strategies in order to register a political position. Despite their diverse professions as *ulama*, professors, lawyers, judges, human rights activists, and writers, they all agree on a common project, namely representative government, accountability, and justice. Some of them are veteran Islamists associated with the 1990s Islamic Awakening such as Sheikh Salman al-Awdah, Professor Abdullah al-Hamid, Judge Suleiman al-Rushoudi, and Dr Muhammad al-Ahmari; but others are younger, and their names only became known after 2010, when they began to publish their books. Differences in age have not created serious obstacles in the way they seek a reinterpretation of the Salafi tradition, as they have worked to bridge the gap between generations of reformers. Older Islamists rely on the enthusiasm of the younger ones to spread the message, rework aspects of the project, and circulate the spirit of reform beyond the reach of books, petitions, and pamphlets. They are all active online, which gives them ample opportunities to propagate their ideas and enlist an increasing number of Saudis in their project of moving beyond the limitations of Salafi thinking. Above all, the so-called Tanwiris represent mutations within the Saudi Islamist scene that are bound to be relevant to the future of the country.

Mutations of Saudi Islamism

In this book the Islamist modernist project is considered a mutation that has consolidated against the dogma of the official Salafi tradition. The latter is characterised by obsessive insistence on the legitimacy of the status quo, outlawing any thoughts or actions that undermine the rule of the Al-Saud. Its mission is to enforce particular interpretations associated with obedience to rulers, legitimate advice, and the criminalisation of any peaceful protest or criticism. It is no surprise that the modernists discussed here reinterpret concepts such as *wali-al-amr* (ruler), *fitna* (chaos), *khuruj ala al-hakim* (rebellion against the ruler), *thawra* (revolution), and *shura* (consultation). The modernists deconstruct these important political concepts and offer a nuanced reinterpretation that seeks to legitimise certain peaceful political actions considered subversive. Sheikh Salman al-Awdah went as far as justifying the Arab revolutions as an inevitable outcome when all peaceful means fail to change the conditions of oppression and marginalisation such as those perpetuated by the Saudi Salafi tradition, which abhors revolution and criminalises those who engage in revolutionary action. Other Islamist modernists such as Abdullah al-Hamid consider collective protest as *nasiha*, 'advice' to the rulers, thus moving beyond the Sunni Salafi insistence on advice that should be offered only privately by learned *ulama* to correct the ruler's misconduct and warn against deviation from the rightful Islamic teachings. Others, such as Muhammad al-Abd al-Karim, focus on a critical evaluation of many Islamist projects that do not prioritise political agendas. He remains critical of acquiescent Salafis who preach morality and propriety as commanders of virtue in a repressive environment where there is no free will. He reinterprets the duty

INTRODUCTION

of *hisba* (commanding right and prohibiting wrong) as civil society activism that goes beyond the Saudi bureaucratisation of the Committee for Commanding Right and Prohibiting Wrong. For him, *hisba* fails as a government project because it is concerned only with personal morality, at the expense of public good. These reinterpretations of many Islamic concepts and the impulse to associate them with modern political terminology remain at the heart of a modernist project seeking to anchor divine politics in modern political thought with its non-religious language and underpinnings.

My analysis of the Islamist mutations situates the new modernist critical voices and their field of mobilisation in the changing Saudi local and Arab regional contexts. In Saudi Arabia itself, Islamism reached an impasse after 9/11, when official public discourse associated it with terrorism, intolerance, and backwardness. Lumping all brands of Islamism together was a government strategy to stifle debate and facilitate the end of a diverse dissident religio-political movement. Increased pressure and repression pushed a fringe Jihadi movement to adopt violent strategies, causing a terrorism crisis between 2003 and 2008, but many other Islamists searched for new meanings to define an Islamist project that is both peaceful and modernist. The Tanwiris have never called for violence as a strategy for political change. They strengthened their articulation of an Islamist project that remains within the realm of Islam but goes beyond the limited spaces that the dominant Salafi tradition allows for political actors. They have produced a discourse that has mutated over several years, becoming hybrid in drawing on Arab modernist thinkers and their own reinterpretation of the Islamic body of knowledge on politics. They have gone even further by engaging with international discourse on democracy, pluralism, civil society, and human rights. These Islamist mutations are better seen from a new angle, namely contextualisation within debates on democracy, civil society, and human rights, rather than how they correspond to the authentic Islamic tradition. These modernists call for rights that are currently denied, and act in ways that continue to be prohibited. From establishing civil society movements to calling for peaceful protest, they face two challenges. First, mainstream Salafi scholars and activists unsurprisingly reject their discourse and actions. They accuse them of subverting the authentic Islamic tradition by impregnating it with alien concepts such as civil jihad, democracy, human rights, and civil society. They also accuse them of seeking Western approval as 'moderate Islamists' or 'democratic Islamists' who are not concerned with substantial issues relating to purifying creed, fighting religious innovations, and defending Islam against a range of enemies such as liberals, Shia, Sufis, and others considered by Salafis to have abandoned true faith. The modernists' overt focus on political reform through a reinterpretation of old religious treatises on government makes them suspect as subversive actors and intellectuals.

Second, the Saudi regime sees a new discourse on political rights, anchored in Islamic sources that may lead to real mobilisation and activism, as a potential threat. Since the Arab uprisings many modernist intellectuals and activists have been put in prison following lengthy trials in Saudi courts presided over by government-appointed Salafi judges determined to criminalise their actions and thoughts. For the first time, the trials of such activists have become the focus of debate and controversy, reported in the local and international media. Long prison sentences followed, but the defence of the prisoners, images of the trials, and the regular Twitter feeds of the activists watching the theatrical performances of the detained activists in the courts circulated among wide audiences, thanks to new online media. At the time of writing, several modernist thinkers and activists are serving long prison sentences, but their followers continue to remind audiences of their intellectual arguments in favour of political reform and the reinterpretation of sacred texts; these remain a way out of the rigid Salafi doctrines and an attempt to inject Islamism with a blueprint for future peaceful action. Both objectives remain loyal to divine politics, but with the flexibility to turn it into a source of inspiration rather than dogma and rigidity. For many modernists divine politics is not simply a reiteration of Quranic verses and Hadith sources but an application of reason to arrive at interpretations that support political transformations leading to just government in this world.

The second context relevant to the consolidation of the Saudi modernist voices is the Arab region and its turmoil since 2011. Saudi modernists assess these uprisings through the prism of the quest for democracy rather than an ideal Islamic state that applies sharia. They are not under the illusion that the Arab masses rose against dictators to force people into submitting to sharia law, increase the Islamisation of society, and banish manifestations of immorality from the public sphere and space. Many modernists have argued that the reassertion of personal and public piety was not the driving force behind the uprisings. They all considered the uprisings as a political movement calling for freedom, dignity, and equality. Some of the Saudi modernists discussed in this book advocated not alienating the Arab masses or burdening them with the immediate application of sharia, thus criticising those Islamists who jumped at the opportunity to return to a dogmatic divine politics that ostracises sections of Arab society. Others justified revolution using Sunni theology, and

INTRODUCTION

wrote about its inevitability following decades of repression and marginalisation. A critique of the main Islamist movement, the Muslim Brotherhood, in its short-lived experience in power in Egypt was provided, in addition to warning against the trappings of power and victory. In general, the Arab uprisings pushed Saudi modernists to assess the prospect of societies succumbing to Islamist pressure and the desire of regimes to hold onto power after decades of persecution and repression. This critique stemmed from their realistic consideration of the pluralism of Arab societies, especially in places such as Egypt and Tunisia. This position was surprising, as it originated in a country where debate about the sharia and its application had always been taboo. But Saudi modernists stretched the limits of interpretation and analysis, and deployed reason in their assessment of the future of neighbouring countries. Many amongst them were disenchanted both with grand slogans propagated by Islamists in Arab countries and with their own government, which insists that its legitimacy stems from applying sharia. They saw no freedom, dignity, or equality under these slogans, and warned against replicating the Saudi political model in other Arab countries. But they all lauded the initial peaceful uprisings for their civility and legitimate struggle.

Islamism Reconsidered

Despite the proliferation of academic studies, there are some scholars who argue that 'Islamism remains an unquestioned category of instant political analysis. The term lumps together movements seeking to change everyday behaviour with those seeking violent overthrow of regimes.'[5] This general critique does not take into account the recent nuanced literature on Islamism and the critical stances adopted to explain both the concept and the diverse groups that are often labelled Islamists. There is, however, a consensus among scholars that Islamism promotes a certain kind of divine politics. Islamism is understood as a set of ideologies and movements 'that strive to establish some kind of an "Islamic state"—a religious state, sharia law, and moral codes in Muslim societies and communities'.[6] In another account, Islamism 'is a neologism that has come into popular and pervasive use. It usually refers to those Muslim social movements and attitudes that advocate the search for more purely Islamic solutions (however ambiguous this may be) to the political, economic and cultural stresses of contemporary life'.[7] Broadly understood, Islamism, as Emmerson argues, 'should refer to Muslims who valorize Islam in public space as a source of tolerance, moderation and democracy'.[8] The focus on the quest to establish an Islamic state may reduce Islamists to one aspect of their project. Therefore, it is better to seek a broader definition of Islamism as a diverse worldview with multiple projects and actors with different histories and localities. Roxanne Euben and Muhammad Qasim Zaman broaden the understanding of Islamism beyond the quest for the state to include reference to a critical project. They define Islamism as 'explicitly and intentionally political as engaging in multifaceted critiques of all those people, institutions, practices, and orientations that do not meet their standards of this divinely mandated political engagement'.[9] The political, however, encompasses both the person and the community. Needless to say that definitions of Islamism must take into account the historicity of the concept through the prisms of which actors are perceived, understood and explained at a specific moment in time.

Moreover, the political project does not inevitably involve a quest for a caliphate-style state. The Islamist modernists discussed here, including veteran *ulama* such as Salman al-Awdah, insist on a civil state (*dawla madaniyya*), based on a re-reading of the historiography of the old imagined Islamic state without reference to an over-arching multi-national and multi-ethnic caliphate. This does not make the thinkers discussed here advocates of secularism. They simply navigate the past models of the historical state to push for a break from this past and move on to a future in which the civil character of the state triumphs over any project to establish theocracies. Al-Awdah clearly writes that there is no theocracy in Islam (chapter 3). His version of divine politics tends to promote the civil aspect of government.

It is common in scholarly work and policy reports to highlight the diversity of Islamism, which includes a broad spectrum of positions, strategies, political trends, and parties. Scholars distinguish between the kind of radical global Jihadi groups that mushroomed after the Soviet occupation of Afghanistan in 1979 and moderate local trends seeking accommodation with their regimes, adopting peaceful strategies to Islamise both society and politics, such as the Muslim Brotherhood.[10] Yet others consider global Jihadism as an offshoot of the original Muslim Brotherhood movement without identifying any serious differences.[11] The limitations of these classifications led to focusing on how Islamism plays out in everyday life. The Islamists who remain embedded in material conditions of class are classified as militant (lower middle class), conservative, and moderate (both middle class).[12]

With respect to the conditions that gave rise to Islamism, scholars identify the ongoing Western domination of Muslim countries, the failure of secular nationalist and leftist ideologies in the post-independence period, and the

INTRODUCTION

thwarted promises of economic development since the 1970s as conditions that gave rise to diverse Islamist movements across the Arab and Muslim world.[13] Sociologists consider Islamism a response to conditions of postmodernity in which societies experience anxiety over globalisation, consumerism, loss of authenticity, and hybridity, thus pushing them to promote a religio-political agenda detached from culture.[14]

Since 9/11 scholarly classifications of Islamism have become more grounded in a desire to distinguish between good and bad Muslims, itself a normative position improvised to separate friends from foes, especially from the perspective of legitimate security concerns.[15] While classifications offer clear categories to be understood by policy makers and others, they are by no means sufficient to understand Islamism as theory and practice in the diverse societies of the Muslim world and among Muslims in non-Muslim-majority countries. Scholarship has become hostage to policy agendas to the detriment of clear, rigorous interpretative frameworks that allow an assessment of social, religious, and political movements at specific historical moments. The focus on Islamists' strategies that oscillate between 'quietist' and 'activist' positions may be justified in security and terrorism studies, but it can obscure the assessment of Islamism as a complex and diverse moral, religious, and political process.

Classifications of Islamism remain grounded in theoretical positions emerging from Enlightenment intellectual categories specific to their Western historical contexts. The term Tanwiri is in fact an exponent of this tendency. These categories fix religion and politics in separate spheres of human action and thought, marked by *a priori* clear-cut distinctions between two realms that should remain forever separate lest they create the kind of chaotic conditions that Europe experienced centuries ago. This rigid approach to the study of Islamism has been challenged by recent complex debates on religion, secularism, secularisation and secularity, all seem to be a product of the return of religion, or its persistence, as an important factor in the public sphere and even international relations.[16] The quest for the separation between religion and politics may have become an illusion even in societies that pride themselves on pursuing secular disenchanted politics such as the USA, Russia, and countries in post-communist Eastern Europe. Many hope that the unique historical transformation of European politics and Christianity, now considered a universal model to be replicated in other societies with different religious histories and contemporary trajectories, would prevail in countries far removed from this specific history. The intellectual heritage of the Enlightenment insists that politics is a secular domain emerging from the need for disenchanted decisions in which the management of resources, competition, confrontation, and policy are formulated on the basis of a set of humanist values that one may argue remain grounded in belief, a survival of a Christian age yet without clear acknowledgement.[17] The so-called secular politics of the West conceals religious values that persist in the rhetoric and practices of governments and opposition parties. On the other hand, the so-called religious politics of the Muslim world is seen as a reminder of Islam's and Muslims' resistance to secularism. These interpretative frameworks fail to capture how religion, politics, and secularism are vague constructs of our academic classifications that are obsessed by demarcation lines and boundaries rather than by the overlapping and messy reality of the real world.

Like Christian, Jewish, and Hindu fundamentalisms, in Western scholarship Islamism, the ultimate fusion between religion and politics, becomes an aberration, deviating from the expected allegedly universal and historical norm. Islamists call for an enchantment of politics while the expectation is now to persevere in the disenchantment of public life. The understanding of Islamism, therefore, continues to be framed within the prism of Christian historical lenses, European Enlightenment microscopic intellectual landscapes, and wishful thinking.

Interpretations of Saudi Islamism have not been detached from this academic heritage. Historical and contemporary studies of Saudi Arabia highlight the role of militant Islamists in state formation, as a security threat, or as a failed challenge to the state.[18] Those categorised as moderate Islamists are perceived through the prism of 'liberalism', no matter how loosely defined or how obscure it may be in the Saudi context.[19] The resort to Western terminology to capture a 'liberal' impulse within a certain Islamist trend illustrates the challenge that Islamism itself poses to scholars who cannot go beyond the theoretical frameworks of the founding fathers of Western social sciences, themselves a product of late nineteenth-century European disenchantment of knowledge.[20] In the debate about the genealogy of Islam in the West, Joseph Massad insists that Islam is at the heart of liberalism, at the heart of Europe: it was there at the moment of the birth of liberalism and the birth of Europe.[21]

Past and current Islamism is better understood as part and parcel of that Islamic discursive tradition, defined by Talal Asad as seeking to instruct practitioners about the correct form and purpose of a given practice in an ever-changing world.[22] Like Islam, Islamism is embedded in controversy, debate, and transformation, each of which is grounded in specific historical contexts and power relations. This theoretical position allows us to move away from

INTRODUCTION

imposing terminologies and classifications that obscure rather than illuminate our understanding of Islamism. In addition to it being a moral worldview that draws on specific interpretations of Islamic texts and history, Islamism is also a blueprint for personal and political action and utopian visions. Like all blueprints it experiences internal tensions arising from trying to reconcile community and individual, theory and practice, aspiration and reality, men and women, past and present, and rhetoric and practice, not to mention the negotiations, compromises, and contradictions that activists with utopian visions encounter in pursuing their agendas.

Islamism is, therefore, multiple texts, contexts, and practices, each of which is embedded in real historical and political situations. Its ideologues, practitioners, and followers may insist on the unity and single interpretation of a set of revered textual sources—among the Salafi variant of Islamism these are the Quran, Hadith, and the tradition of the pious ancestors. But the exploration of the interpretation and reinterpretation of Islamist discourses over time reveals that even their supposedly monolithic and limited textual sources are in fact diverse, multiple, and, instead of consensual, contradictory. Islamists are above all political actors who draw on specific old and recently produced texts to seek an enchantment of their personal life and the world. They draw on the discursive tradition that is 'Islam', but also on their own manuals and pamphlets, produced by writers and thinkers who are grounded in specific contexts. They are modern practitioners and visionaries who want to change the world by action to achieve certain goals, from Islamising societies to overthrowing regimes by peaceful means or military struggles. Like all other Muslims, Islamists seek conceptually to link a past and a future through a present.[23]

Contemporary Islamists are totally immersed in late modernity and its vibrant debates, controversies, and syncretism, which they have internalised without openly admitting it, let alone celebrating or boasting about it. They make choices like any other actors. They may uphold their principles, preach what they do not do, compromise themselves in the pursuit of political goals, and negotiate with their opponents. In real life they make choices, although they may appear to be determined to limit other people's choices. Politically, they may even ally themselves with their declared enemies.[24] They raise grand slogans such as the unity of the Muslim *umma*, Islam as the solution, the application of sharia, and the resurrection of the caliphate.[25] Many of these slogans come and go, depending on concrete historical moments.

In Saudi Arabia, Islamists engage in battles with their opponents with regard to alcohol consumption, mixing between the sexes, the veiling of women, and the legitimacy of insurance in Islamic economies. Moreover, they are also notorious for their battles with fellow Islamists who do not subscribe to their particular version of the Islamic blueprint for action. The fiercest battles are with those who defect from their faction, share the same ideological foundations, or belong to competing trends. Islamists continue to wage war against competitors in a closed political system in which all are denied open political contestation, such as in Saudi Arabia. Inter-Islamist political and economic rivalries are clothed in debates about public morality and religious dogma. They repeatedly invoke the *umma* as a transcendental and transnational order whose political management becomes a sacred task upheld by actors totally immersed in the reality of resource distribution, power brokering, conflict resolution, and negotiation. But in the majority of real situations Islamists who promote divine politics are immersed in a profane world with its challenges and opportunities.

To continue to see the diversity of Islamism through the prism of radicalism, on the one hand, and moderation or liberalism, on the other, aims above all to fix and frame Islamism in eternal ambiguous categories against the fluidity of social and political life. Scholars can only identify Islamist transformations and mutations by focusing on the underlying conditions that prompt one strand of Islamism to change its discourse, interpretations, and strategies in the pursuit of specific goals, which are themselves situational and in a state of flux. We can identify which grand Islamist projects are abandoned, failed, delayed, or replaced by more immediate ones in an attempt to trace how specific actors who are committed to politico-religious visions interact with this messy reality of everyday profane politics. Islamists may become dogmatic, opportunist, or oblivious to pressing changing realities. It is this reality that should become the field of scholarly reflections.

Post-9/11 Saudi Islamist Mutations

After 9/11 Saudi Islamists known as advocates of an Islamic awakening (*al-sahwa al-islamiyya*) entered a hibernation phase imposed on their outspoken members by the regime as it struggled to combat the worst terrorism episode in its modern history. By 2001 important religious activists who had been imprisoned in the 1990s following sporadic contestations with the state were free to return to their preaching roles or jobs under new rules. Some remained marginalised and suspended from their government jobs in education and religious institutions, while more important figures were incorporated as key

INTRODUCTION

agents in efforts to combat terrorism. Public appearances and forums under the auspices of the regime became readily available to 'reformed' Islamists who from now on were expected to engage in regime efforts to defeat radical violent Jihadis and defend the state against armed rebellion. They were expected to help combat terrorism in educational and media institutions, promoting three important agendas. The first was undermining the intellectual and religious foundation of terrorism by defeating the ideology of terror from within the Islamic tradition, a task that required religious scholarship to fix the interpretation of contested Islamic texts and highlight the misconceptions of Jihadi interpretations. Second, promoting a moderate Islamic *wasatiyya*, a centrist position on social and cultural issues in the area of public life such as gender. And third, pledging allegiance to the regime and adopt the discourse of reform instead of rebellion against the regime. This coincided with the regime's reformist rhetoric about the need to introduce evolutionary and gradual change to safeguard against a sudden implosion of Saudi political and social life. While many Islamists celebrated their return to public life after a long absence in prison cells, some key figures thrived under new state patronage networks and venues, and played an important role in deconstructing Jihadi discourse on violent struggle against unjust rulers allied to so-called Western infidel powers. Others abstained from being 'co-opted', and went into voluntary exile either at home or abroad, retreating into preaching morality and criticising Western influences that aim to undermine Saudi Islamic society and values. Others gradually drifted towards clandestine Jihadi circles and played a pivotal role in justifying the terrorist attacks that swept Saudi cities between 2003 and 2008. Yet many activists clandestinely escaped to other 'hot' Jihadi destinations, mainly Iraq after the 2003 American invasion, where they infiltrated the resistance against the USA, thus facing death or imprisonment.[26]

Saudi Islamists faced additional challenges after 9/11. They became the target of criticism and denunciation by several groups within Saudi society. Loyal Salafis, Jihadis, and so-called liberals focused on undermining Islamism. Traditional Salafis, the backbone of the Saudi Wahhabi religious establishment who continue to support the government, the Jihadis sprung from their ranks in the context of the 1980 jihad in Afghanistan, and Saudi loyalist liberals authorised by the state to denounce religious radicalisation in the media focused their attention on criticising Islamism, albeit for different reasons.

As the official Salafi religious establishment criticised organised Islamist activities, especially those associated with imported Islamist ideologies such as the Muslim Brotherhood or the Sururis (a fusion of Salafi and Muslim

Brotherhood ideologies), Islamists struggled to absolve themselves from any wrongdoing and clarify their earlier positions on the legitimacy of rebellion, armed struggle, and confrontation with the regime and infidels. The religious establishment had always denounced Islamists as promoting an illegitimate partisan position (*hizbiyya*) within the Muslim community, leading to divisions within the *umma*, fragmentation of society, dangerous politicisation of the youth, and eventually military confrontation with established political authority. These views have always been central among official Saudi Salafis who claim that the Saudi state should not be challenged publicly, for example in demonstrations and the media, or even criticised in open forums transmitted by new information technology such as the fax machine in the 1990s, the internet after 2000, and recent social networking media such as Twitter and Facebook.

Outspoken members of the official Salafi establishment resented the popularity of certain Islamist *ulama* who had been lecturers in Saudi Islamic studies universities, and other Islamist intellectuals who combined solid training in the sciences of sharia with knowledge in medicine, engineering, and the social sciences, thus enabling them to reach out to young Saudis in study circles, university lecture halls, and debating forums in addition to mosques. As most Islamist thinkers combined religious knowledge with training in secular sciences, they blurred the boundaries between the *alim* (religious scholar) and *mufakir* (public intellectual). Their critical and challenging discourse on the regime's strategies and policies competed with that of traditional *ulama*. Islamists reached much further than most traditional Saudi religious scholars had ever been able to, namely a young generation disenchanted with the subservience of the official Salafi *ulama* to political power. This generation searched for a new empowering discourse that promises authenticity and emancipation while remaining grounded in tradition. Many Saudi Islamists had to defend themselves against the onslaught of traditional *ulama* who held the early 1990s activism responsible for laying the foundation for deviant interpretations of Islamic texts and later encouraging the violence that erupted in 2003.

After the state authorised Islamists to reappear in the public sphere through media channels, internet forums, and study circles, they struggled to re-explain their position and distance themselves from violence, in both its ideological and real manifestations. Some famous Islamists were invited to state-sponsored forums to declare their allegiance to the state and shed their image as radical and violent activists, with the hope that the message would reach their followers lest they drift into the wave of terror that swept the coun-

INTRODUCTION

try. They offered their services to the state to mediate between the violent fringe Jihadis and the regime, calling upon Jihadis to repent and give themselves up to the security services with the promise of pardon or lenient prison sentences. The Saudi Islamist scene after 2001 resembled that in Egypt in the 1990s where from prison cells famous Jihadis, in a process known as *tarajuat*, recanted previous political and religious interpretations and wrote treatises denouncing their early positions and endorsing a peaceful path. With the exception of the state-sponsored televised repentance of Saudi Jihadis after 2003 most Saudi Islamists avoided losing face by clarifying their early positions, which they claimed had been far from calling for violent struggle against the regime. They denounced suicide bombings, the killing of infidels, and military struggle at home and abroad. They dissociated themselves from Osama Bin Laden and al-Qaida branches across the Muslim world, including those in the Arabian Peninsula. They also denounced the Saudi Islamist opposition abroad and called on it to reconcile with the regime, while demonstrating its erroneous and misguided path to political change from the safety of exile abroad.[27] They, however, remained watchful of the constant denunciation by the official Salafi *ulama* establishment, who continued to see them as suspicious and divisive.

While Saudi Islamists struggled to regain their credibility and win the battle against quiescent official Salafiyya, they faced another challenge from those Jihadis who had sprung from their own rank and file. Islamists were expected to denounce and condemn Jihadis as misguided Muslims with superficial understanding of Islamic texts. Having reconciled with the regime and denounced the violent tactics of Jihadis, Saudi Islamists fell prey to Jihadi critiques, most of which concentrated on undermining their new role as defenders of the regime. Jihadis reminded audiences of the recent co-optation of some Islamists by the regime after they were released from prisons, the lavish lifestyle they began to enjoy as a result of engagement with regime agendas, and most importantly the early 1990s sermons of key Islamist figures in which they opposed the regime and exposed its un-Islamic policies. In Jihadi retaliation discourse many Islamists were described as hypocrites who had been tamed by their experience in Saudi prisons in the late 1990s. While the regime was waging war on terrorism, another battle was unfolding between Islamists and Jihadis, which found a niche in the newly introduced internet services and in published pamphlets and responsa. If Islamists in the 1990s dubbed the official Salafi establishment *ulama al-salatin* (the sultan's *ulama*), after 9/11 they themselves were characterised as *ulama munafiqin* (hypo-

19

crites) and *ulama al-fadhaiyat* (satellite television *ulama*) who had not only made peace with a blasphemous regime but played the role of security and intelligence services, promising to entrap Jihadis on behalf of the regime as a service to the state to regain recognition and rehabilitation in the Saudi religio-political sphere.

In addition to the official Salafi *ulama* and the Jihadi ideologues and activists demonising the Islamists, under the pressure of terrorism and in accordance with regime agenda, Saudi intellectuals embarked on an open confrontation with all those who were dubbed radical within the religious sphere. This included the official *ulama*, the Jihadis, and the Islamists. The public sphere was saturated with articles, speeches, lectures, and conferences where any religious position that criticised government policies was attacked for being radical, or responsible for radicalisation. From rulings on gender issues to restrictive labour laws, selected intellectuals under the patronage of the regime confronted so-called radical religious positions on all issues of concern in the public sphere. The regime enlisted men, women, journalists, and intellectuals to undermine the credibility of those who opposed its general social and religious reform policies and questioned its anti-terrorism strategies. These enlisted writers went as far as blaming radical Islam and Islamists for all social ills, from unemployment and spinsterhood among young women to restrictions on personal freedom, terrorism, and violence.[28] Article after article was published in the Saudi press attributing all problems to religious radicalisation, which became a ready-made cause for all psychological, social, political, and economic problems experienced in the country. Such discourse obscured the reality of the political oppression, economic deprivation, injustice, and corruption that had been an obvious characteristic of authoritarian rule in Saudi Arabia. Faced with this onslaught, Islamists began to promote a discourse absolving Islam and its interpreters from any wrongdoing, attributing some of society's ills to cultural and social factors or to misunderstanding of key Islamic texts and sources. They opted for an interpretation that is anchored in an acculturation (*tathqif*) of all social problems. It was rare to find any public discourse that attributed some of the problems facing Saudi Arabia in the twenty-first century to misguided foreign and domestic policies or authoritarianism, not to mention how the regime nourished and sponsored the discourse that inspired one of the most violent militant movements in Islamic history, global Jihadi Salafism. Islamists themselves began to point to flaws in the Saudi education curriculum that many students had followed in public schools. No academic or public figure reminded his

INTRODUCTION

audiences of how in the 1980s jihad was an official foreign policy strategy of the regime, and a strategy in the Cold War devised by the USA and other Western powers such as Britain.

The first decade of the twenty-first century can therefore be considered a decade of intense debates, accusations, soul-searching, and controversies among Islamists in Saudi Arabia. After 9/11 the regime allowed this debate to flourish, and in many instances it sponsored controversial forums with a view to intensify the debate within society. As a result Saudis blamed each other for the many ills that their society was experiencing, terrorism being only one of them. As long as the regime remained sacrosanct, above criticism or scrutiny, old and new activists were able to exchange accusations and counter-accusations in an attempt to resolve one important question: who was responsible for terrorism abroad and at home? Islamists remained cautious while trying to regain their credibility among their own followers and reach out to the regime for reconciliation and recognition after an impasse.

On the eve of the Arab uprisings many Saudi Islamists had already reinvented themselves as peaceful activists seeking the reform of the regime from within, working closely within the parameters of acceptable activism. Once again Islamists reclaimed their space on the religio-political map of Saudi Arabia. They had their own strategies to remain relevant and central to any debate about the future of the country, its political development, and its public policy. The Arab uprisings reinvigorated them when two Islamist parties, al-Nahda in Tunisia and the Muslim Brotherhood in Egypt, came to power. Peaceful mobilisation in the form of demonstrations, sit-ins, pamphlets, and critical statements publicised on the new forums of internet social networking sites increased with a view to press their discourse and enlist new followers. At the same time, they closely followed developments in the Arab world and supported the struggle of Tunisian, Egyptian, Libyan, Yemeni, and Syrian rebels, which many amongst them considered it to be an Islamic awakening. This description, however, obscured the fact that Islamists in Arab countries had not been the first or the only groups to mobilise people against the authoritarian regimes in 2010–11. Many Saudi Islamists saw the Syrian uprising through the lens of sectarian politics, and considered the Syrian rebels as defenders of a Sunni revival against the hegemony of a minority Alawite regime. On the Bahraini uprising Saudi Islamists remained silent, adopting the regime's description of this ongoing conflict, which was dubbed a Shia–Iranian conspiracy to undermine the security of the Gulf, spread Iranian hegemony, and unsettle the Shia eastern region of Saudi Arabia.[29] They also condemned the

2011 Saudi Shia uprising in Qatif and Awamiyya, which had claimed the lives of more than twenty young activists at the time of writing this book.[30] In fact, they blamed the Shia for delaying their own Islamist mobilisation and increased government oppression and arrest among their own activists. After 2011 the Saudi authorities increased their surveillance of the public sphere and curbed dissenting voices, especially after calls to demonstrate were issued on the internet in March 2011 under what was called 'The Day of Rage'. Saudi Islamists remained cautious and refrained from calling for open protest in Saudi Arabia or endorsing outside calls for such mobilisation.[31]

This recent history of state–Islamist relations and Islamist–Islamist debate and controversy is the background that allows an analysis and appreciation of the nuances of the modernist project in Saudi Arabia. This is a mutation among a minority of Islamists who emerged before the recent Arab uprisings but became more focused under its pressure. The uprisings only helped to accelerate their intellectual contribution to how political change can be achieved without bloodshed and without abandoning Islam altogether. Their reinterpretation of divine politics as democracy and human rights is expressed against a Saudi Salafi background that still refuses to recognise the urgency of these reformist projects.

The early manifestations of the Saudi Islamist modernist project had already been the subject of analysis. Scholars have identified the project as an Islamo-liberal trend that seeks to reinvent Islamism as a moderate project. Such a term remains contentious in the Saudi context, and must be carefully scrutinised. In Saudi Arabia it is often believed that this trend remained unable to mobilise people or overcome Salafi resistance. This is attributed to the excessive intellectualism of its advocates and its failure to enlist famous religious scholars.[32] The Saudi context remains hostile to the modernist project because several groups, including the religious establishment, other Islamists, and Salafi populists, resist its discourse, launch criticism against its approach, and even brand it as a deviation from Islam. The trend tried to strike alliances with non-Islamists and enlist nationalists, leftists, Shia, and others in its project, but without much success. Under government pressure alliances fragmented and withered away. But recent developments in both Saudi Arabia and the Arab world may have reinvigorated the trend and increased its followers at a time when radical groups are mushrooming and making news as founders of Islamic states and caliphates.[33] The Saudi project to establish a civil and political rights movement and the imprisonment of the main founders gave the modernist trend new impetus during the Arab uprisings. The trend

INTRODUCTION

is particularly popular among new, connected young activists who have contributed to circulating its demands and arguments beyond the limited number of founders and intellectuals. Today its supporters are lawyers, journalists, publishers, and professionals. Repression may have been counter-productive, pushing a greater number of ordinary citizens to see the merit of the modernists' peaceful advocacy.

Like other modernist Islamist projects that emerged in places such as Egypt, Iran, Indonesia, and Pakistan, the Saudi modernist trend is often described as a post-Islamist movement,[34] advocating rights rather than duties and engaging with cultural and artistic productions to articulate new freedoms within the Islamic tradition. Post-Islamism was first coined as a historical rather than an analytical category by Asef Bayat in 1996 in his study of Iranian Islamism, and later developed by other sociologists. It is considered a process of metamorphosis in which Islamism represents an endeavour to 'fuse religiosity and rights, faith and freedom, Islam and liberty'.[35] This fusion is both a condition and a project, following disenchantment with the grand Islamist projects of the past in which duties superseded rights.

In this book I avoid clear associations between the Saudi Islamist modernists and labels such as liberalism or post-Islamism for many reasons. First, it is more accurate to situate this trend within a discursive Islamism that mutates as it collides with historical contexts and local developments. Islamism and post-Islamism coexist rather than being clearly successive historical phases. The Saudi trend is a mutation in a Salafi context rather than a deliberate move towards liberalism or post-Islamism. Its advocates are anchored in an Islamic context, although they may have sought alliances with liberals and others to widen their circle of followers. What remains important for them is the project to reinterpret the Islamic tradition and deconstruct the roots of authoritarian government from within. This project was a process that accompanied the rise of Islamism in Saudi Arabia rather than a late development or a post-Islamist phase. Second, the modernists discussed here return to scriptures and excavate them in order to find solutions to the entrenched repressive political context in which they live. The only difference between them and other Islamists is the solutions they provide and their appreciation of other political experiences around the world. Their engagement with modern political concepts such as democracy, civil society, and human rights makes them modern. But their modernity remains anchored in Islam and its texts. Democracy for them is not necessarily secular, but can be infused with faith. Civil society is not an alien concept but a new version of commanding right and prohibiting wrong. Freedom is an important aspect of Islam that seeks to liberate people from repression. Sovereignty means the ability of the community to represent itself in elected parliaments. It is important, therefore, to analyse and understand Saudi modernism in its own terms and on its own territory. By describing them as modernist, I emphasise their focus on the ability of human beings to create new conditions for freedom and reform through a re-examination of Islamic sources.

Methodology

The book relies on analysis of textual and oral sources produced by a selected number of Islamist *ulama* and intellectuals. The choice of sources was determined by the reaction that they received upon publication of their treatises. The sources consist of a range of books, pamphlets, internet sources, audio-visual and media appearances. I selected a number of books written by Salman al-Awdah, Abdullah al-Maliki, Muhammad al-Abd al-Karim, and Muhammad al-Ahmari because of the controversy they have generated in the Saudi Salafi context. All of them remain controversial figures who engage with new interpretations of Islamic sources. They are, however, not the only ones to engage in this reinterpretation; the choice was based on the novelty of their ideas and their coherence.

In addition to written sources, moving away from textual analysis to a consideration of activism highlighted the importance of a group of reformers who have been engaged in formulating ideas relevant to civil society and acting on these ideas in the context of engaging in activism. As a case study, the Saudi Association for Civil and Political Rights (ACPRA), known in Arabic as HASM (Jamiyyat al-Huquq al-Siyasiyya wa al-Madaniyya), embodied the activist side of the modernist trend and had to be included in the analysis. HASM emerged as a culmination of the ideas of both its founders and of its sympathisers, who supported its approach and justified its actions. As HASM was criminalised and banned in 2013, it became difficult for many supporters to talk to researchers and the media, yet many remained active online to inform audiences about its project and activism. Combining textual analysis of a number of publications with analysis of the activism helped bridge the divide between intellectual arguments and action as both became interrelated, with one enforcing the other. The intellectual modernism embodied in the textual sources was translated into action based on the ideas that activists and others within the trend had formulated and presented in books and pamphlets.

INTRODUCTION

Textual sources became readily available as a new publishing house, established in Beirut, published several of the books discussed here. The Arab Network for Research and Publishing,[36] founded by Saudi journalist and Islamist Nawaf al-Qudaimi, assumed great importance as a platform committed to publishing books that interrogate the Islamic sources, promote new thinking about political and religious matters, and embody the new perspectives of a modernist trend. The publishing house presented its collection of books every year in Saudi Arabia during international book fairs until March 2014, when its corner in the fair was raided and the books were banned.[37] The publishing house included, in addition to revisionist political, historical, and religious books, translations of highly acclaimed academic studies on Saudi Arabia. The publisher's collection was deemed subversive as it undermined the Salafi tradition and criticised theological arguments that had been taken for granted in the country. It offered what the Saudi regime feared most, namely the deconstruction of what is often referred to as *fiqh al-taa*, the jurisprudence of obedience to rulers. This jurisprudence is central to perpetuating the status quo, criminalising a range of peaceful activities, and giving a religious excuse for authoritarian rule.

Interviews with key activists and intellectuals were carried out in 2013 and 2014. I carried out telephone interviews, and met a small group of writers and activists when they travelled to Beirut and London. The interviews proved to be difficult given the wave of repression that was sweeping Saudi Arabia. The trials and long prison sentences passed on founders of HASM, activists, and human rights defenders, in addition to the travel bans, made many activists hesitate to openly voice any criticism or dissent, let alone communicate with researchers and the media. But I was able to reach several activists and interview them. Many spoke on condition of anonymity. In order to protect their identity, I have not referred to all of them in the footnotes. Those who agreed to be identified are mentioned in the references. I corresponded with a large group by email, Skype, and Twitter. In fact, Twitter became an important source for information and opinions, especially during the trials of HASM founders. While many activists avoided public communication with me, direct messages on Twitter allowed them to respond to my questions and send me lengthy commentaries on their activities. Images and statements by activists in court were circulated, and I was able to track specific individuals, identify their political opinions and interview them. Direct messages were sent to me with detailed and unreserved statements denouncing repression. I followed these up with telephone conversations with activists who sympathised with the accused and provided me with details that were censored in the media. The reader will notice that not all statements and citations are attributed to individuals as I had to conceal the identity of many activists, who volunteered statements on condition of anonymity. This applies to some young activists' Twitter accounts and statements. It was so common among some activists to post statements on Twitter which are later deleted simply because they fear that they will draw attention to themselves by keeping them on this social media. Sometimes, it is also difficult to trace the precise date of individual tweets given the rapid nature of this medium of communication, the frequency of re-tweets and the appropriation of statements by others. When I used Tweets as a source, I only did that when I was able to verify the content of the statement after an interview or after I spoke to its author or his entourage. This allowed me to eliminate suspicious tweets as an inaccurate source of data.

I do not claim that this research is grounded in an illusory academic objectivity. I have written several books on Saudi Arabia, given political opinions to the media, exposed the plight of reformers, and defended prisoners of conscience. This has made me a 'dissident' from the perspective of the Saudi regime. I have never identified with any political trend in Saudi Arabia, whether Islamist, leftist, nationalist, liberal, or secular. However, I remain accused of being a subversive voice, in addition to many others inside the country and abroad. In one trial an activist was accused of reading my books and articles—all banned in Saudi Arabia. Writing this book is perhaps a way of highlighting the plight of intellectuals and activists in an authoritarian state. By delving into their thoughts and observing their actions, I was able to document what repressive regimes fear most. Violence and terrorism are real threats to human life, and can push people to support the most repressive governments. But intellectual reinterpretations of Islamic texts proved to be more challenging as repressive governments cannot count on mass support when it prosecutes writers and peaceful activists.

I cannot claim that I occupy the same position as a foreign social scientist who visits Saudi Arabia for the purpose of 'objective' research and publications. As an academic of Saudi origin, I am committed to research that exposes, undermines, and highlights the detrimental consequences of suppressing opinion and criminalising intellectual journeys that challenge repression. I do not agree with some of the political demands of the modernists. Nevertheless, I present these demands to readers in impartial ways that allow them to judge the aspirations of a group of brave intellectuals living under

INTRODUCTION

circumstances so different from those I have chosen. Their modest demands reflect constraints that I have come to understand. My exile in London has afforded me freedoms denied to all the intellectuals and activists discussed in this book. It offers distance and proximity simultaneously. I was distant enough not be involved in competing local projects, and as a result gained the trust of many activists, yet close enough to understand their dilemmas and plight. This trust had been established as a result of people reading my previous books, following my media appearances, and more recently surveying my opinions on Twitter. I was surprised by how activists and dissidents favourably responded to requests to interview them although they knew that contact with me might lead to interrogation on their return to Saudi Arabia. Meeting them in public places in London and other Arab capitals, and exchanging emails or Twitter messages, was fraught with apprehension. Yet all of them were eager to reach out to my readers and me at a time when the Saudi regime was determined to silence dissenting but peaceful voices.

The voices in this book are all masculine although many amongst them venture to propose reformist agendas that encompass serious reflections on the woman's question in Saudi Arabia. I have dealt with this question in a previous publication and captured women's voices, mainly embodied in fiction and commentaries, that seek multiple solutions to the persistent exclusion of Saudi women, inequality and marginalisation.[38] The debates that preoccupy the men discussed in this book are unfortunately not prevalent in the writings of women. Saudi women excel in writing fiction that capture their aspirations and dreams but very few venture into writing treatise on political issues related to general political reform. The liberals amongst them want more freedoms that allow them to study, work, travel and participate in development without restrictions on their role. The Islamist women, however, want to see more respect for sharia, especially those areas that grant them their rights as defined by Islam. Both rely on the state to honour its promise to provide for them welfare services and spaces for participation in the well-being and progress of the country. Questions raised by women tend to be gender focused, seeking reinterpretation of Islamic texts in matters related to their own status. The wider picture of the application of sharia, democracy, elected government, and other topics I discuss in the book do not seem to feature strongly in their intellectual productions with very few exceptions. Women, however, have signed reformist petitions (discussed in chapter 1) and participated in activism in defense of political prisoners, lifting the ban on driving, and other modes of mobilisation that became prevalent after the Arab uprisings. Some of the modernists discussed in the book reflect on women's issues, their exclusion and inequality, but they remain men's voices on women's issues and cannot be considered representative of women or their aspirations in general.

This book is both an academic assessment of Islamist mutations and a recognition of the importance of a trend that may become the only alternative to violence and terrorism practised by opposition forces and regime repression in Saudi Arabia.

The Organisation of the Book

This study focuses on the latest contributions of Saudi modernist Islamists, especially their responses to the Arab uprisings of 2011. The first chapter analyses the Islamist scene on the eve of the uprisings and traces the limited activism that became apparent in Saudi Arabia itself immediately after they broke out. Faced with repression and greater restrictions on activism, Saudis initially resorted to the old method of submitting petitions to the leadership in which they articulated reformist visions. While not all the petitions expressed democratic impulses, several pamphlets articulated impatience with repressive practices and a desire to alter relations between rulers and ruled. Calls for constitutional monarchy and real political representation coexisted with those advocating reform of the state to facilitate stricter application of Islamic law. Limited protest was initially expressed online, followed by confrontations with the regime in various regions. The first chapter documents these sporadic protests that swept the country among various groups, highlighting the reasons behind their failure to develop into serious challenges to the regime. This failure also inspired Saudis to rethink their strategies for putting pressure on the government, with a small minority augmenting its challenges to the regime through demonstrations and engagement with civil and political rights associations.

In chapter 2 I discuss the unique experience of the Saudi Association for Civil and Political Rights (HASM), as an embodiment of the modernist project that had already been fermenting in the country prior to the Arab uprisings. It was invigorated as it witnessed the mass demonstrations across the Arab world, and borrowed some of the strategies and tactics of this protest. HASM struggled to mobilise society within the context of a nascent civil society, calling for peaceful protest in support of human rights and prisoners of conscience. The chapter narrates how the language of rights permeated the struggle of HASM activists and spilled over to a wide circle of followers

INTRODUCTION

thanks to new social media. HASM supporters engaged in Hashtag activism during the trial of its founders and reached a wide audience. The trials ended with very long prison sentences for its founders and young supporters. The chapter documents the experience of civil society in an authoritarian state, drawing attention to the hybridity of its discourse and strategies.

Chapter 3 considers the responses of one of the most popular religious scholars, Sheikh Salman al-Awdah, to the Arab uprisings. His analysis and justification of revolution from within the Salafi tradition is worth considering as a serious mutation prompted by the uprisings. Peaceful mass protest, which is abhorred in al-Awdah's Salafi context, becomes an acceptable strategy placed within a reinterpretation of traditional Islamic texts and borrowing from Western intellectual heritage. While many Saudi Salafi *ulama* condemned the Arab revolutions as a source of chaos and upheaval, al-Awdah celebrated their liberating potential, which reversed the decade of accommodation with the regime that he had enjoyed. Surprisingly, al-Awdah's writings on revolutions warned against the immediate application of sharia in post-revolutionary countries, a theme that a younger Islamist intellectual, Abdullah al-Maliki (chapter 4) develops in a controversial book published immediately after the Arab uprisings. Like al-Awdah, al-Maliki surprised his Saudi audiences when he rejected the immediate application of sharia by force in post-revolutionary Arab countries and instead called for this to be a matter of choice. The modernist project reaches a new level with al-Maliki's hybrid discourse that reinterprets traditional Islamic texts while incorporating Western intellectual trends. Unlike Salafis who insist on authenticity and purity, al-Maliki represents a new generation of Islamist intellectuals who draw on sources outside the Islamic tradition to express the importance of choice rather than compulsion in religious observance. Like others, he was enchanted by the Arab uprisings, which pushed him to reconsider Islamism in general, offering a critical assessment of its projects and strategies and prioritising the sovereignty of the *umma* before any debate over the application of sharia.

Al-Maliki's criticism of Islamism is further developed by Muhammad al-Abd al-Karim in chapter 5. The latter is prepared to stretch the limits of interpretation in order to deconstruct the religious roots of oppression, injustice, and absolute rule. He sees in Islam, a form of monotheistic awakening, an opportunity to free people from servitude and repression. By reinterpreting well-known Islamic concepts such as obedience to rulers, chaos, *hisba*, and justice, he infuses the tradition to undermine the hegemony of Salafi political jurisprudence with modernist impulses. This project is not complete without a discussion of the intellectual contributions of Muhammad al-Ahmari (chapter 6), who goes beyond Salafi reservations on democracy to advocate it as the only solution. In his writings, democracy is no longer an abhorred Western concept but a universal spirit that is located in multiple historical and geographical sites. His book on democracy represents one of the strongest Saudi endorsements of a political system that has long been rejected by mainstream Salafis. It is ironic for democracy in Saudi Arabia to be defended by an Islamist rather than a liberal.

By introducing the intellectual debates and contributions of well-known Saudi religious scholars and younger religious intellectuals in this book, I hope to demonstrate the mutations that Saudi Islamism has undergone in recent times and under pressure from local and regional contexts. Islamism can no longer be considered a form of dogmatic divine politics. Rather, it is best understood as a series of mutations that anchors Islamism itself in a profane world with its multiple challenges and changes. I hope my analysis of the various contributions of a small circle of Islamists proves that Islamism is neither dogmatic nor flexible. In fact, it is a form of politics that engages not only with the divine but also with the messy profane reality of the world, the complexity of religious texts, and the incredible power of humans to interpret and reinterpret the past and the present. In their commitment to constructing both person and community, some Islamists such as those discussed in this book may offer a vision for the future that combines commitment to Islam with an appreciation of other intellectual traditions. As modernists, they represent in my opinion a serious challenge to authoritarian government, perhaps greater than that posed by those Islamists who resort to guns.

1

PETITIONS AND PROTEST ON THE EVE OF THE ARAB UPRISINGS

Faced with the repression that followed the events of 11 September 2001, Saudi Islamism was destined to split into multiple trajectories. While it had always been diverse and multi-layered, 9/11 widened the gap between different Islamist groups, commonly known as al-Sahwa al-Islamiyya (the Islamic awakening).[1] Many activists fled the country to engage in jihad abroad, for example in Iraq after 2003, while others returned to Saudi Arabia, mainly from Afghanistan.[2] Members of al-Qaida in the Arabian Peninsula remained at home and launched terrorist campaigns in many Saudi cities. Hundreds of Jihadis and ideologues were either shot by security forces or imprisoned.[3] Many others repented and abandoned Islamism altogether. They started exposing the excesses of Islamism, and warned of its future impact on a new generation of Saudi youth. Many of these were rehabilitated in the Saudi public sphere and became writers and journalists, documenting their troubled journey with radical Islamist groups.[4] In the heated and volatile post-9/11 context Islamism became in the state-sponsored public discourse the cause of many problems, from radicalisation and intolerance to unemployment, gender discrimination, and violence.

In this tense atmosphere the regime tightened its grip on radical activists and enlisted many other Islamists in its 'War on Terror'. Islamists were expected to contribute to government efforts to combat terrorism. As preachers and educators, they were regarded as well equipped to de-radicalise the youth, and appear in the media preaching a different message from the one that had encouraged many Saudis to seek martyrdom abroad or at home. Amidst shootouts in Saudi cities between security forces and Jihadis in 2003–8, Saudis struggled to identify the causes of violence. Many blamed radical preachers, educational textbooks, mosque sermons, and al-Sahwa al-Islamiyya in general. Consequently, Islamists of all persuasions faced a heated battle to defend themselves against accusations that they were responsible for violence not only in New York but also in Saudi Arabia and beyond. Many Islamists distanced themselves from radical Jihadis and, under constant government pressure, they volunteered to help combat terrorism by propagating alternative interpretations of Islamic texts, especially those that justified armed rebellion against 'unjust and blasphemous rulers'.

A small group of veteran Islamists who came from the 1990s Islamic Awakening reasserted themselves as reformers seeking political change after 9/11. The impulse towards reform had already been embedded in the language of protest that swept the country in the 1990s,[5] but after 2001 the Saudi context had changed dramatically. Jihadi terrorism was now becoming more of a domestic challenge, not only for the government but also for the Islamists themselves. Faced with this, many Islamists became preoccupied with two main objectives. First, they defended themselves against accusations of terrorism; and second, they developed new strategies and discourses that push for political reform, adopting a new language that draws clearly on global human rights discourse, democracy, civil society, justice, and political participation. Those who adopted this stance became known as reformers, a loosely defined category of activists who belonged to different political and ideological positions, including the Islamists.

Government propaganda initially tried hard to depict radicalism as an outside trend that had infiltrated Saudi society with the arrival of exiled Islamists, mainly Egyptian and Syrian Muslim Brotherhood cadres who had found refuge in Saudi Arabia in the 1960s. Many reformers were not convinced that the language of terror that draws on Islamic sources is alien to the Saudi context. The reformers condemned terrorism but searched for more convincing explanations that anchored terrorism and radicalisation in the Saudi political and religious contexts. In the reformers' view, government repression, marginalisation, and foreign policy, including the export of young Saudis to Jihadi destinations as part of its cooperation with the West during the Cold War years, was part of the problem. Such interpretations of terrorism were unsurprisingly resented by the government as they implicated it in the terrorism crisis. Many reformers put the blame on the repressive political context of Saudi Arabia itself. The government's policies in Afghanistan, where it had supported jihad against the Soviet Union in the 1980s, needed a religious gloss to justify them and promote them among Saudis—which, according to many reformers, resulted in the local terrorism crisis after 2001. The established Saudi religious tradition contributed to justifying foreign policies that had returned home to threaten the domestic scene. The government had enlisted the support of the *ulama* in the 1980s when it promoted the pan-Islamic commitment to intervene in Afghanistan and sent Saudis to fight there. The reformers were not convinced that religion alone could explain the subsequent outbreak of terrorism at the local and global levels. This realisation was central to the thinking of some Islamists, struggling to explain the traumatic experience of 9/11 and its impact on the Saudi domestic scene.

Unlike the majority of Islamists, who took refuge in educational and preaching programmes after 2001, abandoned activism altogether, or travelled abroad to participate in global jihad, the reformers were primarily concerned with local politics and how to change it using peaceful means. They had no specific interest in promoting causes abroad, defeating the West in the Muslim world, or saving the transnational Muslim *umma* around the globe. They were mainly concerned with the conditions of their own country, especially those that had given rise to radicalisation and violence, both of which were regarded as the outcome of decades of alliance between an authoritarian state and an equally authoritarian religious tradition. Their second concern was with the relationship between government repression, unlawful detention, and torture in prisons, on the one hand, and radicalisation, on the other. They saw authoritarian rule and excessive repression as part and parcel of the trend that had resorted to violence in its confrontation with the government, and held state violence against its citizens responsible for the counter-violence of sections of society against the rest. Moreover, authoritarian government meant that the ruling family did not observe a clear separation of powers. The reformers specifically identified the Interior Ministry under the leadership of Prince Nayif (d. 2012) as responsible for excessive repression and the abuse of human rights. In their opinion the ministry's domestic policies and repressive practices undermined the security of most Saudis and pushed a minority towards violence. This theme remained central in the thinking of many reformers whose activism is discussed in the following chapters.

These concerns found expression in the many petitions that the reformers wrote and presented to the leadership between 2003 and 2008, at the height of the wave of terrorism that swept the country.[6] During this period, reformers submitted more than twelve petitions to the leadership, amounting to what Joseph Kechichian calls the 'petition industry'.[7] In 2004 Saudi Arabia appeared as if it was experiencing a Riyadh Spring, in which there was a heightened sense of hope and expectation that the government would respond to the demands in the petitions under the pressure of the domestic terrorism crisis. There was a sense of urgency that only political reform could contain the crisis. In their petitions the reformers clearly called for a constitutional monarchy and respect for civil, political, and human rights.[8] Many well-known Islamists and liberal activists became associated with this round of activism, which immediately followed 9/11. They included, among others, Abdullah al-Hamid, Matruk al-Falih, Ali al-Damini, and Muhammad Said al-Tayib. But the euphoria of the so-called Riyadh Spring did not last for long. Many reformers who were involved in writing petitions and encouraging others to sign them were sentenced to several years in prison.

This first wave of post-9/11 activism ended in 2008 with the reformers failing to achieve the transformation of the Saudi monarchy into a constitutional one and with reformism struggling to attract a strong social base. Instead of weakening the government, the terrorism crisis eventually strengthened the Interior Ministry, the very institution that the reformers wanted to weaken and reform. Reformers remained an elite professional group, with professors, lawyers, judges, and others dominating the reform agenda. Society was aloof from their discourse, especially at a time when Saudi cities felt the pressure of terrorism. Moreover, the idea of a constitutional monarchy as demanded by several petitions failed to appeal to Salafi Islamists, who were suspicious of both the concept and the reformers—a mixture of veteran Islamists, socialists, and nationalists.[9] Suspicion of the reformers was also triggered by the fact that they included Shia personalities such as Tawfiq al-Saif, Jafar al-Shayib, and Muhammad al-Mahfuth. Traditional Salafi loyalists among the Wahhabi establishment opposed the reformist programme, now known as al-Tayar al-Tanwiri, the enlightenment trend. In the Salafi milieu the name carried a pejorative connotation as diametrically opposed to the authentic Salafiyya with its insistence on literal interpretation of sacred texts. Traditional Salafi Islamists were also suspicious of the reformers whom they considered as having abandoned the Islamist project when they endorsed a new political discourse that is difficult to keep grounded in the Islamic tradition.

When Abdullah became king in 2005 he pardoned several constitutional reformers who had been imprisoned by the Interior Ministry, following the circulation of the reformist petitions. Their release from prison was dependent on signing pledges not to engage in future activism. Many of them were banned from travel after their release. By 2008 the reformist trend appeared to have fragmented under the pressure of repression and its failure to gather support from a wide circle of Saudi activists. The reformists who fused Islamism with notions of justice, rights, and even calls for a constitutional monarchy were labelled Islamo-liberals who tried to appeal to a wider constituency than that of the Islamists.[10] Their focus on rights rather than responsibilities of citizens made them correspond to what Asef Bayat describes as post-Islamism.[11] Yet neither label fully explains the intellectual and activist agenda of this group, as mentioned in the introduction. Preaching rights in the Salafi context of Saudi Arabia, where the responsibility of citizens towards their rulers is overemphasised at the expense of these rights, proved to be difficult. Reformers faced the resistance of Salafi *ulama* who attacked them for corrupting the Islamic tradition with alien political concepts such as international human rights, civil society, and freedom of expression. While it is obvious why traditional official religious scholars did not appreciate the reformist agenda, no important religious scholar from among the Sahwi Islamists openly adopted their agenda, thus contributing towards their further isolation and limited support.

However, the ideas and language of rights that reformers propagated throughout 2001–2008 and highlighted in their many petitions remained under the surface, attracting more activists. After the Arab uprisings, reformers returned to writing petitions that benefited from the proliferation of social media. The Arab uprisings and the advent of social media, especially Facebook and Twitter, allowed the reformers to reach beyond their limited intellectual niche. In the following sections I trace the impact of the Arab uprisings in the Saudi context in general and analyse the new round of petitions and protest.

New Saudi Petitions on the Eve of the Arab Uprisings

The Arab uprisings pushed many reformers to start a second round of petitions, hoping that the king would respond under the pressure of the turbulence in the region. In February 2011 several new petitions were circulated online, calling for political reform. The regime moved very quickly to censor the sites, but hundreds of new young activists and old reformers whose names had been associated with previous political mobilisation rushed to circulate them and increase the number of signatories. Three petitions were focused on political reform and youth issues, and a fourth one had an obvious traditional Salafi orientation.

The first 2011 petition, called 'The Declaration of National Reform', demanded the gradual evolution of the regime to a constitutional monarchy, echoing the earlier petitions of 2004.[12] The 119 signatories aspired towards a federal political system that would free the various Saudi regions from Riyadh's centralised political and administrative control. Those who prepared the petition clearly reflected fears that, in the light of the Egyptian revolution, the Sunni Islamist opposition, especially that based in London and the new trends emerging in Saudi Arabia, would take the initiative and dominate the Saudi street.[13] The petition, with its call for gradual political reform, was inaccurately considered a 'liberal' document.

The petition contained twelve points demanding fundamental political, economic, social, and judicial reforms. It insisted on the urgency of implementing the rule of law, equality, the protection of civil and human rights, political participation, equitable development, eradication of poverty and corruption, and national elections for an assembly. Most importantly, petitioners wanted a written constitution, a really independent civil society, and elected local government in the provinces. While the first demand was not new, the second indicated that in the minds of the reformers the existing organisations such as the government-appointed human rights associations are simply bureaucratic governmental agencies. The third demand indicated a desire for regional autonomy, especially after corruption scandals related to land development and confiscation, in addition to the mismanagement of development projects, led to serious flooding and deaths in several Saudi cities. In February 2011 Jeddah was the most affected by flooding, resulting in rainwater and sewage creating stagnating lakes where ten people drowned, and hundreds of houses were swept away. The petition concluded by asking the king to announce his intention to start political reform, release all prisoners of conscience from prison, lift the ban on travel imposed on reformers, and reinstate freedom of expression.

Immediately after this petition, a second document was released in February 2011, this time reiterating commitment to Islamic principles and without openly calling for constitutional monarchy or regional government. This petition was the work of Islamist reformers who wanted to avoid the controversial 'constitutional monarchy' in order to appeal to a wider circle among those associated with the Islamic Awakening. The new petition, entitled *Nahwa dawlat al-huquq wa al-muasasat* (Towards a state of rights and institutions), asked for an elected national assembly, separation between the office of king and prime minister, an end to administrative corruption, freedom of speech, independent associations, release of all political prisoners, and the lifting of the travel ban imposed on activists. Within days this petition attracted over 9,000 signatories, thus reflecting a growing Islamist trend calling for political reform with specific demands.[14] The wide circle of signatories reflected a strong Islamist constituency, and included famous Sahwi names such as Sheikh Salman al-Awdah, Judge Suleiman al-Rushoudi, Muhammad al-Ahmari, and Abdullah al-Maliki, discussed later in this book. This petition was the first in recent times to move beyond important activists and reach a large number of ordinary Saudis. It benefited from online activism, which made it generally accessible despite government efforts to censor the sites on which it was posted. The two petitions were clearly the work of well-established activists, intellectuals, and religious scholars.

However, a third 2011 petition originated among unknown youth, and was certainly triggered by the Arab uprisings. A long document entitled *Matalib al-shabab al-saoudi* (Demands of the Saudi youth) attracted more than 10,000 signatories and included fourteen points.[15] This detailed petition focused on concrete economic and political demands. The youth introduced themselves as educated voices from various Saudi provinces. They claimed that their demands reflected those of the majority of the youth. The petition requested the government to deal with unemployment as a matter of urgency, and increase unemployment benefits to 5,000SR and the minimum wage to 7,000SR. Housing, inflation, and supporting the private sector were considered a priority to empower the youth. On political reform, the petitioners demanded the lifting of the ban on independent associations, reform of the judiciary, and the release of political prisoners. They also demanded an elected national assembly that would form future governments and elected provincial local councils in ways that would return local government to the people. Empowering women, reforming the education system, and eradicating crimes that undermine social security were also mentioned.

In contrast to the above-mentioned three petitions, signed by a mixture of lay reformers, religious scholars, and youth activists, a fourth petition, *Bayan dawah lil-islah* (Call for reform), was most notably signed by sixty-five Salafi religious scholars, including the famous Sahwi Salafi sheikh Nasir al-Omar.[16] The petition was framed as traditional *nasiha*, advice to the ruler, and reminded the Saudi leadership of the pact between the founder of the first Saudi state, Muhammad ibn Saud, and Muhammad ibn Abd al-Wahhab, the eighteenth-century founder of Wahhabiyya. The demands centred on fighting corruption, freeing political prisoners, dealing with unemployment, protecting property and lives, and ridding Saudi media of secularists and those who corrupt public and private morality. Unlike the previous petitions, this overtly Salafi document does not call for the major transformation of the Saudi state into a constitutional monarchy or for national elections. Moreover, it is concerned with returning the Saudi polity to the original model of the first Saudi state, established in the eighteenth century, and the alliance between the Wahhabi founder and the Saudi rulers. The petition clearly considers the current state to have deviated from applying sharia by its introduction of new laws and decrees, all considered to have deviated from the historical Saudi–Wahhabi state model of the eighteenth century, and calls upon the leadership to honour its commitment to Islamic principles.

While the above petitions and online activism were primarily concerned with local Saudi issues, regional concerns were expressed in a new document that denounced the removal of elected Egyptian president Muhammad Morsi by the military in July 2013. The petition, *Bayan al-muthaqafin al-saoudiyyin*, representing Saudi Intellectual Support for the Egyptian People attracted 1,700 signatories.[17] It was intended to denounce the Saudi government's alleged intervention to remove the Egyptian Muslim Brotherhood from power. While the petition did not mention the Saudi government by name, it clearly condemned foreign intervention in Egyptian affairs.[18] After the Egyptian coup in July 2013 the Saudi government offered generous economic subsidies to the Egyptian military that ousted Morsi.

The petition started by citing Quranic verses encouraging believers to lend each other mutual support and cooperation. In this spirit, the petitioners insisted that the Saudi people respect the legitimate elected Egyptian government, denounce the shedding of anti-coup protestors' blood, reject foreign governments' intervention in Egypt, support the protestors in Rab'a Square where Muslim Brotherhood activists gathered, and condemn the suppression of freedom of speech in Egypt following the coup. After the circulation of this petition the Saudi authorities called in several Islamist activists, including the well-known sheikh Muhsin al-Awaji, who was believed to be one of the main organisers of the petition, and Muhammad al-Oraifi, known for his support for the ousted Egyptian government, for questioning. The latter was banned from travelling to Qatar to deliver sermons, and al-Awaji was released after several days in prison.

It is worth mentioning that all petitions invoked the Arab uprisings as the context that should encourage the leadership towards implementing serious political reform. With the exception of the Salafi petition and the petition concerned with Egyptian matters, the documents included a list of political and economic demands that had already been articulated in the first round of post-9/11 petitions. The petitions did not call for the overthrow of the regime, but they pointed to serious shortcomings, and disappointment with the government. None of them called for peaceful demonstrations like those that had already started in Arab capitals. In order to avoid direct confrontation with the regime, the authors and signatories made sure that opposition outside Saudi Arabia was not openly involved in the preparation of the documents. In private conversation with many reformists, it was clear that they refrained from taking a radical stance to avoid arrest and accusations of causing chaos and coordinating their efforts with 'outside agents'. Signatories insisted on previous reform agendas expressed throughout 2003–8, and pledged allegiance to the Saudi king. In fact, most of the activists were either well-known old veterans of reform such as Muhammad Said al-Tayib and Abdullah al-Hamid, or new *shabab*, young netizens, who played an important role in organising the dissemination of the petitions and publicity on Facebook and Twitter.

However, unlike in previous reformist petitions, there was a sense of frustration and disappointment with King Abdullah (d. 2015), who had so far failed to implement a single political demand from the previous petitions—above all, an elected national assembly. Reformers who belonged to a wide range of political ideologies, including Islamists, nationalists, leftists, and liberals, were extremely worried about the future given the age of the king and the opaqueness of the succession process. The timing of these petitions immediately after the Arab uprisings focused attention on an emerging reformist trend in Saudi Arabia that is still loyal to the government but demands an opening of the political system to include a wide social base. In particular, the petitioners were concerned that corruption, economic problems, and political marginalisation can be overcome if the leadership agrees to inaugurate a new era and transform the absolute monarchy into a constitutional one along the lines of those in Morocco and Jordan. They were dismayed by the Interior Ministry's repressive strategies, abuse of human rights, and its extended control over the judiciary. A decade of repression under the pretext of the War on Terror left many Saudis lingering in prisons without the prospect of fair and open trials. While the regime considered those in prison as terrorists or sympathisers of radical ideology, many reformers thought that only fair trials could resolve their cases. Many of the reformers themselves had experienced prison. Appointed judges simply passed long sentences on many prisoners whose crimes were ill-defined. The cases of those prisoners became central to the mobilisation that coincided with the Arab uprisings.

The Establishment of the Umma Party

The Arab uprisings encouraged a group of politicised Salafis to announce the establishment of the Umma Party in February 2011.[19] Although political parties are banned in Saudi Arabia and abhorred by official Salafis, who describe them as *fitna* (discord) leading to chaos, nine activists sent a letter to the king on 9 February 2011 announcing the formation of this new party. The founders included professors in Islamic studies, businessmen, lawyers, and human rights activists. Amongst them were Ahmad al-Ghamdi, Saud al-Dughaythir, Abd al-Karim al-Khodr, Abd al-Aziz al-Wuhaibi, and Muhammad al-Mufrih. After the arrest of all founding members following the announcement,[20] al-Mufrih, who was outside Saudi Arabia at the time, became the spokesman of the group. He began to popularise the party's programme on YouTube and issue statements regarding the arrest of the co-founders.

The party's foundation statement (*nitham asasi*) coincided with the events in the Arab world, although its founders must have been working on this document prior to the uprisings. They described the party's main programme as to establish government according to the Quran and Sunna (tradition of the Prophet), elect the legitimate ruler, and establish the oath of allegiance (*baya*) on the basis of consent. They also called for an independent judiciary, the separation of powers, respect for human rights, and propagation of Islam worldwide. The party considered the sharia as the only source for legislation, the Muslim community as the source of government, and the unity of Muslims as an Islamic duty. The party described itself as working towards strengthening the rights of citizens, women, workers, children, and the disabled in society.[21] The preservation of Islamic heritage and the promotion of research and scientific knowledge are also mentioned as part of its foundation statement.

Other demands focused on establishing social equality, and creating job opportunities and a strong economy able to absorb the impoverished youth. While these demands were embedded in religious language and justified by reference to Quranic verses and the Hadith tradition, they also invoked an engagement with the wider global discourse on human rights, entitlement, and consultation in politics.

The foundation statement remained grounded in Islamic principles with a view to establishing *al-hukum al-rashid* (righteous government) in Saudi

PETITIONS AND PROTEST ON THE EVE OF THE ARAB UPRISINGS

Arabia. The party used the slogan of establishing the Islamic caliphate as one of its main long-term objectives.[22] In statements about Saudi Arabia the party used the term *hukuma* (government), but in its outreach to the wider Islamic world it invoked the caliphate. It seems that the Saudi Umma Party was linked to the Kuwaiti mother organisation, founded by Hakim al-Mutairi.[23] Another branch of this organisation emerged in the United Arab Emirates at the same time. Ideologically, the Saudi Umma Party endorsed al-Mutairi's political theology, which represented reinterpretations of Islam and Salafi sources with a view to promoting political change suitable for contemporary Muslim societies. The Umma Party was an attempt to politicise the Salafi tradition and push towards peaceful mobilisation that avoids being labelled as a rebellion against rulers. The theme of the establishment of the caliphate to unite Muslims makes the party a Salafi version of Hizb al-Tahrir, despite many ideological differences.[24] News of the Saudi Umma Party and its programme were advertised on the web pages of "Muatamar al-Omah" (the Umma Conference), thus linking this Saudi party to the wider global network of similar organisations.[25]

While most founding members were put in prison, between 2011 and 2013 al-Mufrih, the party spokesman, regularly commented on current events, denouncing the Saudi regime for arresting its founders and other activists. Outside media claimed that the party was seeking 'democratic change in Saudi Arabia'. This prompted al-Mufrih to issue a statement clarifying his party's position on Islamic government and democracy. He stated that the party sought government based upon the example of the righteous caliphs and that the principles of such a government are freedom, consultation, justice, and the right of the people to choose their rulers. Such principles are part of the Islamic system and there was no need for Western democratic theory.[26]

In February 2011 the party congratulated the Egyptian people after they ousted President Mubarak, urging them to seek 'freedom, justice, and equality', and called upon Saudis to support the Libyan uprising. It criticised Saudi Arabia for hosting the exiled Tunisian president, Zine al-Abdine Bin Ali, and for supporting the Yemeni president, Ali Abdullah Salih. In 2013 the party condemned Saudi support for the Egyptian coup against President Muhammad Morsi. The party's position on Saudi interventions in the uprisings echoes that of other Islamists in Saudi Arabia, especially the petition mentioned above.

This unexpected, short-lived experience of party politics must have been encouraged by the Arab uprisings. Many activists in Saudi Arabia expected the domino effect to reach their country. The petitions and the establishment of the Umma Party must have been a pre-emptive step to fix the future of change and the multiple aspirations of the various sections of society. The demands were varied, and ranged from calls for constitutional monarchy to returning to the model of the righteous caliphs. Some activists did not shun 'alien' political concepts or systems of government, for example constitutionalism, democracy, and separation of powers, while others preferred to remain faithful to the Islamic tradition and its familiar political concepts such as consultation, the oath of allegiance, and justice. There was only one common ground that all activists shared: the call for political reform. While initiatives seeking such reform were gathering momentum, especially in the virtual world, real sporadic protest was beginning to reach Saudi Arabia.

Sporadic Protest: Saudi Arabia's Digital 'Day of Rage'

Surveying the Saudi virtual protest world throughout January and February 2011, it was noticeable that cyber warfare between opposition groups, young netizen activists, and non-ideological young men and women, on the one hand, and regime security cybernauts, on the other, was raging on the internet. Digital groups such as the National Coalition and the Free Youth Movement suddenly emerged on Facebook and Twitter without prior warning or real and documented organisational presence on the ground. Their specially designed web pages disappeared after censorship, only to reappear at different links with instructions about proxies to surpass Saudi censorship of the internet. Many web pages gathered thousands of supporters, but it was difficult to claim that they were all created by Saudis.

The virtual voices included a mix of Islamist, liberals, and others whose supporting comments cannot easily be classified. No doubt there were also non-Saudis contributing to the virtual Saudi opposition. Some youth had clear political vision about what the outcome of protest should be, but others were simply frustrated at their limited economic opportunities. There was an obvious generational conflict between young activists and those whom they perceived to be tribal, religious, and royal elders. They all directed their anger at either specific members of the royal family or their technocrats and bureaucrats, who are seen as corrupt and morally bankrupt. Young women in particular expressed frustration over their marginalisation. The online digital protest was a prelude to calls for mass demonstrations.

Days after the resignation of Egypt's Hosni Mubarak on 12 February 2011, Saudi digital activists announced the 'Day of Rage', dubbed *thawrat hunayn*

PETITIONS AND PROTEST ON THE EVE OF THE ARAB UPRISINGS

(the Hunayn revolution), invoking a symbolic battle between belief and blasphemy at the time of the Prophet Muhammad. The new generation of Saudi netizens designated 11 March as the day for their mobilisation, despite the knowledge that demonstrations are forbidden in the country. In the past, activists who announced an intention to demonstrate were quickly arrested.[27] While the Saudi calls for demonstrations were gathering momentum in the virtual world,[28] a different situation was unfolding on the ground in nearby Bahrain, which had an important impact on the Saudi domestic scene, especially in the Shia Eastern Province.

In February 2011 digital calls for demonstrations attracted a heterogeneous group of Saudi activists. The Shia of the Eastern Province and their activists in the country and abroad called for protest to free their prisoners and demand equality with the Sunni majority. One of their religious scholars, Sheikh Nimr al-Nimr, who in 2010 had called for the secession of the oil-rich Shia region from Saudi Arabia as a last resort, played a leading role in mobilising Shia protestors.[29]

On 14 February thousands of Bahrainis across the King Fahd causeway linking this small island with Saudi Arabia marched to Manama's city centre and took over Pearl Roundabout. Of course Bahrainis had been demonstrating in their marginalised small villages for decades. But with the euphoria of the Arab Spring becoming difficult to contain by the rulers of the region, Bahraini demonstrators felt empowered to take over an important part of Manama's road network and disrupt access to its financial and banking sectors.

After Bahraini security forces killed six protestors at Pearl Roundabout on 17 February there was more determination to continue with the protest.[30] The Al-Khalifa rulers of Bahrain felt helpless, so they called for help from the Gulf Cooperation Council (GCC) and in particular Saudi Arabia, equally nervous about the impact of the Arab uprisings. Meetings between several Gulf foreign ministers and GCC officials quickly resulted in sending mainly Saudi troops, supported by an insignificant but symbolically important United Arab Emirates, Qatari and Kuwaiti forces, to rescue the Al-Khalifa from one of their worst ever confrontations with opposition forces. Desert Shield, a military GCC force, was to be tested for the first time—not to defend the six founding member states against external threat, but to rescue the ruling family of one of these states. Kuwait, Oman, and Qatar refrained from sending troops but voiced their support for Manama. Al-Jazeera television depicted the pro-democracy movement in Bahrain as a sectarian Shia uprising and refrained from reporting on it during the weeks that followed, thus lending media support to the threatened Al-Khalifa rulers. Kuwait was hesitant, as its loyal Shia population needed to be appeased at critical times when relations with Iran were tense. Qatar was busy micromanaging a Libyan transitional council and brokering the transfer of Libyan oil on Qatari ships. Within weeks the GCC states were busy concocting an acceptable solution to another revolution, one more deadly and significant for the security of the whole of the Arabian Peninsula, namely that against an old Saudi ally, the Yemeni president, Ali Abdullah Salih.

On 14 March Saudi troops crossed the Saudi–Bahrain causeway. Their fingers appeared with victory signs from holes on top of their tanks. It was difficult to assess over whom the victory was achieved—the peaceful Bahraini protestors, Iran, or both. Red four-wheel-drive vehicles carrying intelligence and security personnel followed to protect the Bahraini rulers and enforce their control over the protestors.[31] A day later the protestors were chased out of Pearl Roundabout at gunpoint. Within a week bulldozers had flattened the roundabout.

Saudi Arabia emerged triumphant. In a self-congratulatory mood, the official Saudi press articulated how the regime wanted the episode to be understood and remembered: the defenders of the world of Sunni Islam had saved the whole of the Gulf from an Iranian Shia takeover. Having mobilised the population around a well-managed and orchestrated campaign of Iranophobia, the Saudi regime proved not only to its subjects but also to watching Western governments that it would be tough on future protest. The regime wanted all to believe that the majority of Saudis are happy and that any protest demanding political reform is an Iranian–Shia conspiracy to undermine the Sunni heartland of Islam. More importantly, it wanted its Sunni subjects to applaud its determination to expel Iranian and Shia influence from the Arabian Peninsula. A strong message was sent to American president Barack Obama, who would from now on think twice before issuing slogans in support of democracy and human rights, especially in the Arabian Peninsula. Such slogans did not go down well with an ally like Saudi Arabia. The regime temporarily halted the spread of revolutionary sentiments across the GCC states and crushed the Bahraini pro-democracy movement. The consequences of suppressing the Bahraini uprising gave way to serious confrontations between the Saudi Shia and the security forces across the bridge in Saudi Arabia itself.

PETITIONS AND PROTEST ON THE EVE OF THE ARAB UPRISINGS

From Virtual to Real Protest

With the wind of the Arab uprisings reaching the Arabian Peninsula, mainly in Oman and Yemen, and the Bahraini pro-democracy movement still keeping the cause alive, Saudi Arabia came face to face with its own Shia demonstrators in the oil-rich Eastern Province. From February 2011 Saudi Shia demonstrators staged peaceful real protests in Qatif, Awamiyya, Sayhat, and other towns and villages. Their first demand was the release of political prisoners, mainly those detained in 1996 after the Khobar bombing.

Reporting on the Shia protest was initially scarce, as the government limited media access to the areas where demonstrations were taking place. Those journalists who were allowed into the Eastern Province went there with heavy government escort.[32] Security forces quickly moved to suppress the demonstrators; extensive arrests followed. Religious scholars Tawfiq al-Amer and Nimr al-Nimr, who had called for the secession of the Eastern Province from Saudi rule and later supported demands for constitutional monarchy, were arrested, together with several young activists. Limited reports from foreign journalists quickly emerged, revealing the scale of the security measures, while Shia social media activists flooded the internet with images and video clips of the demonstrators. Later images of dead or wounded demonstrators became more horrific, reflecting the heavy-handed repression of the regime. In an attempt to calm the situation, Eastern Province Shia notables rushed to Riyadh to express their allegiance to the king and demand the release of their political prisoners. Some prisoners were released, but newer arrests were held in prisons.[33] The Shia, especially in Qatif and Awamiyya, continued to demonstrate until 2014. By 2014 twenty-one Shia activists had already been killed by the Saudi security forces, which had also lost a number of agents during the confrontations. The government issued lists of wanted activists and continued to raid the Shia areas in search of them. The confrontation often led to the shooting of the wanted activists, and some of them began to use petrol bombs and resist arrest. The funerals of those killed often sparked further rounds of demonstrations.

At night in the Shia city of Awamiyya heavily veiled women started what is called the Zaynabiyya processions, carrying candles in memory of martyrs and prisoners. The name derives from that of the Prophet's granddaughter, Zaynab, whose brother Hussein is a symbol of Shia martyrdom. They supported their Bahraini Shia co-religionists, demanded the end of what they called Saudi occupation of Bahrain, and remembered young men who had disappeared in Saudi prisons almost sixteen years before. The government imposed a siege on the Shia city of Qatif and issued the names of activists who were on wanted lists. It arrested many young activists and killed several others in raids on their homes. The Shia protest movement failed to attract sympathy from mainstream society; by 2014 suspicion of the Shia had already become well entrenched among mainstream Saudi society. This began to change slightly in late 2014 when a Shia prayer centre was attacked by radical Jihadis, leading to the death of more than seven worshippers. In general the Awamiyya and Qatif demonstrations remained part of a local uprising, confined to Shia areas and without the prospect of cross-sectarian solidarity developing in other regions in Saudi Arabia.

In Riyadh, Muhammad al-Wadani, a young netizen, posted a YouTube video clip in which he read a statement calling for democracy, human rights, and employment. Echoing the Egyptian slogan, he called, 'The people want the downfall of the regime.' On 7 March 2011, while Shia demonstrations were just beginning in the Eastern Province, he emerged from al-Rajhi Mosque in central Riyadh with a group of followers, with the intention of staging a peaceful protest. Young and smiling, al-Wadani carried his black rucksack comfortably over his immaculate long white shirt, freeing his arms to hold a sign announcing a peaceful demonstration. He was soon overwhelmed by plain-clothes security officers, who dragged him away from the crowd into their car and drove him to an unknown destination. It later turned out that he had been arrested and put in prison. Like some Shia notables, his Dawasir tribal elders rushed to Riyadh to renew their allegiance to the leadership. They immediately issued a statement disowning their irresponsible son who they claimed had fallen prey to outside propaganda and agitation. Defying the ageing Saudi leadership amounts to defying parental authority and God; the consequences are banishment, and withdrawal of family support, protection, and financial help.

On the day of the planned 'Day of Rage', helicopters flew low in the skies over Riyadh, mirroring the intimidation of protesters in Cairo's Tahrir Square and Pearl Roundabout in Bahrain, while security forces spread throughout every corner and street in the main cities. A de facto curfew loomed over Riyadh and Jeddah. At noon Saudis prayed as usual, then they quickly got into their cars to drive home for lunch. One lone demonstrator, Khalid al-Juhni, dared to defy the unofficial curfew. He turned up in front of BBC journalist Sue Lloyd-Roberts and her camera crew to tell them that he had had enough of living in a large prison. He wanted to live in dignity, he told the journalist. He anticipated that he would be followed by the watching security forces and

PETITIONS AND PROTEST ON THE EVE OF THE ARAB UPRISINGS

eventually arrested. 'The royal family don't own us. ... I need freedom, all the country is a jail. ... We need a parliament. ... I demonstrate because it is worth it, I am doing this for my four children,' he said. He gave the journalist his mobile number after he asked her to accompany him to his car. Al-Juhni was later arrested and put in prison.[34] He disappeared, but his friends and those of al-Wadani have kept their memory alive on Facebook.

Those lonely demonstrators were followed by real small-scale protest after 2011. After the abortive 11 March 'Day of Rage', daily protests in Riyadh, Jeddah, and Buraiydah became regular events. Small groups focused on specific issues, and stood in front of various government buildings with cardboard signs on which they posted their demands. As in the Shia areas, the release of political prisoners dominated their slogans. Relatives of prisoners marched to the Interior Ministry asking for the release of their fathers and sons, many of whom had been held for over ten years without trial. In February 2011 more than forty women marched to the Interior Ministry in Riyadh asking for fair trials for their husbands and relatives. Relatives of Islamists in prison chanted 'Fuku al-ani' ('Release those subjected to injustice). Veiled women raised signs asking 'Where are our children?' The protest of prisoners' relatives gathered momentum in Buraiydah, in Qasim. On one occasion a group of women with children stood in the street and burned a portrait of Prince Muhammad ibn Nayif, who became interior minister in 2012. Several of the women were arrested. The protest moved to other Saudi cities, where small crowds assembled to call for fair trials and the release of prisoners. 'Freedom sit-ins' became regular events attracting a small number of relatives of prisoners and supporters in Jawf, Hail, and Riyadh. In June 2012 protesters chose a new location, a shopping mall in Riyadh, to stage a protest in support of political prisoners. The protesters posted video clips of these small-scale demonstrations on YouTube and circulated the news on Twitter under names such as I'tiqal (detention). Security forces monitored the demonstrations, and eventually surrounded them and arrested outspoken organisers, including women.

Demonstrations demanding economic rights were also observed in Saudi Arabia during the Arab uprisings. Unemployed female teachers asked to be appointed in fixed and secure jobs. Female students assembled in university halls protesting against unfair marking of their examinations and called for the 'downfall of the principal', thus echoing Egyptian slogans calling for the downfall of Mubarak.[35] While most of the protestors voiced their anger at low-level government civil servants, there were signs that such regular protests were now common practice among employees in the private sector. The Saudi press dubbed the wave of small-scale demonstrations 'protest fever'.[36] Unemployed male graduates regularly assembled around the Ministries of Labour and Education asking for jobs. They were told to go away, but returned with the same demands. Officials were videoed telling protestors to come as single individuals and demand jobs rather than as part of a big crowd, which they described as disrupting access to ministries and causing 'chaos'. Such minor protests were astonishing in a country where trade unions, civil society, and other modes of organisation and mobilisation are banned. They were certainly encouraged by the sight of thousands of protestors all over the Arab world that had gathered momentum since 2011.

Saudi women emerged as capable of getting together in small numbers to pursue their gender-specific interests and rights, evidence for which is their increased willingness to protest and confront government employees in various ministries and businesses. Yet their mobilisation was initially grounded in the digital sphere, where they have been able to get both local and global support. Early in 2011 a group of Saudi women launched a Facebook page 'Teach me How to Drive so I can Protect Myself' and fixed 17 June as the day of a driving demonstration. Several activists became known as prominent among the campaigners, including Wajiha al-Howaider and Manal al-Sharif. The latter was arrested on 30 May 2011 after posting a video showing herself driving in the Eastern Province. On the designated driving day, only thirty or forty women had the courage to defy the ban on driving. The police arrested some but not all of them, and one was sentenced to ten lashes for driving in Jeddah. The king soon overturned the verdict.

Female activists found that few women were willing to move from digital mobilisation to the real world. While in 1990 Saudi women violated the ban on driving and drove their cars to a Riyadh shopping centre, after which they were all arrested, in 2011 the situation was different. Several digital electronic campaigns in support of lifting the ban on driving were announced between 2011 and 2014, with sporadic reported cases of women driving their cars in various cities. Some were arrested, while others escaped the attention of the police. Unlike in 1990, they filmed their driving episodes and posted video clips on YouTube, hoping to normalise the practice and encourage other women to follow suit. Although still unsuccessful in leading to the lifting of the ban on driving, these successive electronic campaigns raised awareness of the problems women face under the driving ban.[37] The minor protests moved the gender-equality debate beyond driving to fundamental rights such as employment, voting in municipal elections, and lifting the guardianship rules in which women have to rely on men to represent them.

PETITIONS AND PROTEST ON THE EVE OF THE ARAB UPRISINGS

One interesting strategy that women campaigners used to avoid arrest was to raise slogans in support of the king while demanding that bureaucrats respect his promised reforms on empowering women. Anger was therefore channelled towards low-level civil servants without challenging the status quo or addressing big issues that cannot be resolved without royal intervention. Security forces usually turned up at the sites of protest, surrounded protestors, and forced them to disperse.

Faced with successive women's electronic campaigns and sporadic driving incidents, in 2013 117 religious scholars issued a statement against permitting women to drive. Others gave interviews to the press citing 'damage to women's ovaries',[38] 'loss of shyness, uncovering of the face, and increasing the time of women outside the house' as reasons for upholding the driving ban. The king appointed thirty women to the Consultative Council in January 2013 and promised that they would participate in future municipal elections as voters, which angered a group of religious scholars, who gathered in Riyadh with the intention of meeting the king to express their opposition to the presence of women on the council.

The sporadic protests that gripped Saudi Arabia after the Arab uprisings spread to immigrant workers as the government tried to regulate their status and expel those who stay and work without permits. In 2013 the government announced that it would remove anyone working illegally in an attempt to increase employment opportunities for Saudis. Illegal immigrants were given until November 2013 to leave the country. In clashes in Riyadh and Jeddah, several Ethiopians were reportedly killed in the crackdown. Ethiopians staged mass protests in poor Riyadh and Jeddah neighbourhoods on a scale that no Saudi city had ever seen. Many immigrant protesters were rounded up and placed in detention camps while awaiting deportation. While indigenous protests by Shia, relatives of political prisoners, and women divided Saudi society between those who condemned them and those who supported them, the immigrants' protest was a truly unifying event. Many Saudis put aside their own frustration and anger at lack of jobs, equality, and fair trials to support the government and condemn Ethiopian and Yemeni illegal immigrants as 'thugs' and 'criminals'. The official press defended the deportations and promoted quasi-nationalist sentiments against foreign immigrants at a time when rising discontent among Saudis was obvious, as described above.

After the Arab uprisings the highest religious authority, Mufti Abd al-Aziz al-Sheikh, increased the frequency of his tours around the country, giving lectures to students at colleges and universities highlighting the sinful nature of peaceful protest and reiterating the obligation to obey the rulers.[39] Any protest, even a short article posted on the internet that questioned royal decisions and policies, was branded as causing dissent and chaos.

While the Saudi regime suppressed the Day of Rage on 11 March, it seems that local protest of the kind described above was hard to contain as small groups came together, assisted by the speed of communication in the virtual world, to suddenly appear in the streets and outside government buildings. As long as the protests did not question the policies of senior members of the royal family they were tolerated, perhaps as a cathartic way of venting anger and frustration. The heavy policing led many young Saudis to vent their anger and frustration in the virtual world. Both security agents and young netizens were active in the virtual world, but unsurprisingly the former seemed to have the upper hand. The propaganda potential of the regime was by far the strongest in a battle between anonymous activist netizens and organised and well-trained security agents.[40] While real coercive force remained extremely important, the regime boosted its capabilities with virtual means of propaganda, spreading counter-arguments and rumours against calls for potential protests. The official media contributed by exaggerating calamities, chaos, crime, and real deadly violence in areas where the Arab uprisings were gathering momentum. News of bloodshed in the countries of the Arab uprisings served to demonstrate to Saudis the heavy price of political change, resulting in chaos, dissent, and rebellion.

Containing Protest

On 18 March 2011, a week after the aborted Day of Rage and in order to prevent the spread of Egyptian-style protest, King Abdullah announced a package of twenty economic benefits to the population, at an estimated cost of $93bn.[41] While many Saudis had expected serious political announcements, there was only economic largesse offered as gifts from the leadership to a population intimidated into submission. A package of economic, social, health, and educational benefits was meant to absorb immediate frustration at the lack of housing, jobs, and health facilities and other mediocre welfare services. Immediate handouts involved extra two-month salaries to public-sector employees, promotions for all military personnel, unemployment benefits for a limited period, a minimum monthly wage of approximately $300, and the promise of thousands of new hospital beds. Future benefits included an undertaking to construct 500,000 housing units and create 60,000 new

PETITIONS AND PROTEST ON THE EVE OF THE ARAB UPRISINGS

jobs in the security and military services. These economic benefits were considered important to absorb the potential for unrest, especially during the Arab uprisings.

The king did not forget the loyal religious establishment, which ensured through *fatwa*s banning demonstrations that no one would dare take part in the future. The king's benefits package allowed for the expansion of the religious bureaucracy known as the 'the people of knowledge'. The *ulama* were rewarded with new centres from which to spread the Wahhabi message, Hanbali jurisprudence, Quran memorisation, and missionary work inside and outside Saudi Arabia. The religious police, who play an important role in monitoring public morality, were rewarded with more recruitment and expansion. Employment in the religious bureaucracy would definitely absorb religious graduates. Rewarding the religious bureaucracy was an important gesture of gratitude for the support of the religious establishment during the Arab uprisings and the wave of minor protest that swept Saudi Arabia from the early months of 2011.

The regime relied on the religious establishment to help protect it against protest. It mobilised its main religious figures to support it at the critical moment of the Arab uprisings in two different but complementary ways. First, Wahhabi religious scholars used mosque minarets to warn against the wrath of God, inflicted on the pious believers if they participated in peaceful demonstrations. On 7 March the Council of Higher Ulama, the highest official religious authority, issued a *fatwa* (religious opinion) against demonstrations.[42] The old opinions of respected *ulama* such as Abdul Aziz Ibn Baz and Muhammad al-Uthaymin regarding obedience to rulers were resurrected to give impetus to recent religious opinions against demonstrations. All local newspapers favourably reported on the current *ulama*'s *fatwa* against peaceful protest. Thousands of hard copies were distributed in mosques and neighbourhoods, in addition to dissemination on the internet. Internet discussion boards infiltrated by intelligence cybernauts posted the *fatwa* on many web pages with several supporting statements.

Second, Saudi official religious scholars warned of an Iranian–Safavid–Shia conspiracy directed by Saudi exiles in London and Washington and the Shia in the Eastern Province to cause *fitna* (chaos) and divide Saudi Arabia. They relied on a repertoire of Wahhabi opinions against the Shia, historically depicted as heretics and more recently as a fifth column acting as agents of Iran. They reminded Saudis of the need for *ijma* (consensus) around the pious rulers of the country and warned that fragmentation, tribal warfare, civil war, and bloodbaths could be expected if people responded to calls for demonstrations. Wahhabi scholars who are not directly associated with the official Council of Higher Ulama, and known as the neo-Wahhabis, for example Muhammad al-Oraifi and Yusif al-Ahmad, had more freedom to denounce the Shia in local mosques, lectures, and sermons, all recorded and publicised on YouTube. Old veteran Sheikh Nasir al-Omar joined the battle against the Shia, thus giving an added force to the opinions of the young generation of *ulama*. While many of those scholars are critical of the regime regarding its gender policies, they support it against the Shia, seen as alien, heretic, and loyal to Iran. The Saudi regime mobilised its digital intelligence services to spread rumours that the Iranians were behind the demonstrations and that if the Sunnis wanted supremacy and victory they should not respond to suspicious outside calls for protest. The Saudi religious strategy consisted of enlisting divine wrath and invoking sectarian difference and hatred to thwart the prospect of peaceful protest demanding real political reforms.[43] So-called independent religious scholars served the regime's interest as much as the official religious bureaucracy. While official *ulama* played the expected role, other preachers found an opportunity to denounce the Shia and boost their popularity among their followers. Facebook, YouTube, and Twitter became the new digital battlefield against the 'heretical' Shia and their alleged Iranian backers.

In summary, the Arab uprisings baffled the Saudi regime, but when protest reached the small island of Bahrain and its own oil-rich territory in March 2011, three classic regime strategies were deployed. First, the Saudi regime unsurprisingly relied on religious discourse that glorifies obedience to rulers and Wahhabi sectarian teachings against the Shia to suppress protest. This obedience to rulers is one of the concepts that many Saudi reformers tried to reinterpret, as the authors discussed in this book will demonstrate. Second, heavy deployment of security forces frightened the population ahead of the scheduled Day of Rage and acted as a deterrent against future mass protest, but did not eliminate the small-scale mobilisation described in this chapter. Repression led to reluctance to respond to calls for protest and lowered the cost of controlling the population. And third, economic benefits tailored to reward the population, especially the military and security forces and the religious establishment, played an important role in absorbing a possible confrontation between the regime and potential protestors demanding employment opportunities.

The Arab uprisings had an important impact on Saudi Arabia. They momentarily demonstrated the power of the people in resisting oppression and offered Saudis free lessons in mass mobilisation that overcomes class, sectarian, and ideological divides. While these categories persisted in the construction of Saudi political identities, the petitions that reformers and activists circulated proved that many Saudis agreed on a set of political demands The post-Arab uprising petitions articulated reform in the language of constitutionalism, separation of powers, independent judiciary, freedom of expression, human rights, and political entitlement. The only exception to these demands was the Salafi petition that focused on calling the government to return to the principles of the pact with the Wahhabi tradition and to the spirit of the first Saudi–Wahhabi polity of the eighteenth century.

The reformers' petitions proved that while ideological divisions may continue to persist, both non-Islamists and non-Salafi reformist Islamists were concerned with fundamental questions about the future of Saudi Arabia as an absolute monarchy. The push towards an elected national assembly by both reformist Islamists and non-Islamists called into question the widely accepted view that the two camps never agree on a common set of demands. Reformers and the young petitioners were drawn from both the Sunni majority and the Shia minority. Moreover, reformist Islamists among the reformers supported these calls and overcame some of their reservations about human rights, democracy, and the constitution. They agreed on the urgency of political reform that would increase people's freedom and participation in government through elected institutions and a well-defined constitution. In contrast, the Salafi petition called for the regime to return to the original pact between the Al-Saud and the founder of the Wahhabi movement.

The failure of the sporadic protests to gather momentum in Saudi Arabia during the Arab uprisings points to the limitations of online activism. The government celebrated their failure, which it claimed demonstrated the loyalty of Saudis and their unwillingness to engage in mass protest at a time when the country was being targeted by outside rivals and their internal agents. Reformers interpreted this failure as a function of weak civil society and the fragmentation of a Saudi public that is increasingly dominated by sectarian, regional, and ideological divides. These divides may be too strong to overcome, but the language of urgent political reform was a unifying factor as signatories of petitions were drawn from a wide cross-section of Saudi society. Consequently, the impulse to strengthen civil society concerned with human and political rights became a priority for some reformers across the liberal–Islamist, regional, and sectarian divides. In the following chapter I trace the origins of this important development in a society that has not been accustomed to engaging with these rights in the framework of civil society activism.

2

CIVIL SOCIETY IN AN AUTHORITARIAN STATE

Before the Arab uprisings, a quiet revolution had in fact been taking place in Saudi Arabia since 2009. It manifested itself in serious calls for *al-mujtama al-madani* (civil society) among reformers and intellectuals. These calls sprang from the early reformist agenda and petitions, discussed in the last chapter.[1] The mutations of Saudi Islamism after 9/11 gave birth to the Saudi Association for Civil and Political Rights (ACPRA), known hereafter by its Arabic acronym HASM (Jamiyyat al-Huquq al-Siyasiyya wa al-Madaniyya).[2] HASM reinvented Islamism as civil society activism and adopted the cases of political prisoners, activists of all political persuasions, and immigrants, in addition to outlining a vision for political reform. Its political message was concerned with calls for political representation, elected government, accountability, and respect for citizens. HASM endorsed the call for the transformation of the absolute monarchy into a constitutional one. Its name reflected its dual concerns, namely civil and political rights.

HASM was an independent civil society, different from those established by the regime and the many independent online organisations that appeared immediately after 2001.[3] Unlike other non-governmental organisations in Saudi Arabia, especially charities and educational foundations, HASM has, unsurprisingly, no royal patron.[4] As such, the regime was from the beginning suspicious of its activities and mobilisation. Also, HASM was different from the other independent online organisations that appeared after 2001 and had no real presence on the ground. HASM differentiated itself from these initiatives because from the very beginning it was a collective effort organised jointly by well-known Islamists and non-Islamists who were ready to openly declare their association and involvement with the organisation.

Its founders engaged with the global discourse on human rights while anchoring this discourse in the Islamic tradition. HASM's commitment to human rights in Islam was not an obstacle to engaging with international human right charters, conventions, and organisations. Its founders encouraged dialogue and communication with both international human rights organisations and the media, thus constituting itself as a local initiative engaged with the concern of similar organisations.

The association's concern with political reform eventually attracted the attention of the regime, and in 2013 led to the imprisonment of most of its founding members.[5] As such, HASM may have been a short-lived experience (2009–13), but its language of civil rights and political reform permeated public discourse in unprecedented ways. The detailed trials of its founding members in Saudi courts infiltrated the public sphere and became the focus of debate and controversies that ensured the survival of the ideas for which those founders struggled, and eventually led to them serving long prison sentences. HASM moved the struggle for political reform and civil rights to the courts where its founders, their lawyers and supporters continued to appear over a long period of time. The details of the charges and the defence of the accused spread beyond the courts to a wide circle of followers who could only support it online in an authoritarian and repressive environment. This was a new development in Saudi Arabia facilitated, by the advent of social media that amplified the experience of HASM and its founders. While there is no way of finding out how many supporters HASM had, it is this amplification that is worth considering when discussing a nascent civil society in an authoritarian context such as that of Saudi Arabia.

From the very beginning HASM's political discourse was inevitably confrontational with the Saudi regime and official Salafi scholars and judges, despite the fact that all its statements pledged allegiance to the king. HASM considered the regime and its official scholars as obstacles to political reform and accomplices in repression and the abuse of human and civil rights. From 2009 it regularly petitioned the king to remove Prince Nayif from his position as interior minister and called for him to be put on trial for the systematic abuse of human rights, unlawful detentions, and torture in prisons. Moreover, its various communiqués denounced official Salafi Wahhabi scholars who cooperated with the regime to criminalise its activities and hamper its mobilisation. It rejected the official religious position criminalising demonstrations, strikes, and other forms of civil disobedience. It also criticised judges and the judiciary believed to be under the control of the Interior Ministry. In this respect, HASM fought two battles at the same time, one with the state institutions it held responsible for repression, and the other with the religious scholars who justified this repression in their *fatwa*s or sentences in court. The literature that HASM circulated tended to focus on political and religious repression as two sides of the same coin.

HASM was a hybrid initiative that was conceived as going beyond the Islamist–liberal divide. Its founding members included veteran Islamists such as Arabic professor Abdullah al-Hamid and judge Suleiman al-Rushoudi, along with human rights activists who were not associated with any Islamist trend such as Muhammad al-Qahtani, not to mention veteran activist Matruk al-Falih. By the time these founding members were facing trial, a hybrid circle of old and new reformers had already coalesced around this new association. As HASM began to publicise its communiqués on its web page and rely heavily on social media, the circle widened and began to include young supporters who defended it and circulated its messages. Young activists tried to attend the trials of its founding members and raise awareness of their cases, drawing on their skills in new media.

The trials between 2009 and 2013 became known as *muhakamat al-islahiyyin* (trials of reformers), *muhakamat duat al-mujtama al-madani* (trials of civil society activists), or *muhakamat duat al-dustur* (trials of constitutional activists). These names bestowed on the reformers a collective identity distinguished from other political trends or groups. These appellations distanced them from the Islamist label to situate their struggle in a civic culture rather than an Islamic one, despite the fact that their calls for civil society and a constitution were anchored in their interpretation of the Islamic tradition. The names given to the reformers undergoing trial framed them as callers for political reform in which civil society and the constitution were but two aspects of general political change.

A young journalist, Iman al-Qahtani, followed the trials, and distributed statements and photos of the court hearings. Al-Qahtani was unusual as she was certainly the only well-known woman journalist who tried to attend the court sessions and report on the proceedings. She was sought out by outside human rights organisations and global media for information about the details of the trials and the proceedings in the court. In 2013 she was reprimanded by the security forces and banned from giving interviews to the media.[6] She was eventually forced to discontinue her Twitter account, which had become a source of instant messaging for those who followed the details of HASM trials. After a long silence, al-Qahtani published an article in Saudi owned al-Hayat newspaper in which she praised the regime, thus casting doubt about her commitment to reporting on controversial issues with a minority accusing her of clandestinely working for the Saudi government.[7] The trials attracted the attention of international media and human rights organisations worldwide. With most HASM founders in prison in 2013, the association left behind a broad body of literature on political reform, human rights, and civil responsibilities. This literature is bound to remain in circulation with many new supporters propagating the message. More nuanced treatises on political and civil rights appeared in publications written by the founders and supporters of HASM, discussed later in this book.

HASM's hybridity also stemmed from the language it used to publicise its political messages and defend prisoners during their long trials. The organisation anchored its statements in two domains, one Islamic and one global. These statements relied both on Quranic and Hadith sources and on international human rights conventions and UN charters. As such, the organisation fused Islam with this global discourse and demonstrated parallel concerns with the same issues. The hybrid language was meant to appeal to a wider public, both Islamist and non-Islamist. It may also have been a deliberate strategy to emphasise HASM's commitment to demonstrating the compatibility of Islam with modern notions of human rights. The organisation defended all prisoners and pushed for political reform which cannot be easily classified as belonging to the ideology of one group.

HASM took up the cases of imprisoned radical Islamists, accused by the government of being terrorists or sympathisers with radical Jihadi groups, as well as liberals such as Hamza Qashgari, whose tweets about the Prophet Muhammad were considered blasphemous,[8] and Mikhlif al-Shammari, a human rights activist known for his critical views on the domination of religious scholars and rejection of sectarian politics.[9] In its supporting statements HASM aimed to create a new consciousness that helps Saudis to see human rights as for all citizens rather than only for those with a particular ideological or political affinity. When a person is detained for alleged blasphemy or radicalism, Saudi society often finds itself divided over whether to support or criticise the case. Islamists protested at the incarceration of people thought to belong to their camp, while liberals did the same in support of people they counted as their own. Entrenched polarisation between Islamists and liberals, Sunni and Shia, and men and women in Saudi society increased divisions to the detriment of common platforms for achieving political reform or human rights for all. Islamists went as far as calling upon the regime to imprison those considered as disrespectful of religion, ban books deemed immoral, or force the resignation of officials believed to have transgressed and deviated from Islam. On the other side, liberals called upon the regime to punish Islamists or religious scholars for simply registering their objections in the media to certain government policies such as the subject of mixing between the sexes or lifting the ban on women driving. HASM tried to bridge these divides under the common language of rights, from open trials to freedom of expression within the limits of the law.

This polarisation was exemplified in the case of Hamza Qashgari, a young journalist who was detained after tweeting allegedly offensive tweets about the prophet, with Islamists demanding his arrest and rejoicing over his long prison sentence and liberals condemning his conviction and later imprisonment. HASM rose above these entrenched divisions, and issued statements that blurred the boundaries and supported controversial cases. This was a deliberate strategy that led to some criticism. Hardline Salafi Islamists accused HASM of being on the side of liberals, while liberals waited to see whether it took up the cases of those counted as members of their own camp. The hybridity of HASM may have confused many audiences, but it was in many ways responsible for the popularity the organisation achieved over a short period of time and in the context of an authoritarian state. Saudi society had become accustomed to the ideological polarisation that the authoritarian regime promoted and even encouraged. An association that aimed to bridge the divide was bound to be viewed with ambiguity and suspicion.

Regionally, HASM demonstrated its commitment to the success of the Arab uprisings. It praised the North African revolutions and interpreted them as necessary upheavals to reverse a long history of injustice and repression. HASM saw in these uprisings how peaceful mass mobilisation can be a successful strategy to topple oppressive regimes. While HASM shared this assessment with many other Saudis, its position on the Bahraini uprising went against the common opinion in Saudi Arabia, which considered it a Shia conspiracy against Sunni Muslims. Moreover, HASM's condemnation of the shootings in the Eastern Province and the arrest of many peaceful activists after 2011 confirmed it as an association that went beyond the sectarian divide and was willing to risk undermining its popularity when it took on board the cases of the Shia activists.

Foundation statement

Since 2001 Saudi reformers had been calling upon the king to introduce a civil society charter taking into account new initiatives concerned with human rights. On 13 December 2007 the Consultative Council approved a draft civil society law. The law—the first of its kind in Saudi Arabia—calls for the establishment of a 'National Authority for Civil Society Organizations' to supervise the activities of NGOs. The draft law has been under discussion in cabinet since 2007.[10]

The government failed to respond after several drafts of the proposed charter were discussed in the Consultative Council. In October 2009, and after waiting for several years for a royal decree, fifteen activists from Riyadh, Qasim, and Jawf announced the establishment of HASM.[11] Eleven members signed the foundation statement, while the remaining four put their names as co-founders without their signatures (this was because they were on trial and did not want to complicate matters further with their direct involvement in HASM). The association immediately announced its presence on a specially designed web page that listed the names of the founders. They were aware of the ban on unlicensed civil society, but went ahead with their project and issued their founding statement. They presented their project as a response to continuous transgressions against human and political rights and an attempt to push for political reform; most of its details had already been embodied in the many petitions they and others had circulated over several years. HASM insisted that it was working towards building a culture of Islamic human, civil, political, and economic rights. Its aim was to be an independent forum that supports the rights of prisoners to fair open trials, exposes torture in prisons, and engages in educating people in the language of rights. One of its main aspirations was to counter the abuse of these rights under the umbrella of sharia and respect for Islam's teachings. The foundation statement insisted that specific abuses can only be dealt with as part of general political reform and cannot be attributed to applying sharia or respecting Islamic tradition. Therefore, most of its statements insisted on distancing the sharia from what it believed to be abuses committed in its name.

The foundation statement listed several reasons for the urgency of this initiative. They included increased oppression since the Gulf War in 1990–1 and the later abuses that followed the War on Terror in 2001. HASM cited the judges' continuous resort to sharia to pass unjustified sentences on activists. It wanted to expose the religious umbrella under which serious repression was taking place. Furthermore, it promised to expose the judiciary's position, which helped the government to perpetuate serious abuses of human rights in prisons and under the auspices of the intelligence and security services. It insisted on open trials for prisoners to replace the secret ones that had led to so many people languishing in prison for years. Its statement criticised global human rights organisations that focus only on individual cases but overlook the collective punishment that the regime applies to all Saudis, and insisted that only serious political reform would deliver positive outcomes. HASM argued that the prevalence of terrorism in Saudi society between 2003 and 2008 was a function of eradicating the concept of *jihad silmi*, peaceful jihad, which needs to become central to the culture of human rights and mobilisation.

The lengthy foundation statement promised to teach citizens their rights as part of spreading a culture of entitlement. Without widespread acceptance of this culture, it was difficult to mobilise the population to seek justice and stop transgressions. The statement linked the problem of terrorism to the continuous transgressions that pushed people towards violence as they were deprived of other peaceful means to mobilise themselves. It summed up its strategy as an association that seeks to pursue *jihad silmi*, to put pressure on the government and allow citizens to participate in the culture of rights. This peaceful struggle became central to HASM's mobilisation, with several of its founders writing pamphlets and delivering lectures on the subject.

HASM identified a number of its strategies and aims in promoting this culture of rights. It promised research papers, books, pamphlets, lectures, and documentation, all of which were posted on its web page from its foundation in 2009. It also introduced videos of lectures and workshops that it organised on specific topics from constitutional monarchy to the impact of the Arab uprisings on Saudi Arabia and the Gulf in general. These lectures were posted on YouTube and circulated on Twitter.

In its foundation statement HASM promised to establish channels of communication with 'the political leadership and other social activists', thus demonstrating its commitment to peaceful mobilisation and its intention to remain loyal to the Saudi monarchy. It insisted on *tawasul* (reaching out) and keeping the channels of communication open with officials in power. All its statements reiterated loyalty to the king and respect for his intentions to reform the regime. This rhetoric may have protected HASM during the first months of its foundation, but pledging allegiance to the king proved limited as a pre-emptive mechanism to placate the regime. While the king pardoned some of the activists in 2005 who later became HASM founders, after 2009 it was evident that he could not intervene in what appeared to be a battle between HASM and the Interior Ministry. By 2013 the latter was successful in putting the main HASM founders in prison.

HASM held regular informal meetings with small audiences in the private homes of its founders, a function of being an unlicensed association denied a public space in which regular public meetings could be held. The meetings initially consisted of an invited speaker, often one of its academic or activist founders and supporters, and a small circle of sympathisers and guests. But after HASM posted its statements and the lectures' video clips on its web page, uploaded them on YouTube, and continuously tweeted links to its modest events, the circle began to widen with thousands of interested audiences being able to watch them and circulate them on Twitter.

HASM's programme was dependent on core actors who voluntarily worked on the project and dedicated their time to documenting abuses and issuing statements about each case that came to their attention. They served as publicists of cases that were later on taken up by international human rights organisations such as Amnesty International and Human Rights Watch, thus working as a gateway for these organisations that were denied full access to Saudi Arabia. The association sought wider publicity in order to draw attention to cases of abuses and transgressions. Its local actors cooperated with global media agencies in order to reach out beyond the local Saudi context with the hope of drawing attention to abuse and indirectly putting pressure on the Saudi government to act on the cases of prisoners and citizens. HASM's peaceful mobilisation was immediately criminalised, as the charges against its founders demonstrated.

Local Civil Society Actors

Any discussion of HASM must involve an exploration of the biographies of its main founders, who, together with other activists, signed its foundation statement. Abdullah al-Hamid was perhaps one of the main activists whose vision and discourse played an important role in the association coming into existence. I have examined al-Hamid's engagement with Islamism in the early 1990s and his role in the Islamist contestation that took place immediately after the Gulf War in 1990–1 elsewhere.[12] His recent involvement with HASM confirmed him in the position of human rights defender and political reformer.[13] He can be considered one of the main ideologues behind HASM and its later activism.

Al-Hamid graduated from the Arabic language department at Riyadh University in 1971. He subsequently completed a masters degree (1974), and gained a doctorate from the department of Arabic studies in al-Azhar University (Egypt) in the field of literary criticism (1978), after which he worked in several teaching posts. He was one of the six founding members of the Committee for the Defence of Legitimate Rights (CDLR) which was established in Riyadh on 3 May 1993, and was arrested on 15 June of the same year.[14] He was subsequently released and rearrested three times between 1993 and 1996.

Al-Hamid was arrested again in 2004 when he became known as one of the men behind the constitutional reform movement calling for the establishment of a constitutional monarchy. His trial formally began on 9 August[15] and continued through the year.[16] He was sentenced to seven years in May 2005,[17] and pardoned in August that year when Abdullah became king.[18]

In 2008 he was again arrested, along with his brother Isa al-Hamid. Abdullah was sentenced to six months for his support for the peaceful protest in Buraiydah held by prisoners' wives, having been charged with incitement to protest. The case was adopted by Amnesty International at the time.[19] He was released on 28 August 2008.[20] He was also one of seventy-seven activists who signed a letter sent to the king in 2009 complaining about secret trials and requesting reform. In 2012 he was one of several members of HASM who were put on trial, receiving wide media coverage. He was sentenced to eleven years in prison. He has written a number of books and articles on politics and human rights, which can be found on his website.[21] At the time of writing this book al-Hamid was still in prison serving his longest sentence.

Like that of many Islamist activists in the 1990s, al-Hamid's thought mutated over the years, and by the time he founded HASM it was clear that he had fused his early Islamism with the global language of civil and political rights. His writing skills and knowledge of Islam allowed him to reinterpret Islamic tradition and combine it with modern concepts, mainly civil society as a space to defend citizens against the excesses of power and authoritarian rule. Together with Matruk al-Falih he is known for theorising the idea of constitutional monarchy and providing an Islamic justification for it, which is in itself a controversial move in the Saudi Salafi context. He is also known for his elaboration of the meaning of peaceful struggle, *jihad silmi*. In his statements and books this began to correspond to modern methods of peaceful protest such as demonstrations, hunger strikes, and civil disobedience, all banned in Saudi Arabia. Al-Hamid is best described as an Islamic intellectual and advocate. His academic career and scholarship fused traditional Islamic studies with an ability to reinterpret both history and Islamic concepts away from the framework of traditional Salafi tradition.

In 2013, while al-Hamid was in prison, Saudi and Gulf activists launched a digital campaign to nominate him for the Nobel Peace Prize. They circulated his biography and called for electronic signatures in support of the nomination. Many professionals, academics, and activists joined this symbolic campaign, to highlight his contribution and commitment to reform in addition to drawing attention to his long prison sentence. The campaign also drew several Gulf civil society activists and intellectuals who registered their support for al-Hamid's nomination.

Abdullah al-Hamid worked closely with another veteran Islamist judge, Suleiman al-Rushoudi. Born in 1937, al-Rushoudi completed his master's thesis on the topic of 'Women in Islam' in 1971 from the Higher Institution for Judges. He worked as a judge and then in administration within the Ministry of Justice and in the Ministry of Agriculture before retiring from government work. In 1976 he became one of the first people to work as a lawyer in Saudi Arabia. In 1993 he was one of the founding members of the CDLR,[22] and was arrested in 1993 after leading protests in Buraiydah against the detaining of Sheikh Salman al-Awdah, discussed in the next chapter. He was also one of the signatories of the 2004 petition asking the regime for constitutional reforms.[23] In 2005 he played a prominent role in the campaign to free three jailed constitutional reformers (Matruk al-Falih, Abdullah al-Hamid, and Ali al-Damini).[24] He was known to have sent several reports to the UN regarding the incarceration and treatment of the country's political prisoners.[25] On 1 February 2007 he was arrested along with eight other lawyers and academics collectively known as the 'Reformer's Group' while they were holding a meeting in Jeddah to discuss the constitution of a committee for the defence of civil and political rights.[26] He was not brought to court until 2011, during which time HASM was formed (he was a founding member) and proceeded to adopt his case. He was released on bail on 23 June 2011,[27] and continued his work with HASM while at liberty, being elected president of the organisation for 2013. Along with several other activists he was given a fifteen-year sentence in November 2011,[28] but was not re-detained pending his appeal. At the time Amnesty International called for the appeals process to be fair.[29] However, he was detained again on 12 December 2012, the day after he held a public meeting in Riyadh during which he asserted that the rights of assembly, association, and peaceful protest are legitimate as recognised by international law. The same day his family was informed that he had been sentenced to fifteen years in jail.[30] Human Rights Watch was among the international organisations that called for al-Rushoudi's release and for all charges against him to be dropped.[31] His family released a statement to the king in February 2013 calling for the removal of the interior minister and the establishment of an independent commission to investigate the human rights abuses being carried out under his authority, along with other demands calling for fundamental reforms in the country.[32]

Al-Hamid and al-Rushoudi had obvious Islamist orientations, but they worked closely with Muhammad al-Qahtani, who was not associated with Islamism, and because he spoke English he gave interviews to the international media. Born in 1965,[33] Muhammad al-Qahtani was a professor at the Institute of Diplomatic Studies in Riyadh, having earned his doctorate at Indiana University (USA).[34] One of the best-known members of HASM due to his public profile, he was mentioned as the forty-seventh most influential global thinker by *Foreign Policy* magazine in 2012.[35] He had previously hosted a satellite show entitled *Economic Issues* on the Economics channel, which was sometimes used to demonstrate the link between economic development and political reform, for example in a programme where he hosted Matruk al-Falih in December 2006.[36] In 2007 al-Qahtani was one of a number of prominent human rights activists who held a symbolic two-day hunger strike to protest at the arrests of eleven other activists, one of whom was held after producing a report on the poor state of conditions in Saudi jails.[37] He was also one of the seventy-seven activists who signed a letter sent to the king in 2009 complaining about secret trials and requesting reform. One of the founding members of HASM, he was president of the group in 2011 and part of the defence team of another young activist, Muhammad al-Bijadi, during his trial that began the same year.[38] Al-Qahtani was subsequently arrested and put on trial alongside Abdullah al-Hamid, where he faced eleven charges.[39] According to Arab human rights organisations, the charges were 'clearly all related to his work as a lawyer and human rights defender' and he stood 'accused of sending "false information presented as facts to the official international mechanisms [the mechanisms of the Human Rights Council of the United Nations]"'.[40]

Along with his co-defendant Abdullah al-Hamid, al-Qahtani was found guilty and sentenced on 9 March 2013. HASM was also officially dissolved by the court ruling. Al-Qahtani received a ten-year sentence at the hearing, and the widely covered case was criticised by the United States government's Commission on International Religious Freedom.[41]

The founders worked with younger supporters such as Muhammad al-Bijadi. Al-Bijadi was associated with exposing the death of a Yemeni, Sultan al-Daish, who was tortured in custody in 2010. On 21 March 2011, immediately after this incident, al-Bijadi was arrested. HASM issued a statement calling for his immediate release, claiming he had done nothing illegal. His defence team raised a notice to the court in June regarding their client stating that it was the job of the investigation committee to look into any transgressions by the government bodies, asking for visiting rights, and stating that they were afraid he was being mistreated and tortured in captivity. They released a statement after the second court sitting (which the defence team was not allowed to attend)—where al-Bijadi mentioned that the charges against him included disobedience to the ruler, inciting others to protest, and speaking to foreign media. A further statement was released in October, after the sixth secret sitting of the court (held on 3 October) in the case of al-Bijadi, where he was again refused representation. In December 2011 another statement was released saying that al-Bijadi had been told it that was impossible for the defence team to represent him (at a sitting on 4 December), and that they should not continue to attempt to attend (at the next sitting on 13 December). The HASM statement repeated the claim that the secret trial was basically revenge against al-Bijadi for his activism, and they invited all activists to attend the sitting on 13 December. On 15 February 2012 the defence team raised a case against the Interior Ministry as a result of the continued arbitrary detention of al-Bijadi, their lack of access to him, and the fact that his legal rights were withheld during the ongoing trial, which was still being held in secret. On 9 April 2012 HASM released a statement holding the Interior Ministry accountable for the state of health of al-Bijadi, who had been on an open hunger strike since 11 March, which included a moratorium on taking any visits or calls until his rights were respected. They then released a statement condemning the sentencing of al-Bijadi—which took place on 10 April—to four years in jail followed by five years prohibition from travelling. He went on a hunger strike again on 19 September in protest against his treatment in jail, after which he was put into solitary confinement. On 14 November HASM released a statement regarding his worsening health condition. Al-Bijadi's involvement in exposing torture in prison and his work with families of political prisoners to encourage them to hold sit-ins and stage demonstrations in Buraiydah had created new realities on the ground whereby HASM activists moved from issuing statements and communiqués, to mobilising relatives of prisoners to demonstrate.

In addition to the figures mentioned above, HASM founders included lecturers in Islamic jurisprudence and sharia studies as well as activists who became known as *nushata al-mujtama al-madani* (civil society activists). They

CIVIL SOCIETY IN AN AUTHORITARIAN STATE

may have been better known as activists rather than for their writings, but they worked to provide Islamic justification for civil and political rights by drawing on their studies in Saudi Islamic universities in both Riyadh and Qasim. They delivered lectures to other HASM members and posted short research papers on its website. Lawyers such as Abdulaziz al-Husan and activist Fawzan al-Harbi, together with a very young supporter, Abdullah al-Said, who was very active on social media, were collectively involved in defending the founders in court or reporting on the trials online.

The final fate of HASM may have been sealed in the courts, where most of its founders received very long sentences and with no hope of a royal pardon. But the advocacy of these local actors, their performance in Saudi courts, and the defence pamphlets that circulated online from 2009 are bound to change the meaning of activism in an authoritarian state. It seems that HASM founders looked to the court setting to fulfil some of their objectives, mainly the spread of the culture of rights within the existing Saudi law and inside its institutions. They insisted on describing what they do as peaceful struggle, a concept that they regularly invoked in the context of defending themselves in court.

Demonstrations as Peaceful Jihad

Abdullah al-Hamid responded to the judges' list of charges against him in court. His oral performances were supported by lengthy written texts that were disseminated to a wider audience after the court hearings. Together with his books on political jurisprudence, these short statements were posted on his personal web page. On one occasion during his lengthy trial and questioning, Judge Hamad al-Omar asked him to clarify how demonstrations can be a form of peaceful jihad.[42] In his response he argued that peaceful jihad has three features: first, it is shrouded in risk and hard work; second, it is performed for the collective interest of Muslims; and third, a peaceful Jihadi must be void of personal desire to seek wealth and privilege. In the response, al-Hamid cites several Quranic verses and Hadiths in support of *jihad al-kalima* (struggle by word). He stresses that this jihad corrects injustice and should be encouraged rather than outlawed. He argues that, when used to confront an unjust ruler, this is one of the most noble and courageous forms of resistance. He explains that military jihad may be a necessity to defend the country from outside threats, but that internally only peaceful jihad by word can lead to fortifying the internal structures of justice and respect for rights. Demonstrations are like the words praised in the Islamic tradition as a mechanism to change evil and wrongdoing. Peaceful jihad is needed all the time, whereas the military kind is occasional and dependent on temporary threats. He laments that the government bans peaceful jihad and eliminates discussion forums that allow people to express themselves and call for their rights.

In addition to the word, al-Hamid thinks of demonstrations as a form of collective advice to the ruler that is better than *nasiha* (private advice). Saudi official *ulama* insist that privately given advice is the best method for reaching out to rulers and informing them about where they have gone wrong. This has remained controversial and is contested by activist Islamists, who are often prosecuted for expressing opinions. Like other Islamists al-Hamid doubts that *nasiha* is the best method to communicate with the government and its officials, as a powerful ruler who receives a private letter may simply ignore it. However, if he is faced with a collective demonstration he may not be able to overlook it. Al-Hamid gives the example of the unemployed who gather in a demonstration asking for jobs or the families of political prisoners who demand fair trials for their relatives. As they engage in visible and peaceful collective action, they draw attention to their plight, which then becomes difficult to ignore. This peaceful jihad should not be interpreted as action against the state but against general *munkarat* (sinful actions) and the excesses of sultanic power. He argues that people should be allowed to express themselves and demand recognition of their interests. This is preferable to physically destroying these *munkarat* (for example, the buildings of banks that charge interest) or raiding immoral places. Such destruction was symptomatic of the Islamist agitations that followed 1979 when many activists took it upon themselves to destroy video shops allegedly selling immoral material. In his opinion, demonstrations move people from violence to peaceful mobilisation. He warns that governments that ban peaceful struggle face political tensions, frustration, and eventually violence. Violence is but one outcome of banning peaceful collective action.

Like those concerned with the crisis of terrorism in Saudi Arabia, al-Hamid seeks to identify the causes. He asserts that *istibdad* (tyrannical rule) must be the primary cause. The absence of civil society, lack of freedom of expression, and banning of peaceful mobilisation all lead to violence in society. Here al-Hamid moves from the Islamic tradition to political sociology to explain how it should be incumbent on governments to accept the formation of civil society and spread the culture of rights and empowerment as alternatives to the inevitability of violence when these forms of collective action are suppressed. Without a new culture of peaceful activism, violence will become endemic and people will start organising themselves in secret cells the size of which will remain unknown until their actions erupt like a volcano.[43] To forestall the sudden eruption of political violence, only open action can absorb people's desire to protect their interests. He warns that radical groups achieve greater success in closed societies because their courage tends to appeal to people who confuse this courage with being right. The thrill of secretive action among young activists pushes them to become self-contained and absorbed in ideas and strategies that may encourage them to attempt to implement them by force. According to al-Hamid, when there is open space for discussion, radical groups lose their audiences because they cannot defend their ideas and violence in public. Society will ultimately reject this violence if it is given a chance to openly debate, change, and mobilise peacefully.

The Court as Theatrical Performance

The government compiled a set of accusations which it used against almost all HASM activists. The judges simply reiterated these accusations with minor amendments, confirming HASM's claim that the judiciary is under the control of the Interior Ministry. The charges against HASM members and activists often included statements embodied in religious language, such as the list of charges against Muhammad al-Qahtani:

1. Attempting to plant the seeds of discord and strife, breaking allegiance to the ruler and his successor, questioning the integrity of and insulting state officials.
2. Questioning the integrity and piety of the members of the Council of Higher Ulama by—falsely—accusing it of being a tool that approves government policies in return for financial and moral support, as in the case of forbidding street protests.
3. Accusing [the] Saudi judiciary in its regulations and applications of being unable to deliver justice for breaching the standards set by Islamic sharia.
4. Accusing [the] Saudi judiciary of being unjust by allowing torture and accepting confessions extracted under duress.
5. Accusing the Saudi regime—unfairly—of being a police state built on injustice and oppression veiled in religion, and [of] using the judiciary to legitimise injustice to continue its systematic approach to violate human rights.
6. Inciting public opinion by accusing security bodies and their senior officials of oppression, torture, assassination, enforced, and violating human rights.[44]

As soon as judges released these lists of charges, HASM members circulated them publicly. They immediately published their replies to each accusation in detailed pamphlets that were not only used in the courts but also formed the background of their lectures. The charges and the defence reflected the unfolding of an intellectual battle over meaning between HASM founders and the judiciary, with both sides trying to ground their accusations and defence in religious language. The trials and the documentation of the proceedings represented a battle over religious interpretation of important concepts that dominate the Saudi political and legal discourse. HASM's defence statements contested the accusation of *fitna* (discord), insulting *wali al-amr* (the ruler), doubting the merit of the *baya* (oath of allegiance), and lack of *adl* (justice). These contestations over the meaning of concepts used by the judiciary against HASM members became controversial. HASM offered counter-interpretations and circulated them in the public sphere to undermine the meaning that judges wanted to fix and then apply in court. Each trial generated a new set of meanings that circulated in the public sphere with HASM activists popularising their counter-interpretations online. The trials of al-Hamid, al-Rushoudi, al-Qahtani, and many other supporters were turned into opportunities for them to lecture on the meaning of human rights in Islam, the right of prisoners, just government, an independent judiciary, and the *shura* state.[45] When they defended themselves they used language as public speech to deconstruct the domination of the state and the hegemonic religious language of its judges. By offering new interpretations of the same concepts that the judges used to criminalise their activities, they believed that they provided the tools for political change.

The court and its surrounding courtyard were transformed into a site for theatrical performance where HASM actors and their lawyers offered detailed revisionist interpretations of Islamic concepts in replies to the judges. HASM actors hoped that images of them in the court would be transmitted to a wider audience than that allowed to be present. They always insisted on open trials, a request which was partially met by the government who made it very difficult for a large audience to enter the court. HASM always announced the dates and times of the court hearings in advance and called upon supporters to travel from other cities to Riyadh and Buraiydah. Both Abdullah al-Hamid and Muhammad al-Qahtani tweeted from the pavement outside the court and took photos with their supporters who accompanied them. Other HASM members who were not allowed to enter the court or were asked to leave waited in the courtyard and gave updates on the discussion inside the court that they received from those who were able to enter. Those who were not allowed to be present relied on photographs and short statements that were circulated on Twitter by those inside the court. A wider audience was able to watch the accused on their way to the court in high spirits and catch a glimpse of the proceedings inside, while supporters engaged in conversation with the police to try and negotiate access. For several hours on the day of the court hearings, social media activism became common among HASM supporters, who transformed the trials into a virtual forum for all to follow and comment on. Their heavy engagement with new social media functioned to amplify the plight of the founders, disseminate alternative interpretations of the charges, and encourage emotional attachments to the accused. New media offered the opportunity to create rhetorical space to debate issues around HASM founders, their initiative, trials, and later imprisonment.

With each trial the audience became bigger, and the legal discussions spread across sections of society that might not necessarily be aware of the individual cases. This was what HASM and its founders hoped for, mainly the spread of the culture of rights and the contestation of authoritarian rule in its own judicial institutions. The founders' trials were turned into lessons in how to deal with judges by offering counter-arguments and alternative interpretations. The government realised how open trials can be a powerful tool in the hands of organisations such as HASM as it turned them into a performance to defend civil and political rights. Official Saudi media initially ignored the trials, but were later compelled to mention them and the resulting sentences, which had already become well known as a result of HASM's engagement with new media and international reporting on the cases. The official press initially avoided mentioning the names of the individuals facing trial in an attempt to deny them celebrity and publicity. Only fringe electronic media were from the very beginning able to identify the accused by their names.

A large online audience, however, does not necessarily mean that HASM had a wide circle of real supporters who were ready to rally to its defence and stage demonstrations against the long sentences its founders received; in fact, only their close relatives protested against these sentences. The al-Rushoudi family, for example, held an emergency meeting after which they issued a statement against the long sentence Suleiman received in 2013. Several of these meetings were organised in succession, and resulted in the family signing solidarity letters calling for his release on the grounds of both his innocence and old age—he was over seventy-five at the time of his trial. The meetings were immediately repressed by the security forces, and since 2013 only online activists have continued to remind audiences of HASM and its founders. Occasionally international human rights organisations help the momentum by issuing statements about the deteriorating health of prisoners and call on the Saudi regime to release them as they are classified as prisoners of conscience.

Transforming a state institution such as the courts into a platform where the accused deconstructed the meaning of their charges and offered alternative interpretations was part of HASM's strategy. Its founders knew that their activism in an unlicensed political and civil rights association was bound to lead to imprisonment. They aimed to defeat authoritarian rule by offering counter-interpretations of the very concepts that are used against them. Their perseverance in continuing the struggle, while knowing that it inevitably resulted in long prison sentences, demonstrated its founders' commitment to the rule of law, freedom of expression, independent judiciary, and respect for human rights. Their trials were turned into occasions for promoting alternative interpretations of religious concepts and language that had been used in the public sphere to limit activism and criminalise demands for political change and respect for human rights.

With most HASM founders in prison, there remains the language of rights as a reminder of the struggle for justice. There was no doubt that the government would abolish HASM, but it was hard to eradicate the short-lived experiment in human rights activism and the language associated with it. This language survived not only in HASM's online archive but in the memory of those who followed the ordeals of its founders and their daily experience in prison. The Twitter accounts of its imprisoned founders remain live and are operated by unknown supporters, or possibly close relatives, who continue to circulate HASM lectures and disseminate information on their conditions in prison. Images of Abdullah al-Hamid in shackles while preparing for Friday prayers in prison circulate outside his prison walls, with hundreds of supporters organising online campaigns for his release. His lectures and short statements are constantly cited and re-cited as reminders of the causes he fought for. Repetition serves as a reminder of the language of rights. It is unlikely that this language will vanish, especially from the blogosphere, while the founders serve their long prison sentences. The language of rights is most probably destined to gather more momentum in the future as it becomes part of transforming the consciousness of a new generation of activists. These may have retreated into the virtual world at the moment to escape further repression, but at least they have not been totally silenced.

If HASM has left any legacy on the political sphere, it has done so through the interpretation of jihad as peaceful mobilisation that includes among other things demonstrations. The regime realised the potential threat of an association such as HASM; it had previously encouraged small-scale demonstrations by relatives of political prisoners and provided a reinterpretation of the religious tradition in favour of peaceful struggle to pursue fundamental civil and political rights. With the Arab uprisings gathering momentum in 2011, the government outlawed any attempt to peacefully mobilise people and criminalised any call to hold demonstrations.

Conclusion

For the first time, HASM and its founders, together with their language and mobilisation strategies, inspired many Saudis to follow their statements and watch the unfolding of their trials in court. HASM moved the struggle of a nascent civil society to one of the most important state institutions, the judiciary, which is central to enforcing government bans and controlling potential peaceful mobilisation. From the beginning HASM was the culmination of several decades of mobilisation that had historically been associated with the Islamist movement in Saudi Arabia. By 2009 and after several rounds of confrontation with the regime, Islamist reformers struggled to find a platform to mobilise their followers, especially after 9/11 and the wave of repression that followed. The founders of HASM envisaged a new way to remain relevant to the Saudi political sphere, positioning themselves as an association for civil and political rights and widening their reach to non-Islamists. This was an important mutation that promised the consolidation of a national reformist movement, anchored in civil society and seeking to provide a space to defend society's interests against rigid government control and religious justifications for this control. HASM tried to break the entrenched dividing lines between ideological groups that had in the past rejected each other. The Islamist–liberal divide looked rigid, especially after 9/11 when the government encouraged the demonisation of Islamism in all its forms, co-opting liberal intellectuals in its battle against Islamism. HASM envisaged the birth of a reformist agenda that is anchored in real civil society and benefiting from the voluntary work of its founders and their supporters who served it in many ways.

Between 2009 and 2013 HASM trials attracted the attention of international media and human rights organisations while Saudis followed the events online, thanks to its young new media activists. The Arab uprisings encouraged HASM founders to augment their mobilisation, especially in defending the rights of political prisoners and exposing torture in Saudi prisons. It must be acknowledged that their calls to support the small demonstrations of women relatives of prisoners did not attract large crowds, but they were important in the context of Saudi Arabia where such collective action has been rare. The regime remained intolerant of demonstrations, and considered calls for them a crime regardless of the focus of such collective action or its specific demands. But it was keen to show that it respected the rule of law, and allowed the HASM trials to be partially open by admitting some members of the public into the court subject to the consent of the judges. Even with the limited number of people who were able to attend the court, the details were publicised and circulated outside, thus allowing a wider audience to engage with the meaning of the charges and their reinterpretations by HASM founders.

The history of HASM may not have ended with the long prison sentences imposed on its founders and advocates; the organisation has left an intellectual legacy grounded in the language of rights and entitlement. The long defence documents that HASM circulated may not be easily accessible after its banning, but its shorter advocacy letters represented an attempt to reach a wider public that may or may not be conversant in the legalistic language of the court. But HASM framed political rights in religious language that most Saudis are familiar with thanks to their education and upbringing in a country where the public sphere is saturated with religious references. While none of the HASM founders included well-known religious scholars, it benefited from the experience and education of a range of personalities who had knowledge in both religious matters and secular subjects. One legacy of HASM will remain important: the way its ideas were taken up by a new generation of religious intellectuals whose books expanded HASM themes. It seems that the language of rights is difficult to suppress after the short-lived experience of this nascent civil society. HASM's position on peaceful protest had an undoubted impact on one important Islamist, Sheikh Salman al-Awdah, who went as far as justifying peaceful revolution in a Salafi context.

3

ON REVOLUTION

HASM founders were not the only activists invigorated by the Arab uprisings; Saudi veteran Islamists such as the famous scholar Salman al-Awdah were equally enchanted by the historic peaceful protests that swept the Arab world in 2011. Peaceful revolutions such as those that took place in Tunisia and Egypt, where thousands of demonstrators occupied public squares, chanted slogans against dictatorships, and symbolically humiliated their leaders, were a novelty among Saudi audiences. With the exception of the Shia region, mainstream society was not accustomed to the public display of peaceful collective action. As mentioned in the previous chapters, although sporadic protest was visible during the Arab uprisings in Saudi Arabia, this failed to materialise in mass demonstrations across the country. Nevertheless, the Arab uprisings presented Saudis with a different model of collective action, unknown in the Saudi Salafi context. The ease by which Arab rulers such as Zine al-Abdine Bin Ali and Hosni Mubarak were toppled after only several weeks of peaceful demonstrations took them by surprise, as Saudis witnessed for the first time the power of the masses achieving political goals without bloodshed, at least at the beginning of the uprisings. Needless to say, official Salafi scholars abhorred the spectacle of change in neighbouring countries and warned against adopting such strategies in Saudi Arabia itself. Yet a peaceful revolution became an interesting model, appreciated by a limited number of independent Saudi religious scholars against the background of an official Salafi tradition opposed to political change, especially that which happens under the pressure of the masses. In fact, the Salafi tradition had contempt for the *jamahir* (masses), whom they often described as ignorant, mob-like, and in need of guidance. According to this tradition, important matters related to policy and reform cannot be left to the common people and should remain the prerogative of the rulers and the *ulama*. But well-known Saudi Islamists were euphoric about the new mobilisation in the Arab world, to the extent of offering reflections on peaceful change. This chapter examines the reaction of one of the most well-known Saudi Islamists, Sheikh Salman al-Awdah, whose writings on revolution offered a clear example of the intellectual mutations taking place in Saudi Arabia after the Arab uprisings.

Before the uprisings many Saudi Islamists had already begun to develop a new discourse that remains anchored in the general wide framework of Salafiyya while stretching the boundaries of human interpretation to allow for a new vision of the polity, the application of sharia, and the relationship between ruler and ruled. In addition, those amongst them with roots in traditional Salafi education and knowledge, such as the dissident *ulama* of the 1990s, began to produce a discourse that is truly hybrid, reflecting syncretism rather than simply reiterating old slogans about Islamic authenticity. Most Saudi Salafis avoid controversial terminology such as 'democracy' and 'pluralism'. But the Arab uprisings encouraged a minority amongst them to use the word democracy and then to call for it. They began to highlight how old Islamic concepts about a just government can be fused with new meanings. Concepts such as consultation, justice, freedom, human rights, sovereignty of the *umma*, and peaceful jihad began to be hotly debated.

Under the pressure of the Arab uprisings, religious scholars such as Salman al-Awdah seem to have moved beyond the traditional Salafi discourse of the abhorred 'rebellion against unjust rulers' to assess the merit of peaceful protest in a revolutionary context. This new development reflected impatience with the total obedience to political authority prescribed by traditional official Salafi *ulama* and the deadly violence of the Jihadis. Al-Awdah's appreciation and justification of peaceful protest offers a third way between the two religious positions, the obedient *ulama* and the rebellious Jihadis, in which Saudi Arabia had found itself locked. The third way blends Islamic theological concepts with a socio-political analysis of current conditions of oppression and marginalisation. As such al-Awdah bridges the gap between the traditionally trained religious scholar and the religious intellectual, thus creating a hybrid discourse that has the potential of appealing to a wide audience of young Saudis searching for a language to articulate political change.

On Revolution

Salman al-Awdah (b. 1956) was a veteran of the religio-political movement best known in Saudi Arabia as the Sahwa, the Islamic Awakening, that came to dominate the Saudi Islamist scene after the 1990 Iraqi invasion of Kuwait. The Sahwa was born out of a Salafi–Ikhwani fusion, although this was not the only discernible trend among its activists and followers.[1] Al-Awdah's career as a religious scholar started in his home town, Buraiydah, where he trained in its religious institute, following the study circles of famous Salafi *ulama* such as Abdul Aziz Ibn Baz and Muhammad al-Uthaymin.[2] He became a lecturer at Imam Muhammad ibn Saud University until he was dismissed in 1993 after delivering a series of political lectures critical of the regime, deemed revolutionary in the Saudi context at the time of the Iraqi invasion of Kuwait in 1990–1. He had circulated his mosque sermons on cassettes during the invasion, inflaming the imagination of a young generation of followers opposed to American intervention in what was considered an internal Islamic crisis. His political activism at the time led to four years in prison.[3] He was released in 1999. While al-Awdah's religious education was grounded in the traditional Salafi scholarship of the Najdi region in Saudi Arabia, he was influenced by modern Islamist thought, mainly that of the Egyptian Muslim Brotherhood, Hasan al-Bana, Sayid Qutb, and the late Syrian scholar Muhammad Surur Zaiyn al-Abdin.[4] Al-Awdah has always denied membership in an Islamist party or political trend, but his endorsement of the Muslim Brotherhood attests to his intimate relations with mainstream Islamism. In fact, membership of a party might limit his popularity and could lead to discrimination or imprisonment in a country such as Saudi Arabia, which bans independent associations and political parties. It seems that al-Awdah has no formal affiliations, but is in fact extremely influential among a wide circle of Islamists not only in Saudi Arabia but also throughout the Arab and Muslim world. After his release from prison he retreated into his religious scholarship, intensifying his preaching on moral and social issues, which shielded him against controversial political debates. Al-Awdah remains one of the most influential pillars of Saudi Islamism.

After al-Awdah was released from prison in 1999 he went through a short hibernation period. He was later rehabilitated by the regime as part of its strategy to use Islamists in its struggle against a more violent Jihadi trend, which brought the battle to Saudi cities in 2003. In media shows after 9/11 he denounced Jihadis and exposed their misunderstanding of the body of Islamic texts on legitimate jihad, emphasising the illegitimacy of globalising the struggle or localising it where it had killed Muslims and non-Muslims. While his televised ad hoc media appearances were meant to target all Arabic-speaking audiences, his emphasis was on the illegitimate armed struggle of Osama Bin Laden and on dissociating himself from al-Qaida and its thought, which by 2003 may have reached its climax after 9/11 and the invasion of both Afghanistan in 2001 and Iraq in 2003. The regime capitalised on al-Awdah's popularity as a charismatic public figure who combined traditional religious scholarship with an ability to reach beyond the circles of scholastic *ulama*, especially among young Saudis, to enlist him in its battle against dissent. He began appearing first on Arabic Al-Jazeera satellite television, where he dissociated himself from previous positions and called upon Jihadis to repent and abandon military struggle against Muslim rulers. He emphasised that he had never supported the regime in calling upon Saudis to fight in Afghanistan in the 1980s, and reiterated that he continued to oppose their flight to other destinations such as Iraq after its occupation in 2003.[5] After the Syrian uprising in 2011 al-Awdah again opposed calls for young Saudis to join the rebellion, and on several occasions insisted that it should be supported with money and humanitarian efforts.

In 2005 al-Awdah regularly appeared on a Saudi-owned MBC television channel to spread arguments grounded in new interpretations of Islam that would eventually undermine Jihadi theories on armed struggle against both the West and the local regimes in Saudi Arabia and elsewhere.[6] He succeeded in developing his own exclusive programme on MBC called Hajar al-zawiyya (Cornerstone), a weekly television programme, which had aired around 150 episodes by the time it was suspended in 2011 at the height of the Arab uprisings.[7] He used this platform to expose the misguided interpretations of Jihadis, and offered Islamic interpretations on a wide range of topics including social and political issues from personal piety to gender inequality. It signalled the adoption of a new approach, deviating from his earlier robust and revolutionary sermons and pamphlets of the 1990s.[8] After dissociating himself from Jihadism[9] and offering a middle-ground position between Jihadi violence and traditional Salafi acquiescence associated with the official Salafi religious establishment, headed by Saudi Mufti Sheikh Abd al-Aziz al-Sheikh, al-Awdah appealed to new followers who appreciated his innovative discourse, now articulated and presented in his popular mosque sermons, Islam Today web pages, and Saudi and pan-Arab media. Al-Awdah resumed his preaching in his home town and reached new students, followers, and sympathisers in Saudi Arabia, the Arab and Muslim world, and among Muslims in non-

Muslim-majority countries. His early popularity among these audiences was tremendously enhanced with the advent of Saudi and Qatari pan-Arab media in which he became a regular preacher, holding his own discussion programmes. While his audio-visual sermons and discussion programmes since 2005 have been analysed,[10] I focus here on his most recent assessment and endorsement of the Arab uprisings of 2011.

As the Arab uprisings gathered momentum in 2011 and led to the deposing of two Arab leaders, Hosni Mubarak of Egypt and Zine al-Abdine Bin Ali of Tunisia, al-Awdah was one of the first Saudi *ulama* activists to publish his reflections on revolution from an Islamic point of view, yet impregnating these reflections with clear references to Western scholarship, an unusual pastiche that traditionally trained Saudi *ulama* had avoided in the past. While Saudi official *ulama* remained anchored in the Sunni scholastic tradition that denounced any action that might result in instability and precipitate *fitna* (chaos), al-Awdah clearly deviated from this position and offered his praise for peaceful revolution in a language that resonates with a wider public than that reached by traditional *ulama*. Official Saudi *ulama* had always opposed collective action, in both its armed and peaceful manifestations such as demonstrations, strikes, hunger strikes, sit-ins, and civil disobedience, and continued to adopt the concept of *nasiha* (private advice) to the ruler with a view to reforming him and changing those of his policies that they see as transgressing from the right Islamic tradition. During the early months of the Arab uprisings they increased the frequency of their *fatwa*s prohibiting peaceful collective action, especially after Saudi activists issued calls for a Day of Rage, envisaged to culminate in demonstrations across Saudi cities on 11 March 2011. Their *fatwa*s were circulated in mosques and published in official media.[11]

Unlike the majority of official Salafi *ulama* who condemned revolutions, al-Awdah celebrated the success of the Tunisian and Egyptian uprisings. He sited peaceful collective revolutionary action in an Islamic framework, and reached out for humanist interpretations that assimilate Western intellectual positions with his Salafi orientation. He surprised his audiences as he analysed revolution, an abhorrent term that most Saudi Sunni *ulama* have rejected and attempted to outlaw as a leap into chaos and dissent. When his new book, *Asilat al-thawra* (Questions of revolution)[12] was published in 2012, al-Awdah dared to rehabilitate the concept of revolution after it had been associated with instability, chaos, and danger for decades. This book declared his position to be different from both traditional official Saudi *ulama* and Jihadi ideologues. Needless to say, the book was immediately banned in Saudi Arabia, but the author quickly circulated it freely on the internet. After al-Awdah showed his enthusiasm for revolutions, the Saudi regime imposed new restrictions on him. His television programme was suspended and he was banned from leaving the country to attend conferences in Egypt and other Arab capitals. Occasionally, higher authorities cancelled his lectures without explanation. Banning him from travel did little to diminish his popularity and outreach. By 2011 he already had developed his own media empire, consisting of special debate programmes on independent Islamist channels such as Dalil and al-Majd, in addition to his personal media web (Islam Today), YouTube video channel (DrSalmanTv), Facebook page, and, most importantly, Twitter account (@salman_al-odah), which in 2015 had several million followers. His words and images circulate freely online despite the restrictions imposed on him. He remains active as a preacher and scholar with more than sixty books published over the years. Locally, his study circles attract large numbers of young students while he remains active in global committees of Muslim scholars. Combining preaching with commentaries on public affairs and political issues make him unique in the Saudi context where the role of most *ulama* is often restricted to providing guidance on personal piety and worship.

In *Asilat al-thawra*, al-Awdah's engagement with political change from theological and political perspectives brought him back as a relevant figure at a critical moment in the Saudi and Arab public sphere. The eruption of unforeseen and unexpected revolutions needed an Islamic endorsement, interpretation, and justification. Al-Awdah swiftly seized the opportunity and improvised a discourse that moves away from the duality of the permissible and prohibited in Islamic political theology. In this book he went beyond the traditional acquiescent Salafi position and Jihadi justification for violence as a means for political change.

Al-Awdah fuses Western political thinking on revolutionary change from Marx, Popper, Fanon, and Tocqueville with his own Islamic heritage. Relying on world examples of revolutionary change in France, Russia, and China, in addition to Islamic revolutionary moments such as the 'Abbasid revolution', he defines revolution as building on the past, reform and reconstruction rather than destruction. It always starts peacefully (Tunisia and Egypt in 2011), but may later become militarised (Libya) when confronted with oppression and regime terror. Revolution is therefore a social phenomenon seeking political change as a result of collective action.[13] It is born from preconditions that combine political, social, psychological, and economic determinants. Politically, systematic oppression, coupled with absolute rule that combines the legislative, judiciary, and executive powers in the ruler's persona, triggers people to seek a new model of governance; the democratic alternative is currently seen as the best option, with variants that spring out of each country's context. Such absolute power is often riddled with internal rivalries that spread to society in an attempt to co-opt groups and activists, thus delaying unity.

Economically, the deterioration of people's standards of living, coupled with rising youth aspirations and unemployment, lead to collective action the purpose of which is to change the situation. Socially, authoritarian regimes deliberately alter the historical identity of their constituency to cause a break from its own heritage, such as the attempts by the post-independence regime in Tunisia to disentangle the country from its natural Arabo-Islamic tradition.[14] The cumulative fermenting impact of these conditions erupts at the right moment (the event) that triggers off the revolution. He describes revolution as a fruit: 'There is no law that determines when revolution is going to erupt. It is like a fruit that may ripen, dry, or be prematurely picked.'[15]

Al-Awdah situates his analysis of revolution in *siyasa sharia* (legitimate politics), which he considers in need of revisionist reading. This revisionist project requires two steps. First, clear revealed Islamic textual sources such as the Quran and Hadith. Second, human *ijtihad* (reasoning) is needed. According to al-Awdah, Muslims have confused *siyasa sharia* with its theorisation by the likes of al-Mawardi, who justified absolute rule and rendered unconditional obedience to rulers a religious obligation. The interpretations of scholars such as al-Mawardi have regrettably replaced the Quran and the tradition of the Prophet among Muslim scholars. He rejects 'rule of the victorious party' (*hukm al-ghalaba*), which seizes power by military conquest. When such rule is established, the solution is to go beyond the traditional duality of responses, i.e. total obedience to rulers or military revolt. His third way centres on collective action that organises opposition and presses for peaceful change. This solution seems to have been ignored by a previous generation of Muslim scholars.

Al-Awdah draws attention to the importance of civil society because it is an incubator for peaceful collective action. He surveys the opinions of Orientalist scholars who explored the historical presence of such independent associations in Muslim history. He cites the work of Bernard Lewis and others to highlight the prevalence of civil associations in the past while lamenting their disappearance in contemporary societies.

Islamic governance for al-Awdah is grounded in *shura* (consultation). But unlike official Saudi discourse on consultation that limits its circles to a selected elite referred to as *ahl al-hal wa al-aqd*, al-Awdah widens the circle of those consulted to include the *umma*, the collective body through its elected representatives. The focus on the *umma* as the legitimate consultative constituency remains central in al-Awdah's thinking and that of the other religious intellectuals discussed in the following chapters.

The social contract, exemplified by the English Magna Carta, represents in al-Awdah's thinking an early example of limiting monarchical powers and asserting individual rights. Al-Awdah seems to be inspired by the English treaty, and may have aspired towards a new social contract between the Saudi monarchy and the people, which would grant the latter certain political rights thus far denied them.

He concludes that the strategy of collective action is not always violent. Peaceful demonstrations, revolutionary attire, slogans, graffiti, art, and hunger strikes prove to be more efficient and justified in a peaceful revolution, as demonstrated in Tunisia and Egypt. He identifies the actors who participated in and enacted the Arab revolutions. This includes the people (*jamahir*), with all their diversity, and the Islamists, although he acknowledges that the latter did not ignite these revolts. The realisation that the Islamists were not the vanguards of the peaceful Arab protests of 2011 may be regrettable in al-Awdah's opinion, but he acknowledges it as a fact. He highlights the role of the people as they coalesced in an emotional demonstration of rage against dictatorship. The people rather than political leaders or parties were behind the revolutions, and they remain the revolution's backbone, especially when all development projects and promises of prosperity collapse. On the Islamists, al-Awdah argues that their ability to organise themselves was important for mobilisation; but without the people, who may or may not have sympathised with their projects, revolutions in the Arab world could not have happened.

On the sharia in a post-revolutionary phase, al-Awdah calls for gradual application (*tadaruj*) in an attempt not to impose a sudden burden on societies emerging from revolutionary upheaval, thus precipitating its total rejection. As the Arab uprisings took place in countries where a mix of sharia and civil laws had been well established, the question whether to launch an Islamisation of the legal systems became hotly debated in the post-revolutionary phase. Al-Awdah argues that the application of sharia in a Muslim society is taken for granted, but the relationship between politics and religion should be determined by the context of each country. He criticises the focus on simply applying sharia punishments to transgressors such as thieves, sorcerers, and witches while ignoring sharia's main function of establishing justice in its wider social and political meaning. In his view, gradual implementation of sharia is better than imposing it in a society that is far removed in its context from the historical conditions of early Islam. Wholesale and sudden application of sharia may eventually lead to people abandoning it altogether. To move from the theoretical foundation of sharia to application involves the use of individual reasoning or interpretation (*ijtihad bashari*), which is limited to time, place, and man. Therefore, he calls for a historicisation of sharia, taking into account human limitations within a specific historical context. The purpose of sharia should be the preservation of religion, life, wealth, reason, and society; but above all, its application should guarantee freedom and dignity. The latter should become a priority for those who call for the implementation of sharia. He warns against those governments that ignore the principles of sharia and use its application as a slogan for political purposes. Obviously, al-Awadah alludes here to the Saudi situation without naming the country. In his opinion, a country may have an Islamic government simply because it claims to apply the sharia, but sometimes the purposes of sharia, i.e. freedom, justice, rights, and the protection of wealth, are totally ignored. The theme of sharia in the post-revolutionary Arab context remains hotly debated, as will be discussed in the next chapter where an even more controversial view on its application is presented.

In al-Awadah's opinion post-revolutionary justice may overlook applying the *huddud* (Quranic punishments). For example, cutting off the hand of a thief is not advisable, as economic conditions may not be suitable for such drastic measure. Flexibility in punishment means that sharia must be contextualised and applied with careful consideration of the current conditions of specific societies. Consequently, he rejects raising the slogan of implementing sharia as a political strategy designed to capitalise on people's emotions. Sharia is meant to establish justice and protect lives and property with an initial selective application that articulates its broad purposes. This is better than suddenly introducing it comprehensively, which might unnecessarily antagonise people.

Al-Awadah is concerned with the identity of the state after a revolution. He argues that in Islam there is no scope for a theocracy. The Islamic state is a contractual project between people on the basis of a civil contract (*madani*). The worst repression occurs when authoritarian rulers instrumentalise religion to cover or justify their oppression. In his view the only solution is separation of the three powers: the executive, legislature, and judiciary. This guarantees the ethos of the civil state (*dawla madaniyya*). In these reflections, al-Awdah writes as a contemporary political theorist rather than a traditionally trained Salafi *alim* (religious scholar).

Democracy as it manifests itself in many countries proves to be better than autocracy, according to al-Awdah. He defends the concepts of the representation of the people, freedom, and civil society. Rhetorically, he asks why Muslims accept autocracy and reject democracy on the basis of the latter being a Western import, if it proves to be the best option available. Democracy promises to be inclusive, as no *umma* can experience a renaissance by relying on the opinion of one ruler or constituency. Inclusive pluralism is a precondition for just government. He warns against alienating sectarian and ethnic minorities, which he considers a misguided and potentially dangerous strategy inviting foreign intervention, death, and schisms within society. He calls for respecting the rights of minorities within a democratic framework. Revolutionary justice requires reconciliation with all sectors in society, even supporters of deposed regimes; as the Prophet said, 'Go, you are free.'[16] Revolutions will become a necessary strategy if followed by democratic contractual government and without a utilitarian instrumentalisation of religion. Al-Awdah pre-emptively warns against revolutions leading to religious dictatorship.[17]

Has al-Awdah's book on revolutions confirmed his status as a revolutionary zealot, encouraging mobilisation against injustice and political authority? He remains cautious and avoids discussing the Saudi case directly, confining himself to general comments, whose applicability in the Saudi context does not escape the attention of his followers inside Saudi Arabia itself. Had his book been totally irrelevant to Saudi Arabia, the authorities would not have rushed to ban it. Two factors have prompted its banning. First, al-Awdah's discourse is grounded in the Islamic tradition that invokes the Quran, Hadith, and Islamic history. These resonate among Saudi audiences, who have been immersed in religious education under the auspices of state education institutions. After all, al-Awdah was trained by revered Saudi religious scholars from his childhood years in Buraiydah, and later became a teacher and lecturer in Saudi religious institutes and universities. Consequently, his reflections on revolution remain an indigenous attempt to reinterpret political and social history within the normative framework of Salafi thought. Al-Awdah's fusion of this Salafi heritage with Western political theory and historical case studies makes him appeal to a wider audience, thus bridging the divide between the so-called authentic Islamic tradition and imported Western concepts. As a scholar who praises Western authors on revolution and the English Magna Carta, al-Awdah defies what is pejoratively described as *taghrib*, or Westernisation. Second, Al-Awdah's new syncretism promises to bridge the gap between Islamists and non-Islamists. The hybridity of his discourse and the easy and simple style of his book make it reach not only Salafis but non-ideologically committed Saudis searching for new paradigms within which to imagine political change and reform. The appeal of his discourse among the youth stems from allowing them to engage with global world debates on democracy, without totally abandoning their fixation on authenticity and the Islamic heritage. Such young people search for frameworks that allow them to keep Islam as a relevant and authentic paradigm but at the same time look to other world experiences to find solutions to the contemporary crisis in governance.

Despite al-Awdah's attempt to pre-empt the reaction of the censorship authorities by avoiding any reference to his own Saudi context, he once again came to the attention of the regime. After his book on revolution was banned he circulated an electronic version, and posted the news on his web page, Islam Today. He explained to his followers on Twitter how to download the book.[18] Occasionally, al-Awdah tweets that his lectures are cancelled for no reason, thus alluding to the current restrictions that the regime imposed on him after the Arab uprisings.

The intellectual fusion that al-Awdah promotes is destined to create intellectual mutations. He promises his readers that they can learn from the experience of non-Muslims, and encourages them to search for innovative interpretations in their own Salafi heritage. On democracy, pluralism, and the sovereignty of the *umma*, discussion of which dominated the public sphere during the Arab uprisings, al-Awdah depicts Islam as still relevant to the debate on the future of societies. But he shows that he is willing to learn from the experience of those non-Muslims who had dismantled authoritarianism.

However, al-Awdah does not fully break away from Salafi principles and audiences. On sectarian minorities such as the Shia and on gender issues he treads a careful path that oscillates between silence and reconciliation. While his book on revolution celebrates the Sunni Arab revolutionary publics in Tunisia, Egypt, Libya, and Syria, he is silent on the revolt in Bahrain with its 70 per cent Shia majority. In his media appearances he warns against what he calls a Shia political projects-read Iran's expansion, but distinguishes this project from the Shia as a sect among other sects within the Muslim *umma*. He asserts that Sunnis are fundamentally different from the Shia in their creed, and calls the latter *rafidha* (rejectionists), a term pejoratively used by Salafis to refer to the Shia.[19] In his book on revolution he prefers to avoid serious interrogation of the question of the Shia in both Bahrain and Saudi Arabia.

However, al-Awdah is committed to the unity of the Islamic *umma* and may not be prepared to deepen the schisms between the Sunni majority and the Shia minority on the basis of creedal differences, especially at a time when the Arab region is torn by what appears to be sectarian wars, masking real political and economic issues. While he was involved in carefully orchestrated meetings with important Shia religious scholars such as Hasan al-Safar, under the auspices of the regime's post-9/11 National Dialogue Forums, he prefers to discuss the Shia question from a political standpoint. He denounces Iran's attempt to penetrate the Sunni-majority countries and promote its own political hegemony, perceived as a threat to security and peaceful coexistence among the different sects of the Muslim world. Sunni expansion is not considered worthy of discussion, as it is taken for granted as the right path to strengthen national and transnational connections among a predominantly Sunni *umma*. When three attacks on Shia mosques in Saudi Arabia in May 2015 took place and claimed the lives of more than 20 worshippers,[20] al-Awdah condemned the attacks and insisted on the importance of national unity. He also warned against linking these attacks to the wider sectarian regional context of the Arab world as these linkages hinders possible solutions to the Shia question in Saudi Arabia itself.

Gender questions that have recently begun to dominate the Saudi public sphere are central to al-Awdah's thinking. His followers appreciate his revisionist discourse that reconciles Islam with modernity.[21] He dismisses the problematisation of gender in Saudi Arabia under the rubric of *qadiyyat al-mar'a* (the woman question), and absolves Islam from any discrimination against women. While he celebrates women's role in and contribution to society, he sees persistent discrimination as originating in social and cultural practices. In his opinion, the liberation of women is a flawed goal, as in Islam they are considered full believers with both responsibilities and rights. He insists that women are entitled to be consulted in the formulation of public policy. While he is critical of social norms that confirm women in a position of subordination, he asserts that women's emancipation should not undermine society's harmony. For example, in societies where women are expected to cover their faces, women should abide by this cultural tradition in order to prevent a backlash. In other societies where this is not the custom, women should be free to remove face cover, while upholding modest dress as prescribed in Islam. In this respect, societal norms rather than personal choices are respected. Al-Awdah obviously does not go as far as considering the veil a personal choice.

ON REVOLUTION

On the hot debate about lifting the ban on women driving in Saudi Arabia, al-Awdah asserts that there is nothing in Islam that prohibits driving. The ban is sustained by societal pressure. Society considers driving as a threat to patriarchal authority and, until social conditions change, it is better not to provoke a backlash that could result in driving becoming a threat to women's security and safety.

Al-Awdah tries to humanise himself as a father by circulating his personal photos, in which he is captured playing with his daughter, who decorates his hair with little colourful ribbons—a revolutionary step not only as a religious scholar but also as a man: Saudi men prefer to be seen in situations of authority rather than playful paternity. Al-Awdah capitalises on the power of photography to alter society's perception of women and young girls by promoting a different understanding of parental authority. He shifts focus from the traditional control and discipline to protective paternalism, hoping to alter society's perception of women.

There are fundamental unanswered questions within Islamic gender debates, such as the legitimacy of women assuming public roles, for example as political leaders and judges. Saudi *ulama*, along with other Muslim scholars, deny the suitability of women for such high-ranking jobs and responsibilities. Al-Awdah has not spoken in these important debates, which have intensified since the Arab uprisings as women who participated in the overthrow of the regimes began to demand greater roles at the top level of government. Neither has he commented on the appointment of thirty women to the Saudi Consultative Council in February 2013, perhaps because of his doubts about the limitations of this unelected forum. King Abdullah introduced the appointment of women in 2013 with the intention of empowering women, increasing their participation in decision making, and responding to pressure to implement measures in support of gradual social reform.

Can we predict what al-Awdah's position would be if mass demonstrations were to sweep the streets of Saudi cities? So far he has not called for demonstrations in Saudi Arabia, but he has certainly justified the sporadic protest that erupted with the Arab uprisings. However, in 2012–13, as mentioned earlier, increasing numbers of women, the relatives of political prisoners, marched in the streets in Buraiydah, al-Awdah's home town. Small groups of women organised demonstrations in front of government buildings calling for the release of their relatives, some of whom had been detained for several years without trial. The protestors were rounded up and sent to interrogation centres together with their children after an incident where they posted a

YouTube video of themselves burning the portrait of the interior minister, Prince Muhammad ibn Nayif. Such sporadic protest was definitely inspired by the Arab uprisings. It adopted its strategies and imagery. Heavily veiled women carried placards and chanted slogans such as *al-shab urid tahrir al-sujun*, 'The people want to free the prisons'. Men also organised similar events in Buraiydah and Riyadh, resulting in further arrests. By March 2013 these small demonstrations were being held regularly, but without the official media reporting them. They were publicised online through social media, mainly Twitter and Facebook, with special accounts such as Itiqal and Munasiron dedicated to sharing news and images of the protest.

While al-Awdah has not encouraged such regular demonstrations, he must have felt under pressure to support the cause of political prisoners and condemn the arrest and harsh repression of women demonstrators, at least in his own hometown, Buraiydah. In March 2013 he issued a statement entitled 'An Open Letter to the Saudi People' highlighting the danger of suppressing civil society and putting activists and women protestors in prison.[22] He tweeted sections of the statement with thousands of followers re-tweeting and commenting on their content. He broke his silence after several women were detained following a small demonstration in Buraiydah. The tweeted short statements appeared later on his news website, Islam Today, in both Arabic and English as a full letter. In the same letter he addressed Prince Muhammad ibn Nayif, currently crown prince and minister of interior, and warned against the use of excessive force against relatives of political prisoners. Al-Awdah invoked human rights in his defence of political prisoners and stated that 'human rights are not limited to those who agree with us'. This statement referred to the fact that many prisoners were accused of being terrorists or al-Qaida sympathisers. In his opinion only fair, open trials can establish justice for the accused. Long detentions are counterproductive as they galvanise relatives and increase tension in society, undermining the government's legitimacy. He justifies the women's demonstration as a result of people losing hope and resorting in desperation to acts that are outlawed. In his letter he refers to the burning of the minister's portrait and calls it a symbolic act that must be noted as a warning sign of the deterioration of the relationship between ruler and ruled. He said, 'The recent burning of officials' pictures is a symbolic act that should give us some pause to think. What got it started? Where is this all going?'[23] According to him, the personalised nature of the Saudi justice system has reached a dead end in resolving the plight of political prisoners. He lamented that 'there are no clear regulations and institutions to normalize how prisoners are treated. Everything is decided on a case-by-case basis on the strength of a detective's report.'[24] Saudi prisons have become places for vengeance exercised by a government that is obsessed with security to the detriment of justice. These prisons are administered by intelligence services without clear guidelines and rules, thus creating conditions for instability, frustration, and anger among a large section of society. Al-Awdah is aware of his critics among the Jihadis,[25] whose right to fair trials he now tries to defend. Nevertheless, his statements on this issue positioned him as a defender of justice for all, regardless of their alleged offences.

In the same letter al-Awdah criticises the media in Saudi Arabia and the restrictions on free speech. He laments the fact that Saudi media labelled all those calling for political reform as agitators. In his opinion Saudis are now less gullible and are capable of formulating independent opinions. As state-controlled media often attribute mobilisation to the work of external agents and agitators, he rejects these claims and insists that demonstrators are driven by real local grievances. They have reached a dead end with the so-called approachable leadership, thus finding themselves compelled to go to the streets to seek justice.

In the letter al-Awdah invokes the *midan* (public square) as the place where activists would eventually go if their demand to free political prisoners is not met, thus reminding his audiences of the success of *midan* politics in places such as Egypt and Tunisia.[26] He warned that 'when revolutions are suppressed, they turn into armed conflicts. If they are ignored, they grow in reach and in breadth. The only solution is to take wise and timely decisions before violence is kindled.'[27] He says that suppressing peaceful protest will eventually lead to violence, and calls upon the government to free political prisoners, especially those who had been detained for their opinions or attempts to establish independent human and civil rights organisations. Finally, he warns that when peaceful action is suppressed, people often resort to violence.

The image of the public square filled with demonstrators seems to have inspired al-Awdah, who considers it the only solution after all attempts to put pressure on the government to free political prisoners fail. This final solution stands between two opposing positions: the acquiescent Salafi tradition and the Jihadi armed struggle. Inspired by the change in Arab countries, a third way between those two extremes is now visible, and is appreciated for its success.

As expected, al-Awdah's open letter to the Saudi people generated harsh criticism from state-controlled media, with several journalists attacking him for his daring criticism of the government over the issue of political prisoners. In the Saudi-owned pan-Arab newspaper *al-Sharq al-Awsat*, Tariq al-Humaid wrote that al-Awdah was once again seeking celebrity status on Twitter, and that his letter was simply meant to position himself as spokesman for the Saudi people. He reiterated that al-Awdah cannot be trusted given his previous agitations in the 1990s when he criticised the use of foreign troops to liberate Kuwait from Saddam's occupation, which represented a threat to Saudi Arabia. Al-Awdah was depicted as a man capable of changing his convictions to suit the present moment. His statement was described as an attempt to blackmail the government and threaten it with future unrest unless it responds to his radical agenda. He was accused of demanding that the government appoint him a representative of the Saudi people in a country where there is no room for a religious guardian along the Iranian model of government.[28] Another journalist, Salman al-Dowsari, accused al-Awdah of reinventing himself as both a reformist and revolutionary who warns against an uprising in a country that is peaceful. He combines talking about love and peaceful coexistence with revolutionary rhetoric, and seeks to play a leading role in undermining the authority of the Saudi government and the impartiality of its justice system. Al-Dowsari writes that al-Awdah launched a 'bomb' when he warned that anger among the people leads to the leadership losing its symbolic significance and legitimacy, with legitimacy moving to the streets. Revolutionary rhetoric was singled out in his statements as an indication of his radicalism and opportunism.[29]

As long as al-Awdah remained aloof from engaging with the Saudi scene and its many political issues and concentrated instead on preaching he was left to pursue his own projects. But the moment he engaged with the hot issue of political prisoners he was faced with fierce criticism, reflecting the government's fear of this engagement leading to serious mobilisation. Al-Awdah knows that the authorities watch him and monitor his activities and writings. So far he has been allowed to consolidate his media empire and reach out to the youth in study circles, sermons, and on social media. However, any deviation from the acceptable sphere of action or challenge to the government is more likely to be met with restrictions on his activities. Banning him from travel is but one step in that direction. The government may not resort to imprisonment given his popularity, but restrictions can easily be implemented to limit his activism or writings.

From Euphoria to Mourning

Some Islamists such as Salman al-Awdah experienced a momentary euphoria with the Arab uprisings, resulting in serious attempts to comprehend the change, justify its strategies, and celebrate its outcome, which resulted in Islamist parties winning seats in parliaments and moving from opposition to government in Egypt and Tunisia. By the eve of the Arab uprisings many Saudi Islamists, including al-Awdah, had already reinvented themselves as peaceful activists seeking the reform of the regime from within. During the revolts they reclaimed their position on the map of Saudi Arabia. They developed their own strategies to remain relevant and central to any debate about the future of the country. They had at their disposal multiple media outlets which they used regularly to influence public opinion and shape the debate about the political future of their country. Their increased online presence demonstrated engagement with the politics of the region, with many well-known personalities supporting the change. The uprisings reinvigorated them as two Islamist parties, al-Nahda in Tunisia and the Muslim Brotherhood in Egypt, came to power. At the same time they supported the struggle of Tunisian, Egyptian, Libyan, Yemeni, and Syrian activists, which they dubbed *sahwa islamiyya*, an Islamic awakening. Many Saudi Islamists saw the Syrian uprising through the lens of sectarian politics and considered the Syrian rebels as defenders of Sunni revival against the hegemony of a minority Alawite regime, backed by Iran. They pressed for greater Saudi support for the Syrian rebels. On the Bahraini uprising, many Saudi Islamists concurred with the Saudi regime when it described the Bahraini revolution as a Shia–Iranian conspiracy to undermine the security of the Gulf. They also condemned the Saudi Shia uprising in the oil-rich Eastern Province. They accused the Shia of opportunism and blamed them for provoking the regime to increase oppression and arrests among their own activists. While Salman al-Awdah remained silent on the Bahraini uprising, his views on the Shia remain grounded in the Salafi tradition that does not accept them as the equals of Sunnis. Yet, unlike the majority of Salafis, he is willing to tolerate them as a minority within the realm of Islam.

Saudi Islamists were seriously enchanted by the 2011 success of their counterparts in Tunisia and Egypt, who reached power through the ballot box. They were aware that the uprisings were not brought about by Islamists alone, who were but one among the forces that toppled these dictatorships. Nevertheless, they celebrated these revolutions as delivery from oppression, while traditional Saudi Salafis continued to describe them as chaos and dissent. The fusion between Islam and democracy was celebrated as a mechanism to marry Islamic authenticity with political modernity, a position also rejected by traditional Saudi Salafis.

However, Saudi Islamist euphoria proved to be short lived, as the elected Egyptian Muslim Brotherhood was removed from power in July 2013.[30] Under Brotherhood rule in Egypt Islamists enjoyed new opportunities that had been unavailable to them under the Mubarak regime. Between 2011 and 2013 al-Awdah started writing articles in Egyptian mainstream media, offering commentaries on government, sharia, and religious matters. He also supported the policies of the Islamist government. This direct exposure to the Egyptian scene came to an abrupt end when in July 2013 General Abdul Fatah al-Sisi removed the elected president, Muhammad Morsi, from office. At this juncture al-Awdah expressed his anger over the toppling of an elected government, and supported the pro-Morsi crowds that gathered for several weeks in Rab'a Square. When the Egyptian military imprisoned the president and other high-ranking Muslim Brotherhood figures and moved to disperse the protestors, leading to hundreds of deaths in the summer of 2013, al-Awdah supported the Brotherhood from Saudi Arabia with his tweets. He wrote, 'Whoever helps a murderer—whether by word, deed, financial support, or even a gesture of approval—is an accomplice,'[31] a statement that reflected his opposition to the Saudi endorsement of the coup and the later enormous subsidies that the government promised to give to General Sisi. He added, 'It is clear who is driving Egypt to its destruction out of fear for their own selves. I am with those whose blood is being shed and against those who are blindly going about killing people.'[32]

Over several days and weeks in July 2013 al-Awdah tweeted commentaries on the plight of the Egyptian crowds in Rab'a Square, and condemned the coup. Saudi Islamists in general resented their government's welcome of the coup and its recognition of the interim Egyptian government. Several personalities including religious scholars signed a petition dissociating themselves from the Saudi position and condemning the financial support promised by Saudi Arabia to stabilise the new Egyptian government.[33] They called upon the king to reverse his support for the Egyptian coup. On 17 July the well-known Islamist Muhsin al-Awaji was among those who were called for interrogation, following his involvement in writing and publicising the petition, while another famous religious scholar, Muhammad al-Oraifi, was prevented from travelling to Qatar to deliver a lecture. For these scholars Saudi support for the coup confirmed the regime as a counter-revolutionary force that feared the rise of Islamists to power. Their organised anti-coup stand was immediately supported by a Twitter hashtag against the king under the title 'The King does not Represent me', which remained live for several days. The euphoria that had accompanied the Arab uprisings began to fade away, only to be replaced by anger at the Saudi government and mourning of the dead in Rab'a Square.

The Egyptian coup represented in the mind of al-Awdah a return to military rule and an end to the short democratic experiment. He must have reflected on his early enthusiasm for peaceful protest which he articulated in his book, media appearances, and virtual forums, and came to the conclusion that dismantling authoritarian rule involves more than street protest. Yet he remained optimistic that the process had already begun, and retreated into the security of faith in God and his support for the oppressed.

Conclusion

It is too simplistic to argue that Saudi Islamists such as Salman al-Awdah moved from radicalism to moderation or liberalism as an opportunistic position in the context of the Arab uprisings. It is more accurate to describe the process that the case study of Salman al-Awdah illustrates as a mutation under real historical, political, and social conditions. Islamism in Saudi Arabia reached an impasse after 9/11, yet remained a relevant religio-political movement despite regime efforts to co-opt its outspoken activists and undermine their credibility by associating them with terrorism. Salman al-Awdah propagates a new discourse that has mutated under specific conditions, one of which is the transformation of the Arab world since 2011 as a result of peaceful protest. In his publications and media appearances he has fused his Salafi intellectual heritage with modern concepts, while keeping this heritage anchored in Islam. He has not openly identified himself with a specific political party or association; but al-Awdah is certainly preparing for a hybrid discourse that can inspire a new generation of Saudi youth and lay the foundation for future activism. His writings reflect impatience with traditional Salafi views that have affirmed acquiescence and criminalised peaceful protest in the pursuit of justice and political representation. Many in Saudi Arabia, especially among journalists and writers in the official press, continue to demonise al-Awdah, reminding their audiences of his position in the 1990s when he rejected the government's decision to invite foreign troops to defend Saudi Arabia against an imminent invasion by Iraq. In their view al-Awdah represents a radical trend within the so-called Islamic Awakening, and cannot be dissociated from its project to seize the state and impose an even stricter application of Islam. He is regularly accused of encouraging the youth to perform jihad in other countries but, despite his denial of this, he remains a suspect

Islamist. Many of his accusers have failed to provide evidence from his writings and media appearances in support of their claims. It seems that his endorsement of the third way, seeking political change by peaceful means, represent a more dangerous mutation than outright calls for violence. Al-Awdah is banned from travel, and remains on the government's watch list. Restrictions on his freedom and continuous intimidation represent in his view the conditions that prompt people to seek change and eventually revolution. Al-Awdah has summed up this danger: 'There is nothing that prompts us to encourage revolutions as it is enshrined in danger. ... It just comes when profound reform has stumbled.'[34]

Al-Awdah is probably one of the most important *ulama* in Saudi Arabia today. While there are other more populist Salafi preachers such as Yusif al-Ahmad and Muhammad al-Oraifi, al-Awdah remains more distinguished as he combines religious knowledge and engagement with political issues. He presents a new image of the intellectual who blurs the boundaries between the traditional scholar, on the one hand, and political analyst and activist, on the other. He will remain a source of inspiration for contemporary Saudi youth in general, especially those seeking higher education and engaged in political discourse about politics in the modern world. Populist Wahhabi–Salafi scholars such as al-Ahmad will struggle to persuade this cohort of educated youth to follow their path. The latters' audiences tend to be of modest educational background, seeking local solutions to questions about piety, commanding right and forbidding wrong, and gender issues such as women's driving, *ikhtilat* (mixing between the sexes), and women's participation in the public sphere. While al-Awdah may be equally concerned with these issues, he nevertheless has moved beyond limited Salafi solutions to modern concerns and provided political insights that can potentially change the Saudi polity in different directions, all of which ensure some kind of political representation, civil society activism, and greater respect for human rights. Al-Awdah has definitely inspired many younger religious intellectuals who pursue his ideas and elaborate on his concepts. In the next chapter I discuss how al-Awdah's concern with breaking away from traditional acquiescent Salafi interpretations is explored by a new generation of intellectuals such as Abdullah al-Maliki.

4

BETWEEN FORCE AND CHOICE

DEBATING SHARIA IN A SALAFI CONTEXT

The Arab uprisings perplexed many Saudi Islamists, as its slogans did not reflect the quest for the Islamic state or the immediate application of sharia. They were an unexpected moment that paved the way for reflections on the future of countries dismantling decades of republican military rule. Saudi Islamists waited for the unfolding of events in neighbouring countries. While many celebrated the election of the Muslim Brotherhood to parliaments and governments in Egypt and Tunisia, which confirmed their claim that if Arab societies are given the choice they will definitely choose Islamist governments, a small minority carefully warned against rushing into subjecting societies to immediate sharia rule. It is not without irony that this warning came from young intellectuals in a country such has Saudi Arabia, which has always prided itself on applying sharia. One such personality is Abdullah al-Maliki, whose controversial writings on the topic provoked a hostile reaction in Saudi Salafi circles. Al-Maliki moved the debate further by questioning the merit of imposing sharia by force in a post-revolutionary phase. Although the application of sharia is taken for granted in Saudi Arabia, the question of how and when to implement it began to be hotly debated among Islamist intellectuals, especially after the Arab uprisings.

The controversy erupted after al-Maliki published a short article in al-Maqal, a web-based news forum that specialises in publishing controversial and revisionist interpretations volunteered by like-minded young intellectuals, including women and Shia. In 2014 al-Maliki and Sultan al-Jumairi launched a news and analysis website, al-Tagreer, to provide a niche platform for broader Tanwiri perspectives than those in al-Maqal.[1] After the controversy over his short article he published a book on the same topic, in which he explained in great detail his new perspective on the implementation of sharia. Applying the sharia is taken for granted in Saudi circles, and he was vehemently attacked as a misguided Islamist who had become a secular liberal. While mainstream Salafis often use such labels to denounce their opponents, it was rather strange that it was used on al-Maliki, given his deep commitment to the Islamic tradition. This chapter traces al-Maliki's controversial thinking about the application of sharia in post-revolutionary countries.

From Traditional Scholarship to Intellectual Controversies

Abdullah al-Maliki (b. 1978) represents a new generation of Islamists who have truly broken away from traditional Salafi training and thinking simply by questioning established assumptions about the application of sharia in contemporary society. Born in the mountain town of Taif, he had a traditional religious education in the study circle of the mosque. He then went to study at Umm al-Qura University, where he completed a master's degree on the Algerian-French thinker Muhammad Arkoun and his position on the critical analysis of religious discourse. He currently works as an administrator at King Abdul Aziz University in Jeddah, and spends most of his time in research and writing.[2]

His critical moment came after 9/11 and the heated debates in Saudi society that followed this event. He was immersed in these debates, which required a new way of thinking about religion and society. This coincided with greater spaces for discussion that were allowed to take place following 9/11. It was difficult to remain aloof from the intense debates, according to al-Maliki. After 9/11 a chance opened up to discuss and revisit the Saudi religious scene and its political consequences. The government initially encouraged the debating of religion in an attempt to reach out to sections of society that it hoped might help contain the violence that erupted in Saudi Arabia itself between 2003 and 2008. Nevertheless, the short-lived opening of the public sphere led to intense exchanges between activists, religious scholars, and intellectuals. Al-Maliki initially participated in internet discussions, taking part in real forums among like-minded young writers without revealing his true identity. Between 2003 and 2008 he was active in formulating opinions and commentaries on current affairs in internet forums, which were replaced by Facebook and Twitter as means to reach out to wider audiences in

2009.[3] While his virtual outreach has become large due to the great use of Twitter in Saudi society, estimated to be the largest in the Arab world, his real circle remains confined to university-educated activists and religious intellectuals. He admits that this circle is narrow as it does not spill over to wider society, but he acknowledges that discussion among this group is crucial for deconstructing taken-for-granted opinions about religion, politics, and society, especially the dominant Salafi tradition. With the advent of Twitter, the discussion spread beyond real activists who assemble to debate current affairs. In order to circumvent prevalent repression of political debate, al-Maliki insists that he and his group are known as intellectual researchers rather than political activists. This way, their discourse is projected as an intellectual religious research agenda rather than as political treatises that could be seen as threatening by the government. Organised discussion forums about the topics he is interested in are often camouflaged as workshops to discuss 'family and society'. In these workshops the conversation drifts into discussing political and religious issues. This way such workshops and informal discussion salons are held without drawing attention to the forums or their organisers, which would result in cancelling events that have an obvious political title or agenda. But most intellectuals in this loose association disseminate their ideas in short articles posted on electronic media, which have flourished in the past decade: websites such as al-Maqal, al-Asr, al-Tagreer, and other more established ones such as al-Awdah's Islam Today. Al-Maliki and other similar-minded intellectuals have benefited from publishing their books in the Saudi-owned, Beirut-based Arab Network for Research and Publishing under the directorship of Nawaf al-Qudaimi. Both the electronic media and the publishing house became important in consolidating an intellectual Tanwiri trend and making it visible in the public sphere.

While al-Maliki does not attach great importance to labels, he acknowledges that his traditional Salafi opponents refer to him as belonging to *al-tayar al-tanwiri* (the enlightenment trend),[4] which according to his Salafi critics dilutes commitment to Islam. He considers himself as belonging to an intellectual trend that is concerned with offering new Islamic interpretations of current urgent questions about government and Islam. Yet this trend is not organised in civil society, and remains a loose intellectual association of young activists and writers whose membership consists of occasional meetings and intellectual exchanges. They include personalities such as Muhammad al-Ahmari, Muhammad al-Abd al-Karim, Nawaf al-Qudaimi, Abdulaziz al-Qasim, Abd al-Aziz al-Khodr, Suleiman al-Dhahiyan, and many others. While some are religious scholars teaching at religious studies faculties in Saudi Arabia, others are writers, journalists, and professionals. Al-Maliki points out that the enlightenment label is used by Salafi opponents to dismiss a group of thinkers and activists who are simply trying to retain the centrality of Islam in social and political life, while offering ways to deal with the rigidity of the dominant Salafi thought and its implications on Saudi politics and society. The consolidation of the Tanwiri intellectual trend prompted many Salafis to write books and articles denouncing its premises and highlighting its danger to Islam. It is often described as an Islamic bridge to Westernisation and secularisation.[5] Its opponents consider it an attempt to undermine Salafi Islam from within, and reprimand its thinkers for not prioritising the dangers of Westernisation. Instead, Tanwiris turn their deconstruction inward and privilege criticism of Salafi thought. Abdullah Salman al-Awdah, a young writer, describes the Tanwiris as 'those who wanted to escape from being tarnished as innovators by traditional Salafis, and those disenchanted with Sahwa. They created a Tanwir island.'[6]

Abdullah al-Maliki is concerned with the fate of religion under state control, which not only threatens people's freedoms but is in fact detrimental to religion itself. He laments that after 9/11 many Islamists and those labelled liberals in Saudi society launched attacks on so-called radical religious discourse that had prospered and flourished under the authority of the state. They ignored the repressive political context in which this discourse was consolidated. After discussions with like-minded activists and thinkers, he says that they reached the conclusion that religious reform is impossible under authoritarian rule, which co-opts scholars, manipulates *fatwa*s, and stifles debate. He insists that

> Controlling religion creates a hypocritical society similar to the Saudi one. The wealth available to the state enabled it to silence critical thought and prevent people from exploring new interpretations. Religious scholars have become a tool within state institutions. This tool limited the ability of scholars to discuss, debate, and disagree. Some may offer good interpretations while others err. Yet without a free space to debate multiple religious opinions, religious discourse in Saudi Arabia stagnated. We need a dialectical approach to religious knowledge, but this approach is not possible to develop without freedom from state control.[7]

The state monopolises the production of religious discourse, and this prompted many young activists to migrate to the free forums made available on the internet. In his opinion, 'in the past we focused on a more acceptable and familiar concept, namely *shura* (consultation) as a foundation for just government. This was to avoid collision with traditional Salafi thinkers. But after 2008 this newly emerging free space allowed us to dare to coin the term democracy as a priority.'[8] Al-Maliki does not hesitate to call for democracy, which means 'the sovereignty of the *umma*. It is a mechanism that allows the *umma* to vote and choose its leader. It is the antithesis of the rule of a single person or family.'[9] The supreme king who says 'I am the state' is a thing of the past in light of discussions in these gatherings, he says. The shift from calling for *shura* to calling for democracy created unease in Saudi Arabia. In fact, those who call for democracy are totally immersed in religious knowledge, and their conclusions have sprung from their novel reading of the Islamic sources. Al-Maliki argues that the Arab uprisings pushed these discussions to the forefront. He highlights how the events of the Arab world after 2011 encouraged many like him to formulate the quest for democracy in clearer and sharper terms without abandoning the Islamic project. In fact, grounding his quest for democracy in Islamic discourse gave it a stronger momentum, as it ceased to be simply an import from the West. In his view the Arab uprisings are positive developments, as they pushed the Salafis who had previously condemned democracy to reconsider their convictions. His mission has become to prove that democracy is now the only solution to decades of isolating people from decisions under authoritarian and repressive rule.

For al-Maliki, democracy does not only mean elections; it means a free civil society that is able to mobilise and operate without state control or patronage. Such freedom allows 'debate about controversial issues such as the rule of a non-Muslim over Muslim countries, the role of women in public office, pluralism, and sectarianism'.[10] All these hot issues are subject to discussion, which is a by-product of the Arab uprisings. Central to this debate is limiting state interference in cultural and social issues and lifting restrictions on personal liberties. Cultural matters should be left to society to manage. The state cannot also be in control of people's creed. The state should be concerned with matters related to this world rather than people's beliefs. Al-Maliki proposes a minimalist state that is not concerned with controlling every aspect of life. He wants the state to be concerned only with managing the economy to ensure equality and social justice. People should have the ability to decide on their personal choices in everyday life. The functions of the minimalist state should be limited to worldly matters, and should not control society or patronise it. Society must feel free to choose its own course of action and beliefs.

Against the background of the Saudi state insisting that its constitution is the Quran, al-Maliki offers a different perspective. He rejects this claim on the basis that it undermines the status of the sacred book. The claim represents an aberration of the message of Islam that is embodied in the Quran. People reach to the Quran through faith, while a constitution is a man-made document that regulates matters relating to government. As such the Quran cannot be subjected to voting, revision, or change, while a constitution can be amended and altered. Therefore, the constitution is a man-made pamphlet that is necessary to regulate worldly affairs. Where there is a prohibition of a certain act in Islam, one cannot subject this to voting. Take for example the prohibition on *riba* (interest), which is not a matter for debate or voting. The rule of God, in al-Maliki's opinion, cannot be subjected to parliamentary majority opinion. He has faith in the decisions of a Muslim-majority society to prevent making *riba* permissible. In Saudi Arabia, according to al-Maliki, society is not what both the government and its liberal constituency want us to believe. It is not radical, as it is often depicted. But, if given an opportunity to vote, the majority of society would not vote against the rule of God. Society will welcome a constitution that defines its rights and regulates relations between rulers and ruled. Nor is society ready to reject Islam. If this society is given freedom, it will certainly engage in debating religion rather than rejecting it. However, this is not readily available under state control. The constitution is a necessity to limit repression and guarantee political and civil freedoms, in addition to human rights. The delay in achieving these rights is not attributed to the traditional Salafi position that is controlled by the state. In fact, al-Maliki blames the political leadership for delaying debates about the constitution and ignoring several petitions demanding it. He has participated in the petition *Dawlat al-huquq wa al-muassasat* (A state of rights and institutions), circulated in 2011 and discussed earlier in this book. Among other things, it called for an elected consultative council, independence of the judiciary, freedom for prisoners of conscience, and civil society.

He considers society to be vibrant and keen to engage with important debates, but stifled by repression. Once given freedom, it will come to the conclusion that a man-made constitution does not undermine the Quran, as outlined in the above-mentioned petition. Only an opening up of the political sphere similar to the one that took place after 9/11 under local and international pressures will allow new religious interpretations to emerge. Even traditional sections of Saudi society that in the past have rejected aspects of democracy now accept them.

Al-Maliki argues that Saudi society may not really be averse to innovations, despite a history of resisting modernisation. He cites the examples of female education, satellite dishes, mobile phones, and many other new technologies and ideas. After initially treating them with suspicion, Saudi society has come to accept them, and even to use them to promote new visions. He refers to how Saudi Salafis and activists have benefited from new communication technologies after initially rejecting them for their alleged corrupting influence. The same will apply to introducing a constitution; it may seem alien now, but society will eventually endorse it to guarantee its rights and freedoms. Unfortunately, the government felt threatened by the Arab uprisings and reverted to stifling debate. Al-Maliki feels pessimistic about the consequences of the new repression that followed the 2011 uprisings. The repression of reformists and their subjection to long trials reflect a setback that is bound to delay political reform, the only condition for moving forward. Here al-Maliki refers to the trial and subsequent imprisonment of personalities such as Abdullah al-Hamid, Suleiman al-Rushoudi, and Muhammad al-Qahtani, all founders of the Saudi Association for Civil and Political Rights (HASM).[11]

Abdullah al-Maliki is one example of a new generation of traditionally trained religious intellectuals whose upbringing predisposed him to continue to be immersed in the conservative Salafi milieu of Saudi society and educational institutions. However, like many others of his generation, he tries to create space between the politically conservative Salafi tradition and the liberal tradition, seen as a philosophy distant from Saudi culture and norms. Nevertheless, he has gone as far as calling for democracy, and clothing this call in Islamic garb. Although he is not one of the better-known religious scholars and ideologues of the Islamist movement, his writings pushed the limits as far as to incur the wrath of traditional Salafis, simply because he called for sovereignty of the *umma* before the application of sharia.

Sovereignty of the Umma

Abdullah al-Maliki's short article 'Siyadat al-umma qabl tatbiq al-sharia' (Sovereignty of the *umma* before applying sharia), published on the al-Maqal website,[12] generated severe criticism, especially among those Salafis who accused him of being a liberal and a secularist; both accusations represented an attempt to dismiss him despite his religious upbringing and knowledge. This criticism prompted him to write a book under the same title in which he provided a detailed interpretation of his position on the sovereignty of the *umma*.[13]

Al-Maliki admits that political sovereignty is a foreign concept, translated into Arabic as *siyada*. It is often confused with the famous *hakimiyya* (sovereignty of God), which in Islam means that sovereignty ultimately rests with God. He draws on a definition of political sovereignty as the highest authority associated with an independent people represented by their chosen government. Sovereignty allows governments to legislate, apply the rule of law, and protect society. Historically and in many societies its sources have been divine power, an individual ruler, or the people through their representative bodies. His survey of the changing meaning of sovereignty in European history captures debates between classical Western scholars such as Jean Bodin (1530–96), Thomas Hobbes (1588–1679), John Locke (1632–1704) and Jean-Jacques Rousseau (1712–78).[14] If there is a lesson to learn from this survey, it is the long struggle towards people's sovereignty achieved only under democratic government. He criticises those Salafis who confuse the political meaning of sovereignty with their quest for the sovereignty of sharia. The supremacy of sharia as a source of legislation is taken for granted, but this glosses the meaning of sovereignty as a political concept. Political sovereignty is concerned with authority to rule, whereas the sharia may be a source for legislation. God's sovereignty does not exclude people's sovereignty, as it is people rather than God who conduct real worldly affairs. In his view, God in his sacredness does not come down to people and oblige them to apply sharia. If God had political sovereignty, there would be no non-believers or political systems that contradict God's message.[15] Revelation needs people to become reality, and those people are constrained by their own historical moment. Those traditional Islamists who raise the slogan about *hakimiyya* contribute to the creation of a theocratic class similar to the old European model, which combined religion and politics and put itself above everybody else simply because it derived its legitimacy from claiming that it represented God. The authority of this theocratic class rested on divine sources rather than the people. This created conditions for repression in the name of God and the outlawing of any dissent by labelling it rebellion. As traditional Islamists among both the Sunni and Shia propagate the concept of God's *hakimiyya*, they have in their own way created confusion with regard to people's sovereignty. Political sovereignty should rest with the collective *umma*, the people, according to al-Maliki.

After explaining what political sovereignty means and how it should not be confused with the Islamist concept of *hakimiyya*, al-Maliki gives four important conditions for its realisation: freedom; *istikhlaf* (viceregency); the oath of allegiance (contract); and consultation. These are the basic foundation of sovereignty.

According to al-Maliki, freedom is a condition that people are born into, while oppression is a condition to which they are subjected after birth. He lists Quranic verses that assert the priority of freedom, reflected in God telling people that he has shown them truth with the choice of believing or disbelieving. He returns to the story of Satan, who chose to disobey God and, after being given an opportunity to repent, chose not to. Such a story demonstrates that belief is a matter of choice rather than compulsion. To believe in one God means freedom from other forms of oppression such as those practised by people against each other, or that of social tradition and norms, or the oppression of mythologies and instincts. In the context of society, freedom means choosing your beliefs away from oppression. The relationship between this freedom and sovereignty is organic, as one cannot talk about a sovereign *umma* that does not enjoy freedom.

The second important condition for sovereignty is *istikhlaf*, the collective responsibility of people to preserve life as vicegerents. This is not the prerogative of one ruler or a group of religious scholars; it is the responsibility of the *jama'a*, society itself. Here, al-Maliki departs from traditional opinions. Those who are oppressed or forced to follow certain rules are exempt from this collective responsibility simply because they are not free to choose and monitor the actions of government. In Islam, according to al-Maliki, there is no room for absolute authority. Throughout Islamic history scholars have referred to the ordinary people using pejorative terms such as 'the masses', while reserving positive words such as 'the elite', 'the notables', and 'the chosen ones' for the rulers and their circles. This has led to the undermining of the *umma* and its various constituents. The *umma* should not be a society of followers denied the right to freedom, a condition imposed on it as a result of prolonged oppression and marginalisation under authoritarian rule.[16]

Thirdly, sovereignty depends on the oath of allegiance, a contract between the *umma* and the ruler.[17] This is a social contract in which the ruler becomes a representative (*wakil*) of the people and their interests rather than the divine will. The ruler has no legitimacy without the *umma*. The idea of government as a social contract is embedded in the early Islamic experience of the Prophet, regarded by al-Maliki as a model that has been corrupted by successive authoritarian and absolute government throughout Islamic history. In this history the ruler became detached from those who had given him legitimacy to rule, and in most cases had not chosen him themselves.

The fourth condition is *shura*, or consultation, a process that allows the *umma* to exercise the right to choose its leader rather than simply a meaningless process.[18] While in many modern Islamic writings *shura* is seen as the 'functional equivalent of Western parliamentary rule, and as the basis of an authentic Islamic democracy',[19] according to al-Maliki it is a binding principle of Islam. It is binding because it means accepting majority decisions. The highest level of consultation is in the political field, where choosing the ruler is the main priority. *Shura* also includes removing a ruler when he fails in his role. This can be achieved through referendum rather than conquest or violence. Therefore, elections become a mechanism that allows the *umma* to choose its leader and representatives. It is the act of consultation as a right enjoyed by all people with no one group claiming to monopolise the right to be consulted. *Shura* is a collective responsibility that epitomises the sovereignty of the nation.

The strongest attack on al-Maliki was based on his claim that we should respect the choice of a Muslim nation if its majority decides against the immediate implementation of sharia in a post-revolutionary period. Saudi Salafis and others do not consider the application of sharia as a matter of choice subject to discussion or voting. But al-Maliki deviates from this axiomatic principle when he argues that imposing sharia on society negates its right to be sovereign. The duty of a Muslim requires convincing society of the merit of the sharia rather than simply imposing it by force. He argues that a Muslim nation is unlikely to reject the application of sharia although it may reject an Islamist political party for mismanaging the affairs of society. But, if the majority in a Muslim society rejects the application of sharia, it is the duty of Muslims to correct this choice using civil means, and to clarify the merits of returning to the sharia. Sharia should therefore be the outcome of mobilisation in a peaceful, contractual framework using activism, the media, and civil society. He explains that he does not differ from those who call for the application of sharia, as he thinks it is an obligation, but he disagrees with those who seek to impose it by force or compulsion. When a leader imposes sharia without consultation, it is likely that another leader who may come to power as a result of conquest or a coup can equally suspend it.

Al-Maliki uses the example of prayer in Islam. He argues that it is an obligation to pray, but a Muslim may exercise his free will and decide not to pray. Without free will, the obligation to pray becomes meaningless. This also applies to other prohibited acts such as drinking alcohol and committing adultery. Muslims are ordered to respect the prohibition on these acts, but without free will there is no substance to the obligations. In democracies elections reveal what people want, but a democratic government should not be concerned with people's convictions. It should be concerned with their choices. Similarly, if people choose not to apply the sharia, this does not mean that the sharia itself is a matter of choice. It simply means that they have chosen not to apply it. Allegations that democracy pushes people to reject the sharia are misguided. The problem is not in democracy, but in Muslim societies that reject sharia despite its status as an obligation in Islam. The remedy is to educate the Muslim community to apply the sharia as a matter of choice rather than force.

Al-Maliki has concentrated on critiques of the mainstream Islamist movement, especially the Muslim Brotherhood and its short-lived experience in governing Egypt after the revolution in 2011. In an article entitled 'Why has the Muslim Brotherhood failed in government?'[20] he states that removing an elected president by force is wrong, but that society has the right to demonstrate against such an elected president when he ceases to fulfil its needs. When such demonstrations accelerate, an elected ruler has two options: call for early elections or step down. The Muslim Brotherhood in Egypt reached a dead end as President Muhammad Morsi refused both these options. Al-Maliki brings the experience of French president Charles de Gaulle in 1968 when he faced opposition from leftists and students, and eventually stepped down from office. Al-Maliki's personal preference was for Morsi to complete his term in office, but as this was increasingly difficult he was wrong not to accept early elections. Legitimacy in al-Maliki's view is not a solid, unchanged entity. It is 'like fire, it can glow and become bigger but also it can shrink and disappear'.[21] Morsi's handling of the crisis of legitimacy paved the way for the military intervention. Here, the Muslim Brotherhood was opportunistic, preferring the coup to early elections in the hope that it would increase their popularity. They were wrong. They had moved swiftly from a revolutionary movement to one that is embedded in power. They should have understood that ruling a country requires cooperation rather than marginalising other important movements after seizing power, albeit in a legitimate democratic way.

In a blunt critique of the old Muslim Brotherhood slogan 'Islam is the solution', al-Maliki proposes that 'the sovereignty of the *umma* is the solution'. This sovereignty is in his opinion a safeguard against a situation such as the one that emerged in Egypt after the election of the Muslim Brotherhood in 2012. This sovereignty means respecting people's choices and taking notice of their decisions even after they have voted. Elections are not an opportunity to rule without consulting with people or taking notice of their evolving needs. The Egyptian coup of July 2013 is not a conspiracy against Islam, as claimed by the Muslim Brotherhood, but a second revolution to reassert the *umma*'s sovereignty after it had achieved it on 25 January 2011. Al-Maliki argues that no conspiracy is able to mobilise so many people as was claimed at the time; deposing Morsi was a protest against a president and his policies, despite the fact that a majority had elected him.

Salafi Resistance to So-called 'Bearded Liberals'

Al-Maliki's innovative approach in dealing with the role of the *umma* and its sovereignty resulted in an invitation to participate in a controversial forum where many young researchers, professionals, and activists assemble to discuss and debate political issues within the Gulf region, the third meeting of Multaqa al-Nahdha al-Shababi (the Youth Rising Forum), under the directorship of Sheikh Salman al-Awdah[22] and management of Mustafa al-Hasan, a professor of religious studies at King Fahd University for Petroleum and Minerals. The forum had already met twice, first in Bahrain ('Change: Horizons and Perceptions', 2010) and later in Qatar ('Force behind Thoughts', 2011). According to al-Hasan, the Youth Rising Forum is different from the Islamist Awakening, which focuses on worship and does not offer an opportunity for the youth to be engaged in civil action. The forum represents an attempt to reinstate civil action and concern with public affairs in the daily lives of young people by drawing on the Islamic tradition.[23] The forum is described in its own sources as an independent organisation that aims to provide a platform for a new youth unburdened by stale ideologies, tired of being patronised, rebellious by nature, and committed to an awakening that combines different political positions from the Islamists, liberals, and nationalists. It is this mix that created the controversy prior to the third meeting in Kuwait.

The third forum was meant to take place in Kuwait City in March 2012 under the title 'Civil Society: Means and Purposes'. The Kuwait meeting generated controversy both in Saudi Arabia and Kuwait.[24] Thirty-six Saudi Salafi scholars signed a statement warning against the danger of this forum.[25] The signatories included famous traditional hardline Salafi *ulama* such as Nasir al-Omar and Abdulrahman al-Buraik. They attacked the meeting for many reasons. Nasir al-Omar described the conference as 'debauchery', while another sheikh accused the participants of being deviant, without shame. The Salafi statement claimed that the invited speakers were liberals, secularists, atheists, Christians, Orientalists, and Shia. They specifically identified mixing between the sexes in the workshop as an attempt to Westernise the youth under a religious umbrella—mainly the patronage of Sheikh Salman al-Awdah. It was obvious that the conference organisers wanted to widen their audience beyond Islamists, as they invited Shia, liberals, men, women, and foreign scholars to discuss important and relevant topics related to civil society. The *ulama* who attacked the Kuwait meeting were probably concerned that the youth would be exposed to a 'subversive' discourse critical of their vision. They feared a meeting in which intellectuals and youth rather than Salafi *ulama* would take the lead. Salafis were not invited to participate in the forum, which added to their suspicions. These were not allayed by the participation of such an important personality as Sheikh Salman al-Awdah, who had gained large popularity among the youth since his participation in media programmes promoting a modernist vision of Islam. In fact, because the forum had been endorsed by al-Awdah as a supervisor (*mushrif*) many Salafis objected to the event, perhaps out of rivalry with al-Awdah, whose followers had increased in recent years. Furthermore, the diversity of the invited youth threatened to dissolve the boundaries between Islamists on the one hand and liberals and secularists on the other, whom the traditional Salafi *ulama* prefer to remain separate. The gender mixing that was allegedly a feature of the meeting was attacked as unacceptable for its corrupting potential. The forum was criticised for inviting gender activists such as young Hala al-Dosari, who was due to give a presentation on women's issues. The participation of French political scientist Stephane Lacroix and Kuwaiti academics such as Shafiq Ghabra and Ghanin al-Najjar was also singled out as unacceptable. The inclusion of Shia activists such as Saudi Tawfiq al-Saif was also a matter of concern for Salafis.

Salafis had also voiced their objections to the previous meetings held by the Youth Rising Forum. They argued that concepts discussed in the forum such as freedom, openness, coexistence, reform, and enlightenment are unsuitable in a Muslim society. They are considered 'modern' and alien to Muslims, and products of the West and the liberal tradition. Humanism (*insaniyya*) and civil society (*mujtama madani*) are suspect ideas borrowed from the West, and can never be used without knowing their origins, warned Abdul Aziz Abd al-Latif, Salafi professor of creed at Imam Muhammad ibn Saud University in Riyadh.[26] In particular, he singled out civil society as an imported secular concept aiming at separation between religion and state, absolute freedom for society, and the corruption of women. Another Salafi sheikh, Sulaiman al-Kharashi, went as far as to invent the label 'bearded liberals' to refer to those Islamists who have called for the establishment of civil society by drawing on Islamic reinterpretations. They are also known as Asranis (contemporaries), whose aim is to promote secularism in the forum.[27] Salafi critics of the third forum identified al-Maliki's article on the sovereignty of the *umma*, which was advertised on the conference programme, as yet another reason to call for banning the meeting. His article was described as 'an attempt to dilute the sharia, strengthen liberal thought and contaminate the minds of young people'.[28]

Criticism of the Youth Rising Forum was also voiced by non-Salafis, who dismissed it as nothing more than an attempt to reinvent Islamism under new, modern slogans. The enlightenment trend represented in the forum is seen as failing to clearly adopt the concept of the civil state (*dawla madaniyya*), in which equality and freedom are guaranteed for all citizens. The forum was accused of being a political platform rather than simply a space for exchanging academic agendas. The participants are often introduced as activists rather than researchers, thus demonstrating the political agenda of the meetings, according to liberal critics. Saudi writer Mishari al-Thaydi criticised the forum for adopting an ambiguous understanding of freedom in order not to antagonise Salafi audiences. In fact, he accused the organisers of keeping this ambiguity as a strategy so that they could not be accused of collusion with those who reject it in Saudi society, mainly Salafi hardliners.[29]

Kuwaiti Salafis co-operated with their Saudi counterparts to push the government of Kuwait to ban the meeting. Muhammad Haif, a Salafi Kuwaiti member of parliament, criticised the conference and called for it to be banned.[30] Others in Kuwait argued that the forum included participants who could be considered Saudi dissidents, so it might be better to cancel the forum than antagonise a neighbouring Gulf country. The Kuwaiti Interior Ministry issued a statement one day before the meeting, cancelling the licence initially given to hold the conference in one of Kuwait's hotels. The organisers renamed the meeting and were allowed to hold a smaller event in the Kuwait Graduate Association, after three political groups, the Kuwait Muslim Brotherhood, independent Islamists, and liberals, united to proceed with the planned event. A scaled-down conference went ahead, but with many invited guests cancelling their attendance at the last minute.[31]

The controversy surrounding the third Youth Rising Forum reflected the level of competition among various Islamist groups struggling to attract the youth. Moreover, governments in both Kuwait and Saudi Arabia regarded such an independent forum as a threat, which might spread across the Gulf states, especially at a time when they all felt the pressure of mass mobilisation in the Arab world and tried to prevent similar developments in their own back yards. The Salafi opposition to the forum seems to have coincided with the interests of both the Kuwaiti and Saudi governments; both had a vested interest in preventing it from taking place at the time of the Arab uprisings. They saw this forum as a potential subversion, as it promised to reach out to activist youth searching for an independent civil society forum operating beyond the limited boundary of each Gulf country. The transnational outlook of the forum participants and invited youth proved to be threatening, especially at a time when other Arabs were engaged in mobilisation in their own capitals during the Arab uprisings. The forum was seen as an opportunity to create a transnational Gulf youth movement that could gain strength after regular meetings held in various Gulf capitals, thus increasing the cross-fertilisation of ideas and cross-border mobilisation. Support networks had already been noticeable among the youth even before the conference was due to take place, as Gulf youth active on Facebook and Twitter had demonstrated great solidarity with others not only in the Gulf but also in the wider Arab world. News of the arrest of reformers and activists in Saudi Arabia immediately reached like-minded groups in other Gulf countries. The arrest of political activists across the region was debated online, with participants denouncing governments and calling for their immediate release. A real meeting taking place in Kuwait would have had the potential of converting online solidarities into more threatening activism. Banning the meeting was a precautionary measure to prevent activists who had only known each other in the virtual world from encountering each other in the context of a conference. Al-Maliki regrets that he did not attend the smaller gathering that took place after the ban on the forum.

Assessing the Arab Uprisings

According to al-Maliki, Islamism, the largest and most well-established social movement in the Arab world, had an opportunity to lead countries from authoritarianism to democracy after the Arab uprisings. Yet this opportunity was not straightforward. Al-Maliki argues that the Arab masses had suffered under dictatorships, as they were prevented from fulfilling their basic needs and enjoying political and civil rights. They aspired towards a real awakening, wealth, and social justice. In this context, all Islamist trends must ask themselves a fundamental question: what did the Arab masses want and what were the demands in 2011?[32]

Al-Maliki dismisses the claim that the Arab masses mobilised and occupied public squares in order to apply sharia, revive religion, prohibit alcohol, fight un-Islamic behaviour, destroy graves on saints' tombs, force women to wear the *niqab*, or bring back polygamy in countries where it had been prohibited (Tunisia and Libya). Their anger was not directed against nightclubs and dance floors. They did not demonstrate to bring back the rule of the righteous ancestors or the Sunni tradition. His analysis of the Arab uprisings deconstructs the rhetoric of many Islamists who described them as an Islamic awakening. In fact, the Arab masses had simple but urgent demands: freedom, dignity, and justice, all of which can be achieved by regaining the lost sovereignty of the *umma*. The masses wanted to be the sole source of sovereignty rather than a single triumphant ruler or his political party. This does not mean that they wanted to undermine or overlook their Islamic identity, which they have preserved more carefully than their rulers have done. Regaining sovereignty means choice. It is this choice that underpinned the mass demonstrations that swept the Arab world. This assessment of the Arab uprisings, which seems to be more convincing, draws on a realistic reading of the uprisings. Al-Maliki is aware of the diversity of those who participated in the uprisings and the slogans they raised. He is not prepared to gloss over these things, or depict their collective action as an Islamic awakening when in reality it was not.

Al-Maliki does not hesitate to admit that during the uprisings Arabs may not automatically have chosen the application of sharia. If the Arab masses choose the sharia, their choice must be respected. But if they do not, then no one has the right to impose sharia on them in a post-revolutionary period. No good would come out of such a step, as it would bring about hypocrisy and fear. The sharia does not aim to turn people into hypocrites. Preachers have the right to preach morality but they do not have the right to force people into submission. Once the masses become free and sovereign, change by peaceful means is more desirable than violence, terrorism, and wars. Choosing the sharia is better than submitting to its imposition by authoritarian rulers or Islamist parties.

Al-Maliki criticises those who reject democracy, such as traditional Salafis, on the grounds that it allows the people to make decisions with regard to the prohibited and permissible. This is a misunderstanding of both democracy and Islam. Islam rather than the people remains the source for permission or prohibition. The legitimacy of right and wrong comes from the religious system of knowledge; however, the legitimacy of government must come from the people in a democratic system. Consequently, parliaments are not places for issuing *fatwa*s or elaborating on Islamic jurisprudence; both remain the prerogative of religious scholars. He proposes that priority should be given to the sovereignty of people over a hasty implementation of sharia. He insists that there is a difference between the sharia and its application. Sharia is God given and revealed, while its application is a human act anchored in interpretation and therefore not part of religion—in fact, it may sometimes undermine religion, especially when unjust rulers use it for their own purposes, mainly as a legitimisation for repression. Only the sovereignty of the people can guarantee the rightful application of sharia as the people's choice.

Renewing Islamic Thought in the Saudi Context

Although al-Maliki's writings do not refer directly to the Saudi situation, his views clearly resonate in the context of an unelected ruler claiming legitimacy on the basis of applying sharia. This has always been the foundation of the Saudi state. Yet al-Maliki questions such claims to legitimacy by prioritising the sovereignty of the *umma*. He sees no merit in the imposition of sharia by force in the absence of authority that rests within the *umma* instead of a single ruler or a family. The harsh criticism he received from Salafi circles demonstrates beyond doubt that the project of renewing Islamic thinking remains a difficult task in a traditional Salafi milieu like that in Saudi Arabia. His writings imply that Saudis do not enjoy sovereignty, so the application of sharia is not a matter of free will but a function of instrumentalisation by the ruler whose legitimacy depends on such claims. As a religious intellectual, previously unknown in the country except among a small circle of activists, his writings put him in the spotlight. He aspires towards space for free intellectual discussion in the pursuit of political reform. Yet political control over religious discussion hinders the possibility of moving towards debating real issues that impinge on the prospect of democratisation. He sees no opportunity to free religion from this control under political oppression. His critique of the *ulama* as a selected class tied to political authority is bound to antagonise traditional Salafis, especially those who preach obedience to rulers or marginalise the *umma* as a mass of followers rather than people who should be consulted. His focus on free will brings into the equation the individual and his personal liberty to choose within the framework of a Muslim community. This free will is undermined in Saudi society as the ruler and his *ulama* remain the first arbiters, coercing people to conform in ways that can only perpetuate oppression and exclusion. He counts on society, which is in his opinion inclined to debate and argue, and cannot flourish under oppression. Even those who appear to be radical now will benefit from an opening of the public sphere that would free them to discuss their views and reinterpret their convictions. Freedom does not necessarily mean that radical elements in society would benefit and increase their followers at the expense of those more moderate groups who seek real political change. Al-Maliki responds to such claims made by so-called Saudi liberals who have always propagated the idea that society is conservative and radical. The idea of a sovereign *umma* may have antagonised some radical Salafis, but it can become normal and acceptable with time, in his view. The real obstacle to political reform is attributed to the leadership rather than society. In this respect, al-Maliki departs from those intellectuals and activists who blame society for delaying openness and political progress. He considers the leadership as the main obstacle, especially when it arrests peaceful activists and those who call for independent civil society.

In conversations with al-Maliki, it is clear that a critical assessment of the Islamist movement is one of his preoccupations. Those Islamists committed to correcting people's behaviour, preaching morality, and encouraging piety have failed in their duty as activists because they have not prioritised the big questions, mainly political reform, social justice, and empowerment. In short, they have not called for the sovereignty of the *umma*, a task which he had taken upon himself to clarify. He is also disenchanted with those Islamists who have been preoccupied with identity politics at the expense of pushing for political and civil rights, recognition of pluralism, and political questions relating to justice and representation. This critical stance, although not directly targeting Saudi Islamists, is extremely relevant to the Saudi context where historically the so-called Islamic awakening (Sahwa) has not been clearly concerned with adopting an agenda that would strengthen the sovereignty of the *umma*. His support for HASM, led by Abdullah al-Hamid and others, clearly reflects his inclination to move from theorising sovereignty of the *umma* to more active engagement with projects that promote his ideas.

As young religious intellectuals al-Maliki and many others like him are constrained by the limited opportunities available to them to openly propagate these ideas, communicate them to a wide audience, and debate them in established forums. The cancellation of the Youth Rising Forum in Kuwait is an example of how governments remain intolerant of youth activism that brings together intellectuals and activists to debate political issues relevant to the existing circumstances. Such a forum could not be held in Saudi Arabia, and even in the relatively more relaxed context of Kuwait it proved to be difficult to assemble a large number of guests, all ready to engage in discussion of both religious and political matters. Fear of the consolidation of transnational regional youth pressure groups that adopt the language of human rights, civil society, and social justice remains widespread across the Gulf region. This is not surprising given that the demographics of the region show that those under thirty years old exceeds 60 per cent, many of whom have embraced social networking technology such as Facebook and Twitter to deconstruct official agendas, call for rights, and mobilise to denounce excessive political control, poverty, and abuse of human rights. The more this large young constituency engages with the language of rights and anchors these rights in Islamic frameworks, as al-Maliki has done in his writings, the more governments feel threatened by new intellectual mutations that may blur the boundaries between Islam and the global contemporary focus on citizens' rights. Al-Maliki aspires towards formulating a new Islamic vision that moves beyond the strongly cherished dichotomy between Islamic and Western concepts. In his discussion of sovereignty he fuses the Islamic historical tradition with political philosophy that draws on important thinkers in the West. Like Salman al-Awdah, discussed earlier in this book, there is a clear attempt to go beyond rigid intellectual boundaries that had been guarded by the majority of Islamists in the pursuit of Islamic intellectual purity and identity politics. While these attempts remain confined to intellectual circles, wide audiences are now able to access these debates in simple language that is not totally immersed in traditional theology. The mutations break the rigidity of traditional Islamic scholarship on divine politics and fuse it with a humanist perspective by drawing on other sources of knowledge, long considered alien to the Saudi Islamic context. Neither young religious intellectuals such as al-Maliki nor more well-established *ulama* such as al-Awdah are prepared to fully endorse a Western tradition, but they are willing to draw on it in order to move beyond the current political stagnation of countries such as Saudi Arabia. They have gone beyond the taboo of using Western knowledge and its allegedly corrupting influence to help understand and interpret their current political situation. They contribute to a new hybrid discourse that deconstructs the boundaries between secular and religious politics. Democracy, the most abhorred and resisted political system among most Saudi Salafis, is now endorsed as the best choice for a repressed society after decades of considering the traditional Islamic *shura* as the only viable option. Al-Maliki does not hesitate to use the term democracy, although he admits that initially he was hesitant and preferred *shura*. The Arab uprisings were perhaps still an unfinished project, but they certainly enchanted young religious intellectuals like al-Maliki, who considers them an opportunity to assert the sovereignty of the *umma*, that necessary condition in which sharia is applied as a matter of choice rather than force.

5

DECONSTRUCTING THE RELIGIOUS ROOTS OF AUTHORITARIANISM

A younger generation of Saudi thinkers is determined to deconstruct the religious foundation of authoritarian rule. This process is bound to lead to confrontation with both religious authorities and the government. Critical assessment of traditional Salafi thought, in addition to an evaluation of more politically active movements such as the multiple Islamist trends, reflects serious disenchantment with both groups and an attempt to push the debate about Islamic politics towards new frontiers, thus opening venues for justice, political participation, and representation. This critical assessment, however, struggles to find a legitimate niche in Saudi Arabia. Those who embark on the project of deconstructing the religious roots of authoritarianism have limited options; for example, they publish their ideas outside Saudi Arabia or disseminate them in alternative media. Unlike traditional official Salafis, the new generation of critical Islamist thinkers are not embedded in state institutions such as the Council of Higher Ulama or the judiciary. Neither are they dominant in educational institutions like the traditional Salafi scholars or the more populist Salafi preachers.

The short-lived opening of the public sphere immediately after 9/11 that allowed intense debates about religion in Saudi Arabia was reversed with the Arab uprisings in 2011. With several activists facing trial and imprisonment, many Saudis expressed their opinions in the limited online spaces that were still available to those who articulated controversial opinions on religion and politics. With the Arab uprisings, rumours about Saudi Arabia's intention to censor new social networking media such as Facebook and Twitter circulated, but it was difficult to impose a total ban without the country encountering serious international criticism. Saudi activists and commentators increasingly posted their articles and thoughts on their blog pages and on social media where they followed the Arab uprisings and volunteered their support for demonstrators in Arab capitals. Those who wrote political articles on Saudi Arabia itself were more likely to be targeted by security and intelligence services, especially if their postings reflected reinterpretations of religious treatises that had guaranteed obedience and conformity, or directly engaged with political questions about the future of the country.

One such critical writer is Muhammad al-Abd al-Karim (b. 1971), assistant professor of Islamic jurisprudence at Imam Muhammad ibn Saud University, who was detained in December 2010 for two months after posting an article in which he discussed the unpredictable future of the country if members of the royal family engage in succession struggles.[1] This chapter explores his ideas on the religious foundation of authoritarian rule, the crisis of Islamic political discourse, and criticism of Islamism. Like Abdullah al-Maliki, discussed in the previous chapter, al-Abd al-Karim is a young scholar who is determined to expose the current roots of authoritarianism by delving into its historical foundation in Islamic religious texts. He promotes new alternative perspectives that challenge the traditional meaning of monotheism, the obligation of obedience to rulers and commanding right and forbidding wrong (*hisba*). His ideas represent direct criticism of the religious literature that justifies the 'sultanic state'. He defines such a state as a polity that deprives people of the right to be involved in political matters, governed by a royal family and assisted by loyal religious scholars who justify its actions and decisions. This definition is certainly constructed on the basis of his observation of the Saudi state. His criticism offers a new meaning of divine politics that goes beyond Saudi Salafi assertions and dogma.

From University to Prison

Like many young critical writers searching for free spaces to express their opinions, Muhammad al-Abd al-Karim wrote an article in which he asked a series of questions about the future of Saudi Arabia and posted them on his Facebook page:

- What is the future of the country if members of the Al-Saud enter into a fierce struggle amongst themselves over the leadership?

- Is the existence of Saudi Arabia as a country dependent on the Al-Saud?
- If the royal family falls as a result of internal struggle among the princes or as a result of external international pressure, what would happen to the Saudi people?
- Why do we fear the implications of the fall of the regime, an eventuality that may lead to the fragmentation Saudi Arabia?
- Do the Saudi people have an existence independent of the ruling family?
- Why are Saudis not part of the allegiance committee that decides on succession to the throne?[2]

These are the questions that troubled al-Abd al-Karim, and eventually led to his imprisonment for a short time.

Al-Abd al-Karim describes the Saudi polity as *kiyan souwari*, an artificial creation in which class, tribal, feudal, and sectarian divisions are dominant. His concern is with how Saudis can become a unified nation that is involved in deciding how it wants to be ruled. His Facebook questions proved to be dangerous, provocative, and daring in the Saudi context. Ordinary citizens are not permitted to openly ask such questions or to express their concerns over the fragmentation of the country. But al-Abd al-Karim articulates a series of grievances describing how the state created conditions for social and political fragmentation, alienating citizens not only from each other but from the state. Many citizens are concerned with the speedy accumulation of wealth, as they suspect that the state is not destined to last for long. Saudis, in his opinion, are preoccupied with daily subsistence, health facilities, housing, and employment. Those who praise the government are often hypocrites, looking for more privileges and benefits and motivated by the need for services rather than real citizenship.

In his opinion there is lack of trust between the rulers and the ruled, resulting in weaknesses within the Saudi polity. He reflects on the fragmentation of other Arab countries from Yemen to Sudan, and insists that Saudis may not be immune from such divisions. It is his reflections on the potential for fragmentation of the Saudi polity that proved to be too provocative: if there is a serious struggle between princes over succession, are Saudis meant to side with one branch of the royal family against another? In the absence of real citizenship, which is replaced by narrow identities and interests, the artificial Saudi polity is not exceptional, and nothing will hold it together in the future. He laments that religious scholars do not call for political reform. Instead, they rush to praise the leadership when it initiates any change. They have lost the initiative and become subservient to political leadership. Criticism of official religious scholars is not new in Saudi Arabia, and is unlikely to have been the reason behind al-Abd al-Karim's detention. The fact that he tackled one of the taboo topics, the prospect of royal struggle over succession, was enough to provoke a harsh government reaction.

To safeguard against the disintegration of Saudi Arabia, al-Abd al-Karim calls for political participation, which would allow society to have a stake in the state and monitor the government. This requires dismantling the culture of secrecy, openly discussing the future of internal royal power struggles, and involving citizens in running the affairs of government. Only then can the artificial polity become real, immune, and strong, with an autonomous existence that shields it against divisions. The government would then become the government of the people rather than of the privileged few. Equality between the people is one precondition for just government and the only guarantee against internal strife. Moreover, protecting public wealth rather than plundering resources becomes a priority. Al-Abd al-Karim concludes that this is the only way to preserve unity and protect Saudi Arabia from external powers using divisions to undermine cohesion.

The provocative content of this Facebook article is unusual in the Saudi context. No journalist, intellectual, or religious scholar is free to even allude to internal royal power struggles and their implications for the durability of the Saudi polity. While such speculations have always been addressed by outside observers and writers, the Saudi public sphere is strictly forbidden from engaging with these legitimate questions. Thanks to the availability of alternative media, al-Abd al-Karim was able to circumvent the taboo and make his inner thoughts accessible to a wide public.

He went as far as questioning the meaning of citizenship in Saudi Arabia. In another article, also posted online, he argues that citizenship means total allegiance to the ruler.[3] In Saudi Arabia a citizen is defined in terms of this allegiance rather than by his rights and responsibilities. When Saudis are called upon to develop their citizenship, they are actually invited to offer absolute servitude to political authority. Such calls aim to create 'a citizen totally under political control, fully pacified, and always wishing the leader good long life so he can continue to plunder the nation's wealth'.[4] In his opinion, this distorted meaning of citizenship leads to the highest state functionaries becoming the greatest criminals who are associated with corruption.

On 5 December 2010, within days of posting these provocative articles, al-Abd al-Karim was summoned by the head of the faculty at the university for questioning. Officials at the university wanted to ascertain whether he was their author. Al-Abd al-Karim objected to being interrogated at the university. He told his friend Abdullah al-Maliki that he expected to be arrested following this incident at the university. Four security agents visited al-Abd al-Karim without a warrant, and arrested him with no explanation. His followers immediately set up Facebook fan pages[5] and a Twitter hashtag calling for his release. They posted pictures of his books and wrote commentaries on his scholarship. International and Arab human rights organisations considered him a prisoner of conscience, and criticised the Saudi government for his arbitrary detention. He was later released from prison, but he was suspended from his teaching job. In 2014 he was still under surveillance, but he has continued to tweet short statements on religion and politics. He remains cautious, especially as many activists have been regularly interrogated or put in prison for posting statements online. The experience in prison must have increased his determination to deconstruct authoritarian rule and the ongoing repression that is often associated with it. In his view, 'Saudis live under repression, in fact we breathe repression with the air; it haunts us in our dreams. It is our hell before we encounter hell. Even our appearance, streets and houses are designed by repression. Repression has shaped the media, religion, security services, universities, and institutions.'

Al-Abd al-Karim is concerned with repression, and his writings reflect his desire to deconstruct its foundation. He is not unique in thinking that repression in Saudi Arabia, unlike in the Arab republics, is based on traditional religious thought, mainly the traditional Salafiyya, which insists on obedience to rulers. It is grounded in religious *turath* (heritage), which he tries to reinterpret in order to create a new foundation for just government.

The Crisis of Islamic Political Discourse

It may appear strange for a Saudi religious thinker to find inspiration in the French Revolution to tackle the crisis of Islamic political thought; however, drawing on European history has become a common trend even among those grounded in religious education. Like al-Awdah and many others, the new generation of Islamic thinkers have found in the European past a source of knowledge that may not be totally endorsed but is at least engaged with in an attempt to explain the persistent authoritarianism and political stagnation of their own countries. Like many others, Muhammad al-Abd al-Karim uses the European experience to highlight the centrality of freedom from political and religious oppression across cultures and nations. He sees freedom from oppression as a universal quest. His reconstruction of the French Revolution focuses on the role the Church played in supporting European oppression. Nevertheless, it is viewed through the lens of Islam and its history, rather than the standards of historiography. In his view the Church was central in consolidating and justifying absolute rule. Consequently, the French Revolution was focused on dismantling the relationship between state and religion and creating the first model of a secular state, 'a state without religion'.[6] The revolution led to the confiscation of Church property and privileges, helping to curb its authority over society. The state gradually took from the Church the right to administer birth, marriage, and death. This shift limited the ability of religion to consolidate authoritarian rule. The emerging secularism was the solution in Europe. It is responsible for the development of the notion of citizenship. But al-Abd al-Karim asks whether this European model that separated religion from state is the solution in the Arab world:

> Do we separate religion from state like Europe did in order to achieve justice, freedom, and equality? Do we replace the values embedded in sharia by those based on citizenship, rationality, and natural law? Do we consider the sharia as a relic from the past that has no place in the present given that repression has been clothed by religion? Or do we still find in sharia modern values that have the potential of building a human civilisation?[7]

The modern state has not always evolved to establish justice by separating state from religion, but it has succeeded in rationalising government by a separation of powers. It has freed people from religious authority and sub-identities and has moved away from government by force to government by pressure groups, wealth, and media. In some instances a rational form of oppression replaced religious oppression. Here al-Abd al-Karim offers his interpretations of European history in order to assess whether this European model can inspire Muslims in their struggle against the form of authoritarianism that is supported by religion.

European history and intellectual heritage are not the only sources in which al-Abd al-Karim and many others like him find inspiration. He turns his attention to Egyptian and Moroccan writers such as Rafiq Abd al-Salam, Ahmad Raysouni, Muhammad Abid al-Jabiri, Ali Omelil, and Abd al-Majid al-Saghir. He finds in these writers a source of inspiration, helping him confront the rigidity of traditional Salafi political discourse, especially its subservience to political authority. This is noteworthy given that scholarly studies on Saudi Arabia often emphasise how its Salafi religious tradition is exported abroad and popularised thanks to the petrodollar.[8] Some studies also emphasise how

Saudi Arabia must itself have been shaped by the discourse of radical Arab Islamists rather than Muslim modernists. The thinking of the Egyptian Muslim Brotherhood in the second half of the twentieth century is believed to be the main outside influence.[9] Saudi Islamism is considered an outcome of exogenous forces that eventually developed an internal logic of its own.[10] It is very difficult to find any scholarly work that highlights how Saudis themselves have been influenced by modernist Islamic thinking, especially that coming from North Africa. In the writings of this new generation of Saudi Islamist thinkers, we find that they themselves have been inspired by outside Arab modernist intellectual currents.[11] Therefore, while Saudi Salafiyya has certainly travelled and mutated abroad to influence Arab and Muslim audiences, it is equally important to identify how Saudis themselves have engaged with outside Arab modernist intellectual currents. Muhammad al-Abd al-Karim is but one Saudi intellectual who invokes Moroccan modernist thinkers in order to formulate a critique of traditional Salafi thought.

Al-Abd al-Karim tries to find an alternative intellectual source to help him deconstruct the subjugation of men by other men. More than in any other Arab country, or even pre-revolutionary France, religion justifies authoritarian rule in Saudi Arabia. He therefore draws on ideas that are developed elsewhere but with the intention of investigating the intimate relationship between religion and authoritarian rule in his own country.

He introduces Islam as a monotheistic awakening, *sahwat al-tawhid*, a form of freeing men from oppression rather than simply a narrow obligation to worship one God. This provides the title for one of his books.[12] In his view, the first principle of Islam is to declare *tawhid*, that there is no God but God, thus negating the submission of men to men. But expanding on the meaning of *tawhid*, he offers an interpretation of monotheism that turns Islam into a project to liberate people from worldly oppression that is exercised by men over others rather than simply freeing men from religious innovations (*bida*), worshipping other gods, or seeking ritual and creed purity. According to al-Abd al-Karim it is hard to believe that Arabs, the first recipients of the monotheistic message of Islam, are now the least free in the world, having been subjected to centuries of oppression.

The initial mission of Islam was derailed during many historical phases of authoritarian rule from the Umayyad to the Abbasid dynasties, according to al-Abd al-Karim. The Umayyad dynasty paved the way for the rule of the single man, supported by the *asabiyya*, solidarity of his kin group, while Abbasid rule led to the consolidation of religious thought justifying government without consultation and negating the right of people to change the conditions of their oppression. Contemporary Islamic political thought has perpetuated the situation and produced people who are obsessed with creed but oblivious to the problem of oppression. Here there is a clear but subtle reference to the Saudi context, which has produced preachers overwhelmingly concerned with ritualistic purity and religious practices at the expense of resisting oppression in this world. He asks, 'What is the nature of this man who has pure creed but is subjected to the oppression of a despot? Such a man profess piety but his morality is corrupt.'[13]

The monotheistic awakening associated with the early message of Islam has not produced serious reflections on the conditions of servitude under which people live. Consequently, people are concerned with securing their afterlife without any preoccupation with justice in this world. Al-Abd al-Karim proposes a shift in thinking from concern with an afterlife to concern with this life, *duniyya*, worldly matters that are currently characterised by loss of freedom and entrenched authoritarianism. To return to the original message of monotheistic awakening, one needs to assess the attempts among contemporary Islamists to engage with the oppressive political scene. Here he critically reflects on various Islamist trends that have dominated the Saudi public sphere but have failed to offer an alternative path to provide a solution to the conditions of servitude through a political reform agenda. It seems that the Arab uprisings created doubts among writers such as al-Abd al-Karim with regard to the Islamist agenda. He is aware that people in the Arab world are now occupied by fundamental questions that go beyond Islamising society and educational programmes targeting the youth in order to ensure their conformity to an Islamic way of life devoid of religious innovations and blasphemy.

Critique of Islamists

It is not surprising that Muhammad al-Abd al-Karim's assessment of Islamists starts with criticism of the dominant traditional Salafi trend in Saudi Arabia. Salafis, in his opinion, privilege the purity of religious creed and practices and pay little attention to oppressive political conditions. They insist on a narrow definition of monotheism as fighting religious innovations. In their approach, preaching to the youth is the most important strategy to ensure the purity of creed in Muslim society. Education is highlighted at the expense of political projects; as Salafi scholar Muhammad Nasir al-Din al-Albani (d. 1999) insists, 'politics is to leave politics'. The purification of creed is therefore a priority among traditional Salafis. Democracy for al-Albani is 'a blasphemous project, the contrary of Islam, elections are forbidden, women's participation is outlawed, and all this is detrimental to Muslim society'.[14] Although not a Saudi—he was the son of an Albanian watchmaker—al-Albani had tremendous influence on the Salafi scene in Saudi Arabia and beyond. He is regarded as a great contemporary figure, equal in importance to two Saudi Salafi scholars, Abdul Aziz ibn Baz and Muhammad al-Uthaymin.[15]

In al-Abd al-Karim's opinion, an extreme form of Salafi disengagement from politics is the official trend that dominates in Saudi Arabia, propagated by those who insist on obedience to rulers, whom he calls the 'sultanic jurists'. These have gone to extremes in depicting reformers and activists as rebels, innovators, and instigators of dissent and chaos. Advocates of this school clothe their political position in religious ideas. They are prepared to coexist with dictatorships, the rule of conquerors, and repression simply because they accommodate despotism and refuse to challenge it. This Salafi school considers the participants in the Arab uprisings in both Egypt and Tunisia as *khawarij*, invoking the Kharijites of an earlier Islamic era. The Salafis use their position as judges to enforce obedience to rulers, acting on behalf of the state to cast dissidents as *kafir*s (blasphemers) and passing long prison sentences on activists. Their cooperation with the state ensures that dissent is stifled, and even criminalised as an un-Islamic act. Here al-Abd al-Karim's criticism is no doubt influenced by the successive trials of Saudi activists that have gathered momentum since 2011 and led to judges passing harsh sentences on peaceful activists such as HASM founders, discussed earlier in this book.

According to al-Abd al-Karim, the politically unengaged and quietist Salafi tradition dominant among official Saudi *ulama* has given rise to a violent Jihadi counter-trend, which calls for the use of force against rulers. In this respect, traditional Salafis failed to create an alternative discourse that peacefully challenges authoritarian rule. In his opinion, traditional Salafi resistance to political activism, by outlawing peaceful protest, is responsible for the emergence of violence as a political strategy. The Salafi Jihadis equally reject democracy, but adopt a violent path to change. According to al-Abd al-Karim, the monotheistic awakening is interpreted as violent struggle in Jihadi thought. Unlike traditional Salafis, Jihadis have not concerned themselves with purifying people's creed or piety, but with rebellion against rulers, often accused of not ruling according to sharia. Consequently, wherever Jihadis conquer a territory, they immediately insist on establishing sharia, thus isolating and alienating the rest of society. But al-Abd al-Karim doubts the merit of applying sharia rule 'by the sword'. In this respect, he echoes the conclusions of Abdullah al-Maliki, discussed earlier. If people do not enjoy freedom and equality, sharia remains insufficient to establish justice. When Jihadis insist on applying sharia by force, they blur the boundaries between themselves and those rulers who equally resort to force in their project to gain Islamic legitimacy as a result of claiming to apply sharia. A clash between Jihadis and rulers becomes inevitable. It has led to the elimination of Jihadi ideologues and rebels and the imprisonment of their followers in many countries. According to al-Abd al-Karim violence is symptomatic of the failure of the Jihadi project as people do not want to replace one form of existing state repression by Jihadi coercion: 'There is no scope for one group imposing sharia on others as this contradicts the meaning of sharia which insists on equality.'[16] Establishing sharia in Muslim societies requires people to free themselves from repression and patronage. Those who force the sharia on people seek to impose their rule and will.

While Jihadis have been unsuccessful in resisting repression, other contemporary Islamist movements are equally unclear about the centrality of freedom from coercion under political or religious guises. Although all Islamists are engaged in vigorous activism in education and youth programmes, they have, in al-Abd al-Karim's view, failed to clarify their position on political repression. In fact, freedom from political oppression is not the main priority for many Islamists, in al-Abd al-Karim's assessment of their agenda. The Islamists' relationship with authoritarian regimes often tends to revolve around accommodation and coexistence rather than directly challenging their rule. Al-Abd al-Karim mentions one of the strongest Islamist trends in Saudi Arabia, the Sururis,[17] who have spread throughout Saudi society since the 1970s. His criticism of this strong Islamist movement centres on the inability of its activists to focus on political oppression, with detrimental consequences for society. This Islamist movement

> does not have a revolutionary agenda against the state but also does not have strong allegiance to state institutions. When Sururis criticise the state, they identify the functionaries as responsible for any wrongdoing. They also blame those they call the secularists and the Westernised for corrupting Muslim society. This trend has no political position because its priority is to focus on education above all other priorities.[18]

According to al-Abd al-Karim neither traditional Salafis, Sururis, nor Jihadis articulate an agenda that promises liberation from oppression. Salafis and Sururis are concerned with personal piety and religious education, while

DECONSTRUCTING THE RELIGIOUS ROOTS

Jihadis are primarily occupied with violent rebellion to establish sharia without offering an alternative model of government. At times of crisis, with the exception of Jihadis, many Islamists appear to defend the regime against calls for political reform or peaceful action. This was obvious when online calls for demonstrations on 11 March 2011 were not heeded in Saudi Arabia. The so-called Day of Rage failed to attract protesters amid heavy and intimidating security measures, as mentioned earlier in this book. While the official religious establishment denounced these calls, many Islamists in Saudi Arabia concurred and dissociated themselves from the online protest campaign. While there were many reasons behind the failure of the protest campaign, it has been widely attributed to a lack of support from Islamists.[19]

Al-Abd al-Karim's assessment of Islamism in general reflects a disappointment with grand projects that seem to have neglected the most urgent questions about political reform in countries such as Saudi Arabia. He asserts that 'the success of an Islamist movement should not be measured by the number of religious innovations (*bida*) that it succeeds in eradicating or society's pure creed but by the movement's closeness to achieving justice in this world, which is the ultimate purpose of monotheism'.[20]

Al-Abd al-Karim doubts whether Islamists' focus on education and the purity of faith and practices can lead to political reform under persistent authoritarian rule. He gives the example of Egyptian reformist Muhammad Abduh (1848–1905), whose main mission was to instigate renewal through reforming education. This renewal proved to be difficult to achieve in the context of oppression. In fact, al-Abd al-Karim rejects the idea of the 'oppressive just ruler' (*al-mustabid al-adil*), visualised by many Islamic thinkers as an acceptable transitional ruler leading to better government in the future. The contradiction between oppression and justice in the persona of such a ruler cannot generate conditions where people achieve the latter.

In order to deconstruct authoritarian rule, society needs a clear political reform agenda, which is different from education, preaching, and simple protest or dissent. A political reform movement with a clear vision rather than simply a religious educational programme is a prerequisite for political change. Al-Abd al-Karim thinks that in Saudi Arabia the only Islamist trend that clearly called for political reform and deviated from the traditional Salafi position in its political concerns was the 1990 Movement for Legitimate Rights in Saudi Arabia that emerged in the context of the Gulf War.[21] The movement was subsequently suppressed by the regime. Its activists were put in prison or fled into exile. Throughout the 1990s the government curbed the ability of many activists to disseminate their ideas, precipitating a fragmentation of the movement. However, the impulse for political reform remained alive even after many activists were put in prison. Some resumed their calls for change after they were released, only to face imprisonment again. While this is history, al-Abd al-Karim clearly endorses the political agenda of the constitutional reformists.

In Saudi Arabia, al-Abd al-Karim identifies the constitutional reformists, a loose association of activists and writers such as Abdullah al-Hamid, Abdulaziz al-Qasim, and Matruk al-Falih, as articulating a clear vision for political change. In his opinion many activists are disenchanted with mainstream Islamists such as the Muslim Brotherhood and the Sururis. After such disappointment, young activists eventually abandon these well-known Islamist movements and gravitate towards groups that have a clear political agenda, reaching to activists beyond the Islamist–secular divide. Al-Hamid, who was involved in the Movement for Legitimate Rights in Saudi Arabia in the early 1990s, continued to press for peaceful change after spending several years in prison. Al-Abd al-Karim lists the main petitions submitted by various activists and others since 2003; all have clear political demands, centred on the political future of the country, justice, citizenship in a pluralistic society, and the priority of constitutional reform. The government resorted to the same style of repressive measures as in the 1990s, and put many of the old activists in prison again in 2003–4. The Saudi leadership, according to al-Abd al-Karim, identified their demands as dangerous and threatening to national security, while the religious leadership condemned them for using alien and Western language such as 'pluralism, civil society, citizenship and constitution'. From the perspective of the government, al-Abd al-Karim thinks that reformist demands threaten the very foundation of authoritarian rule as they seek to involve people and their representatives in government and the regulation of the relationship between ruler and ruled under the umbrella of a constitution. Demands for political representation and a constitution are rejected by the religious establishment in Saudi Arabia on the grounds that traditional forms of consultation (*shura*) between rulers and ruled are already practised and the Quran is the only constitution, so there is no need for a man-made document that may take precedence over the holy book. In this respect, the political and religious forces in Saudi Arabia cooperate, to not only dismiss but also to criminalise a reformist movement aiming to deconstruct authoritarian rule, regulate relations between the rulers and the people, and widen political participation. Repression of the reformist movement stems from its clear political demands, all rejected by the political leadership and the religious establishment. In these repressive circumstances there is but one choice for the Muslim *umma*, according to al-Abd al-Karim: 'It is either *shura*, consultation, and the rule of the *umma* to establish real justice and monotheism, or the rule of the single individual, which leads to injustice and repression.'[22]

Towards a Liberation Theology

Freedom from *istibdad* (repression) remains a central theme in al-Abd al-Karim's writings. He defines repression as 'the rule of a man or family without restraints from the political community'.[23] He identifies the worst type of repression as that practised under a religious umbrella. It has a detrimental impact not only on people's lives but also on monotheism itself. For these reasons, he embarks on a journey to deconstruct the religious foundations of authoritarianism, especially those anchored in Salafi traditional thought. This journey leads him to formulate a kind of 'liberation theology', in which a reinterpretation of Islamic concepts and principles leads to establishing the discourse of liberation from repression. He hopes that his effort encourages the realisation that *hukm shuri* (government by consultation) is the only alternative to *hukm al-ghalaba* (government by conquest and force). But before this is achieved, Muslims need *fiqh taharur* (liberation theology/jurisprudence), which is the subject of his book *Tafkik al-istibdad* (deconstructing repression).[24]

In *Tafkik al-istibdad* al-Abd al-Karim argues that the starting point for a Muslim thinker concerned with political theology and liberation from authoritarianism remains the events that followed the death of the Prophet Muhammad. He goes back to that moment when the Prophetic state faced its first challenge of succession after his death. He outlines the various succession disputes that took place in Madina immediately afterwards. The resolution of the conflict in favour of the caliph Abu Bakr is believed to be an example of how family rule was rejected by the early Muslim community. He thinks that

> The companions of the Prophet achieved victory over tribal society when they rejected the possibility of family rule. The worst deviation from this outcome came later when Muslims fell into the trap of families ruling over them. Both caliphs Abu Bakr and Umar were not from the Quraish tribe whose branches had been competing to lead the Muslim community.[25]

After this fleeting moment in Islamic history, *istibdad* became the norm throughout successive historical periods. Among contemporary Muslims it is consolidated as a result of various strategies. First, repression relies on a huge security and intelligence bureaucracy, both of which function to detain, torture, and spread fear. Second, it is dependent on an equally large judicial bureaucracy, whose main function is to cast a religious umbrella over repression so that it appears as if it complies with sharia. Third, repression is justified by media empires that control the public sphere and distort facts. And finally, a network of religious scholars that ensures the submission of the population is a necessary precondition for perpetuating repression.[26] Al-Abd al-Karim's analysis of repression in its historical manifestations and contemporary methods seems to describe a condition predominant in Saudi Arabia itself. Resorting to history and generalising about the Muslim past is an attempt to tackle contemporary conditions in which all four repressive strategies are present. Al-Abd al-Karim describes the Saudi condition without actually naming it.

The official Salafi tradition that is dominant in Saudi Arabia requires Muslims not to challenge repression under the pretext that this would undermine human lives, stability, and peace. The advocates of this position go as far as banning any form of peaceful resistance to oppression such as strikes, demonstrations, and civil disobedience. This theological position leads to negative outcomes:

> Religious scholars grant repressive rulers full control over people in addition to the right of their family members to inherit their position until a new conqueror appears on the scene. This new conqueror is initially described as *baghi*, usurper, but when he seizes power he becomes a legitimate leader, thus making power and might the main determinants of a ruler's legitimacy and right to rule.[27]

Banning peaceful protest by resorting to Islamic theology is a way of perpetuating repressive rule; religious scholars describe anyone who challenges the authority of rulers as 'innovator', 'debauched', and 'Kharijite'. Judges use these descriptions to justify the harsh sentences they pass on peaceful protesters. The victims of such political–judicial cooperation, often peaceful activists or dissidents, are always seen as people with responsibility towards political authority rather than people with rights that should be respected. It is this shift, which turns citizens from people who have rights to people who only have responsibilities towards the leadership, that creates lasting repressive conditions. Al-Abd al-Karim alludes here to the Saudi context, where religious scholars and preachers continue to remind their audiences of the rights of rulers, *huquq wali al-amr*, rather than the rights of citizens. The first set of rights requires obedience and compliance rather than challenging their rule, whereas the rights of citizenry seem to have disappeared from the public discourse of such scholars. Mosque preachers and high-ranking religious figures

1.1: Protest in Buraiydah February 2013 (chapter 1)

1.2: Irhal (leave) protest in Qasim against minister of interior Muhammad ibn Naif February 2013 (chapter 1)

2.1: Abdullah al-Hamid and Muhammad al-Qahtani surrounded by supporters outside the court (chapter 2)

2.2: Abdullah al-Hamid and Abdullah al-Maliki on rasif, the pavement where al-Hamid used to tweet before entering the court, Riyadh (chapter 2)

3.1: Salman al-Awdah (chapter 3)

4.1: Abdullah al-Maliki (chapter 4)

5.1: Muhammad al-Abd al-Karim (chapter 4)

6.1: Muhmamad al-Ahmari (chapter 6)

such as the Mufti continuously remind their audiences of the rights of the ruler, saturating the public sphere with calls for obedience and respect. In this state-controlled environment the rights of citizens are often forgotten.

In order to dismantle the theology that perpetuates repression, al-Abd al-Karim starts with well-rehearsed Quranic and Hadith texts that Saudi religious scholars use in order to remind their audiences of the obligation to obey rulers.[28] These texts are commonly invoked to silence dissent in Saudi Arabia. They are interpreted in the Saudi context as calling upon Muslims to respect their leaders and never challenge them in public. Quranic verses and sayings of the Prophet are central in the Saudi Salafi tradition, and have been used without revisionist interpretations, according to al-Abd al-Karim. The concept of *wali al-amr* (the ruler), which dominates the Saudi religious and political discourse with the assumption that such personalities should remain unchallenged, is central to al-Abd al-Karim's revisionist theology, simply because it is constantly invoked in the Saudi context to circumvent challenging the authority of the rulers. The concept of *wali al-amr* as a single person or group of persons (*wulat al-amr*) has assumed a sacrosanct status given that it is anchored in Islamic texts, thus endowing it with a certain symbolic significance. Official scholars equate obeying God and the Prophet with obeying the ruler by relying on a specific interpretation of one Quranic verse. Moreover, many Saudi religious scholars go as far as invoking a Hadith that asks the community to obey and be patient with those rulers who steal people's money and practise torture. This is justified simply by reciting a Hadith calling upon Muslims to obey their ruler 'even if he steals their money and break their backs'. The Saudi interpretation of this Prophetic saying has become the subject of ridicule in alternative media.

Al-Abd al-Karim refers to Sheikh Salih al-Fawzan, who was asked about how a Muslim should react when a ruler steals his money. Al-Fawzan replied that a Muslim is under obligation to resist a commoner stealing his wealth but that he should be patient with regard to a ruler committing theft of his property.[29] Al-Fawzan justifies his position by claiming that challenging a ruler results in greater danger than stealing someone's money. As such, there is only one path out of the danger of chaos among Muslims: patience. Al-Abd al-Karim rejects the call to be patient, and goes as far as comparing such a ruler to thugs and bandits who should be fought in order to defend people's right to their own wealth. According to him, a man killed defending his wealth is considered a martyr in Islam. He reaches this conclusion on the basis of interpreting another Hadith that mentions the right of a Muslim to defend his wealth, even if this requires violence against those who steal it. Protecting wealth from theft should not be considered an act against the oath of allegiance given to a ruler, but should be a defence of the right to protect property. In many Quranic verses God encourages Muslims to resist *dhulm* (injustice) and describes those who do not as succumbing to fire. The injustice of a ruler should not be exempt from the obligation to resist him.

Al-Abd al-Karim rejects Islamic theology that considers *wali al-amr* as the central point in the Muslim community. He feels that this encourages a culture of absolute authority, especially if *wali al-amr* is not subject to accountability. In his view, *wali al-amr* should be a representative of the whole *umma* rather than a single authority over it.

He reprimands early Muslim scholars for considering an unjust ruler as a legitimate *wali al-amr*. Historically, many Sunni Muslim scholars both within the Salafi tradition and outside it accepted three mechanisms to deal with an unjust *wali al-amr*: obedience, patience, and private advice. Muslims living under conditions of repression are expected to resort to these, but none of them lead to freedom, according to al-Abd al-Karim. He insists that there is an obligation to change repressive conditions. In fact, those who do so are promised victory in the Islamic tradition, while those who simply acquiesce are destined to become weak and are eventually destroyed. A Muslim is required to establish justice and freedom from oppression.

The most suitable strategy to resist repression is peaceful action (*amal silmi*), as obedience, patience, and private advice have serious limitations. Advice is based on preaching to encourage people to do good and warn against the consequences of not doing so. But advice does not embody an obligation to remove injustice or give people their rights. A ruler may not listen to advice, and can even expel those who offer it from his court. Such a ruler has a choice when faced with private advice, and a positive response is by no means inevitable. This kind of advice should be confined to correcting the ruler's personal behaviour in order not to tarnish his reputation by publicly exposing his sins. But when his excesses are public, advice given in secret fails to guarantee justice. Muslims should not wait until a ruler shows clear blasphemy and shuns prayers, the only conditions under which theologians allow rebellion against rulers, as there are worse abuses that justify peaceful protest, such as plundering wealth and oppressing citizens. The Islamic position on peaceful action with a view to changing the conditions of absolute rule should be permissible rather than prohibited. The only way to seek justice and rights is *jihad madani*, by which al-Abd al-Karim means peaceful struggle such as civil disobedience, demonstrations, and strikes. He does not call for violent struggle in order to correct the excesses and injustices of political leadership, but identifies a set of strategies that achieve the objective of peacefully overcoming abuse inflicted on people by an unjust ruler.

Al-Abd al-Karim considers the religious opinions of those scholars who insist on obedience, patience, and private advice as assisting unjust rulers in perpetuating their injustices. As rulers become accustomed to a docile community, they have no fear that their oppression will be challenged. This makes them less willing to change their government and respect the rights of citizens. The *umma* loses its values when it abandons its right to challenge repression and injustice. Al-Abd al-Karim rejects the claim that sharia obliges people to be patient when faced with repression from their rulers.

If the *umma* has the right to peacefully resist a legitimate ruler when he imposes injustice, what is then the position vis-à-vis a conqueror who establishes his rule by sheer force? Al-Abd al-Karim is critical of those scholars who assert that obedience to a usurper is better than challenging his rule. He cites the words of the founder of the Wahhabi movement, Muhammad ibn Abd al-Wahhab, who claims that 'all Muslim scholars reached a consensus that a conqueror should be obeyed'.[30] In other words, Muslim scholars justify succumbing to the rule of a usurper to avoid the upheaval and chaos that are associated with armed struggle. Scholars' fear of bloodshed among Muslims prompts them to insist on obedience, hence perpetuating and prolonging the legitimacy of *taghalub* (government by force). Al-Abd al-Karim considers these religious opinions detrimental to the attainment of justice.

A jurisprudence of liberation requires subjecting several Islamic political concepts to scrutiny and reinterpretation. In addition to the concept of *wali al-amr*, *baya* (the oath of allegiance to the ruler) should also be subjected to revisionist interpretation. According to al-Abd al-Karim, the oath has become the prerogative of those people considered *ahl al-hal wa al-aqd* (people who tie and bind), a selected appointed elite that does not necessarily represent the *umma*. In fact, this elite is often chosen by the ruler himself to give the oath, thus disenfranchising the *umma* and negating its right to freely choose its ruler.[31] He sees no good in appointed or self-appointed notables giving the oath of allegiance to a ruler, as one important condition seems lacking: representation of the community. As long as the 'people' do not select their own representatives who can then give the oath, the principle of representation is not respected.

Another important concept is *shura* (consultation), with traditional scholars leaning towards considering it voluntary rather than obligatory. A ruler is now under no obligation to consult his constituency, since religious scholars have granted those in power, whether by inheritance or conquest, an unbounded legitimacy without resorting to the opinion of the whole *umma*. Al-Abd al-Karim argues that in recent years consultation has become a 'political carnival' with its own rituals, institutions, and buildings.[32] Perhaps here he has in mind the Saudi Consultative Council, established in 1992, with its impressive building. The king appoints all its members, and its decisions are not binding to the government. Under these conditions *shura* becomes meaningless. The leadership is not under any obligation to listen to or implement any policy recommendations emerging out of the consultation debates and advice in the consultative council. In short the ruler 'has become like a god and his community is obliged to obey him'.[33]

Al-Abd al-Karim also has problems with the concept of *fitna* (chaos, strife), which had become a common imprecation in the Saudi context. Judges who deal with detained peaceful protesters, activists, and even writers and commentators on public affairs, often include *fitna* against the ruler in lists of charges. Examples of accusations under the broad title of *fitna* often launched against peaceful activists include 'threatening state security, inciting disorder and undermining national unity, disobeying and breaking allegiance to the ruler, communicating with foreign media, and questioning the integrity of officials'.[34] Judges consider peaceful activists as precipitating dissent and encouraging people to reject their rulers or challenge their policies. This is a crime in Saudi Arabia, as demonstrated by the number of human and civil rights activists who are in prison following accusations of precipitating *fitna*. Al-Abd al-Karim chooses a different interpretation of *fitna*. He asserts that it means a test of people's perseverance and endurance when struggling against injustice. It is an examination of someone's willpower to continue a struggle rather than the kind of criminal act described used by the judges. *Fitna* does not emerge as a result of resisting oppression, but is a consequence of remaining silent when confronted by pervasive injustices. In a direct reference to the Arab uprisings in which thousands of people assembled peacefully in public squares in Tunis and Cairo, chanting slogans about freedom and dignity, al-Abd al-Karim asks: 'Where is this alleged *fitna* when people who want to celebrate life free of oppression assemble peacefully without weapons? Their only weapon is recitations and songs. They raise colourful flags and avoid disrupting traffic on their way to public squares?'[35]

Civil disobedience is not a form of *fitna*, but is embedded as a requirement to resist oppression in a Prophetic saying. Al-Abd al-Karim sees in the

Prophet's words a call for such disobedience, as he advised Muslims not to serve repressive rulers. In fact, he ordered them to boycott such rulers: 'There will be a time when princes become oppressive, ministers debauched and judges traitors. If you find yourself in this situation, do not serve them as tax collectors or policemen.'[36]

In the Saudi context rebellion has assumed a wide meaning, under which all peaceful acts can be listed as causing dissent, instigating rebellion, and encouraging chaos. Al-Abd al-Karim criticises those Saudi *ulama* who call for the killing of peaceful demonstrators because they consider them to be practising a form of *khuruj ala al-hakim* (rebellion). Al-Abd al-Karim gives the example of Sheikh Salih al-Sadlan, who delivered a sermon in which he called upon the ruler to kill demonstrators. Al-Sadlan was not the only one to invite the Saudi leadership to apply the harshest measures against demonstrators, as Saad al-Buraik also called upon the king in 2011 to 'crush the skulls of demonstrators'.[37] In his sermon, al-Sadlan did not make the distinction between those who rebel with arms and peaceful protestors. People who criticise rulers using words are all accused of causing dissent and practising rebellion. Another Saudi scholar mentioned earlier, Salih al-Fawzan, adopts a wide definition of rebellion which includes, in addition to armed struggle, 'words that undermine the ruler or insult him. Also words that encourage people to rebel should be part of rebellion as the beginning of war is often words'.[38] This all-encompassing definition of rebellion makes it unlawful to challenge political authority by words, action, or belief. It is basically a justification for unchallenged absolute rule based on the total disenfranchisement of the population and its total obedience. Al-Abd al-Karim tries to challenge this religious discourse in his reinterpretation of Islamic sources on political action. He resorts to other religious opinions that remove peaceful protest from the category 'rebellion'. The term should be used to describe armed struggle only, rather than a whole range of peaceful acts, often deployed by activists to express an opinion, or to call for a change in policy. As long as these peaceful acts do not disrupt public order, or destroy life and public property, they should be permissible. He argues that widening the meaning of rebellion is a strategy to deter people and intimidate them when they resort to peaceful protest. Scholars who practise this intimidation often want to terrorise people into giving up their right to protest. They magnify the danger of political change so that people are scared of calling for even minor reforms. As a result, people are denied the right to engage in peaceful collective action and are coerced into submitting to unjust government under a religious umbrella.

Al-Abd al-Karim celebrates the sacrifices made by Saudis calling for peaceful jihad, the kind of protest that Saudi *ulama* depict as rebellion even when it consists of civil disobedience, drafting reformist petitions, and demonstrations. He includes human rights activists who were detained simply because they were active in mobilising people in support of prisoners of conscience, establishing civil society organisations, and alerting people to abuses in prisons. Restrictions on the right to protest come with the consolidation of what al-Abd al-Karim calls the 'Sassanid tradition', referring to the Persian imperial rule that is embodied in the work of a famous medieval Arab scholar, Abu al-Hasan al-Mawardi (972–1058). Al-Mawardi's political theology became a standard reference for many later scholars who raised the status of the ruler above the common people. In al-Abd al-Karim's view, people became like a 'herd of animals'.

In al-Abd al-Karim's view, religion itself suffers when the ruler is elevated to a God-like figure. He becomes arrogant, enjoying excessive wealth and imposing servitude on citizens. He invokes French scholar Étienne La Boétie's seminal work *The Politics of Obedience: Discourse on Voluntary Servitude* (1548) to explain why people voluntarily accept domination. When people are born into the conditions of servitude, it becomes easy for them to accept their position, he explains. More importantly, when absolute rule is justified by religion, it leads to associating Islam and its jurisprudence with repression. Such association negates the principles of equality and freedom upon which Islam itself is based. It also allows the politicisation of religion given that the absolute ruler requires that religious scholars support and justify his rule by resorting to sharia sources, which are in turn used to criminalise any attempt to resist this rule. Absolute rulers seek the symbolic power of religion, thus protecting themselves against criticism, unrest, and the prospect of peaceful rebellion.

Reforming the Saudi political system has reached a dead end, with official religious scholars insisting on obedience to rulers, patience, and private advice. Muhammad al-Abd al-Karim searches for peaceful solutions that allow society to pursue peaceful reform. He proposes a new meaning for *hisba* (commanding right and forbidding wrong), commonly known as *al-amr bi al-maruf wa al-nahi an al-munkar*. For him *hisba* is an Islamic duty that should correspond to autonomous civil society under the rubric of *ihtisab madani* (civic duty).[39] In Saudi Arabia the duty to perform *hisba* has been taken away from society and turned into a bureaucratic institution. This results in a superficial application of the duty. Al-Abd al-Karim criticises how in Saudi Arabia the so-called religious police are primarily concerned with immoral behaviour. They are restricted to chasing people in the streets in search of immorality associated with personal conduct or failing to perform Islamic rituals. This reductionist practice of *hisba* leads to trivialising the duty, associating sharia with coercion, and tarnishing the image of Islam. These religious police, in his opinion, give a very bad impression and undermine Islam itself. Moreover, limiting the practice of *hisba* to state employees, known as *rijal al-hisba* (men of hisba), automatically excludes society from participating in its application and entangles commanding right with the state's political project. Instead, *ihtisab madani* should 'allow individuals to establish institutions, associations, and unions in all sectors of life. They should use all peaceful means to express their opinion and exert pressure. They are the ones that should practice *hisba*.'[40] This kind of civil activism should replace the government-controlled institutions responsible for the duty to command right and forbid wrong. Here again, al-Abd al-Karim insists on the peaceful means that can be deployed to achieve the objectives of *hisba*. In its new meaning *hisba* is not the prerogative of a small group within the Muslim community enforcing to the Saudi interpretation of commanding right. It is the duty of all Muslims who can organise themselves in civil associations the ultimate objective of which is to protect society from the excessive abuses of power in political, social, and economic sectors of life. *Ihtisab madani* becomes a buffer zone between society and the state, protecting the former from the abuses and excesses of the latter. In this new interpretation of *hisba*, al-Abd al-Karim reinvents it as civil society and action whose main objective is not to control or monitor personal behaviour, and ensure that Muslims practise their religion, but to protect society from the absolute exercise of power.

Conclusion

Like many other young Saudi religious intellectuals, Muhammad al-Abd al-Karim is concerned with the hegemony of the traditional Salafi thought that has dominated the Saudi public sphere and its political consequences. He considers the Saudi Salafi tradition responsible for perpetuating authoritarian rule. He recognises that specific interpretations within this tradition legitimise repression. He therefore starts with deconstructing the religious roots of repression as they unfold in Salafi thought with the view that more nuanced interpretations will eventually emerge. Sunni political theology, in his view, has developed over centuries to protect leadership, justify repression, and isolate the community from the decision-making process. This is done under the pretext of preventing *fitna* (chaos and dissent). He seeks then to interpret common concepts that are often invoked to ensure the acquiescence of society. His project leads to developing new meanings for terms such as the ruler, obedience, dissent, peaceful struggle, and civil society. Without too much borrowing from outside the Islamic tradition, al-Abd al-Karim turns traditional Islamic concepts into modern blueprints for action that empower society and allow it to find the language to resist being marginalised by excessive control from above. In his writings he is critical not only of official Salafis but also of those Islamists who have emerged in the last three decades. While most of them were keen on educational programmes, he laments that their discourse contains no clear political agenda concerned with justice. Educational programmes that take place in a repressive context are less likely to be successful simply because they can be suffocated by too much control and surveillance from the state. If his mission is to limit the excesses of the state, then al-Abd al-Karim has succeeded in engaging with the Islamic tradition in new ways that allow for creative interpretative frameworks within which contemporary society can free itself from political and religious authoritarianism. The official divine politics that has contributed to disenfranchising the Saudi public is increasingly being contested, the result being the emergence of a hybrid discourse that engages with both Islam and the wider intellectual traditions of other countries. But together with other thinkers who share his concerns, al-Abd al-Karim finds himself marginalised and even punished for his views. Salafi resistance, together with regime fears that this liberation discourse becomes hegemonic and succeeds in replacing the old obedience-focused Salafi tradition, mean that al-Abd al-Karim and many others will remain under surveillance for the foreseeable future.

6

DEMOCRACY AGAINST THE ISLAMISATION OF REPRESSION

The intellectual project of undermining the Islamisation of repression that legitimises and perpetuates tyranny reaches another level of theorisation in the work of Muhammad al-Ahmari, who does not hesitate to use the word democracy as the only viable alternative to authoritarian rule, especially that which flourishes under Salafi justifications.[1] Al-Ahmari aspires to release democracy from its specifically European associations and present it as a spirit that pervades the quest for equality and dignity in many human societies. He is perhaps one of the most outspoken Islamist defenders of democracy in the Saudi milieu, a position that puts him at the centre of controversy and debate. Whilst other Islamists prefer to remain faithful to the concept of *shura* to avoid a backlash from those who reject democracy on the grounds that it is a Western import, al-Ahmari goes beyond these reservations and explores the spirit and practices of democratic government. His approach remains grounded in intellectual arguments, drawing on both Islamic and Western history. He engages with his own Islamic tradition in novel ways that allow him to situate the quest for democratic consultative government in this tradition itself. Al-Ahmari advocates political transformations that lead to the end of despotic rule as seen in the Arab world over the last decades, and enable the people to exercise their right to choose their own government. He offers a glimpse of the debates that gripped the Islamist movement not only in Saudi Arabia but across the Arab world as it was confronted with the rise of the masses calling for a break from past political authoritarian rule and practices.

Like many other Islamist thinkers he saw in the Arab uprisings an opportunity not to be missed. He was aware of Salafi resistance to both the spirit and practices of democracy, and his writings allude to how this resistance can be overcome. This chapter traces al-Ahmari's personal and intellectual journeys in order to map the latest contribution to the debate about democracy and its merits in the Salafi context of Saudi Arabia.

A Controversial Figure

Muhammad al-Ahmari was born in 1959 in the Sarawat mountains in western Saudi Arabia.[2] After primary education in his local village school he moved to Abha, where he studied sharia and religious studies at al-Mahad al-Ilmi al-Shari (the scientific institute). After studying at Imam Muhammad ibn Saud University he worked as a history teacher. His early education in religious studies in Abha was combined with exposure to international intellectual trends in the United States, where he completed a master's degree in modern history. He later obtained a doctorate in Britain on North African history, studying religious endowments in Algeria.

While studying in the United States on a Saudi scholarship, al-Ahmari became known for his critical stance on many Saudi policies. In conversation with Saudi officials responsible for *dawa* (lit. 'call': mission), he often clashed with the mission's vision on the role of Saudi-sponsored students abroad. On one occasion he objected to the mission's instructions to spread Islam in America according to Saudi/Wahhabi interpretations, as taught at the Imam Muhammad ibn Saud University.

In 1990 Saddam Hussein invaded Kuwait, and Saudi Arabia called upon American troops to defend the kingdom. Like many Islamists at the time, al-Ahmari was against this invitation, which served as a catalyst for the consolidation of the Islamist movement in Saudi Arabia, and its development as an opposition trend.[3] Al-Ahmari continued to live in the United States for almost two decades, working with the Islamic Assembly of North America (IANA). After 9/11 the IANA, together with other Saudi-sponsored associations, came under attack for propagating radical Islam.[4] Al-Ahmari moved back to Saudi Arabia in 2003 for a short period and worked as a consultant in publishing and translation at the publisher Obaikan. His return to Saudi Arabia was complicated by the fact that he was married to a Palestinian–Lebanese woman who did not have residence rights in the country. But al-Ahmari wanted to return to Saudi Arabia: 'I had not been involved in organised opposition. All I did

DEMOCRACY AGAINST THE ISLAMISATION OF REPRESSION

was to propagate critical ideas, writing a research paper on the legitimacy of demonstrations from an Islamic point of view.'[5]

While he was in Riyadh, working in translation and publishing, al-Ahmari continued his involvement in debate circles and lectures among friends and other intellectuals, often held in private homes. In 2007 he was critical of the government when Saud al-Mukhtar, an active Islamist, was arrested together with other lawyers and academics whom the court in Riyadh described as *khaliyat Jeddah* (the Jeddah cell).[6] The court accused al-Mukhtar and his colleagues of subverting the government, forming an illegal organisation, and sponsoring terrorism in Iraq. Al-Ahmari wrote about how authoritarian government is the intellectuals' enemy, regardless of their ideological orientation. Commenting on the plight of prisoners and their relatives put him under surveillance by the security agencies. He laments that being an intellectual (*muthaqaf*) who is constantly breaking taboos and bridging divides between East and West, and Islam and other civilisations makes life problematic in Saudi Arabia. Security agents who followed his writings and lectures kept him under constant observation. Al-Ahmari was gripped by a sense of alienation and exile at home.

Al-Ahmari cites an incident that dramatically upset him in 2007. He recounts the story of Omm Saud, Saud al-Mukhtar's eighty-year-old mother, who visited her son in prison in a wheelchair pushed by a companion. He remembers: 'The mother was very old and unable to walk. She was brought to the prison in a wheelchair pushed by her sons. The prison security guards refused to let her helper push the chair and she was forced to enter the prison crawling on her hands and feet. This was an inhumane situation.'[7] She died in 2014 while her son was still in prison.

At the same time, al-Ahmari entered into heated debates with Salafi religious scholars over several contentious issues, particularly their denunciation of the Shia and their position on women's rights. His encounters in Riyadh where he frequented debate circles at the invitation of well-known Salafi scholars confirmed his position as a controversial figure with allegedly subversive ideas that challenge those scholars. On one occasion the Salafi sheikh Nasir al-Omar invited him to give a lecture that coincided with the Israeli attack on Lebanon in 2006. The official Saudi policy at the time condemned the Lebanese Hizbollah for provoking Israel into a full attack on Lebanon by kidnapping Israeli soldiers. It seems that at the time many Salafi *ulama* were instructed by the government to condemn the Shiite Hizbollah and outlaw any support or donations to the Lebanese people affected by the Israeli attack.[8]

Al-Ahmari argued against encouraging sectarian divides, pointing out that Islam does not prohibit sympathy for *mustadafin*, the oppressed and the poor, even if they are Shia. He also warned against sectarianism, as it poses a danger for social harmony and coexistence between Sunnis and Shia in Saudi Arabia itself. He later wrote a famous article, 'Khidat al-tahlil al-aqadi' (The trick of creedal analysis), explaining his rejection of sectarian politics that generated harsh criticism in Saudi Arabia.[9] He called upon people to abandon creedal analysis when assessing a political situation such as the Israeli attack on Lebanon and the plight of the Lebanese people in southern Lebanon at the time, arguing that the Salafis who prohibited solidarity with the South Lebanese Shia were engaging in creedal analysis, based on their condemnation of the Shia religious tradition. Political analysis, al-Ahmari proposed, is much needed in this situation. According to al-Ahmari the Saudi government encouraged intellectuals and religious scholars to denounce the Shia and other groups that were considered as posing a threat to the regime.

Al-Ahmari's proposition to move away from creedal analysis generated heated debate in Saudi media as it was critical of the pitfalls of imposing religious and sectarian opinions to support political positions. Saudi author Ali al-Amim dedicated a long article in the Saudi sponsored-newspaper *al-Sharq al-Awsat* to undermine al-Ahmari's analysis, casting doubt on his commitment to freedom and democracy. Al-Amim considers al-Ahmari as having failed in his historical analysis and use of the early Islamic tradition to call for new frameworks to understand urgent contemporary issues. He regards him as a politicised personality who continues to be embedded in what is known in Saudi Arabia as the Sururi trend, one of the most prolific branches of the Islamic Awakening of the 1990s.[10]

Al-Ahmari was subjected to pressure from official sources to write against the liberal trend in Saudi Arabia. He remembers the time when the Interior Ministry sent him a message asking him to denounce Saudi liberals in his articles. He was told that, given his education abroad and engagement with multiple intellectual trends, he was in a good position to write critical articles on liberalism. Al-Ahmari interpreted this as an attempt to undermine his credibility and add to the fragmentation and divisions between intellectuals. He argues that this was a trap that the ministry set for him in order to inhibit the creation of common platforms for debate among the country's intellectuals.[11] He laments that those religiously observant Saudis have a distorted understanding of liberalism, reduced in most cases to personal freedoms that in Salafi views encourage immoral behaviour and undermine social and religious integrity. Had he agreed to write denunciations of liberalism he would have undermined his own intellectual integrity.

On another occasion al-Ahmari differed with the Salafi sheikh Nasir al-Omar over women's right to drive. He argued that the situation of women in Saudi Arabia was marked by serious discrimination that cannot be justified by going back to Islamic religious texts. He presented a full critique of the Saudi position, especially Salafi resistance to lifting the ban on driving. He claims that he embarrassed al-Omar when he presented him with Islamic evidence in support of promoting women's rights. Al-Ahmari mentions that al-Omar admitted that the Salafi position on women's rights rests on weak Islamic grounds but claimed that it is difficult to change. Al-Omar informed al-Ahmari that if he and others were to change their views in favour of lifting the ban on women driving, he would lose popularity among his followers. Al-Ahmari considers al-Omar's justification unconvincing as it exposes the desire of these scholars to maintain their popularity among their followers rather than fulfil their role as guardians and interpreters of the Islamic tradition.

Al-Ahmari's assessment of the intellectual environment in Saudi Arabia paints a picture of polarisation and adversarial confrontations, encouraged by the political authorities. Lack of freedom, constant surveillance, and interference in debates renders Saudi intellectual life fragmented, adversarial, and difficult. Salafi rigidity and opposition to intellectual freedom seems to help the government close the channels of free debate and discussion. In these circumstances, al-Ahmari feels intellectually alienated as he strives to bridge a divide that has been erected between the so-called liberals and those religiously inclined personalities who dominate the Saudi intellectual public sphere. Described by his father as a mix between a *mutadayyin* (religious observer) and *mutamarid* (rebel),[12] al-Ahmari may have felt restless in Saudi Arabia.

In 2007 al-Ahmari had the opportunity to become the director of a new research centre, the Arab International Affairs Forum, in Qatar. He moved to Doha, where he is now in charge of several Islamic newsletters and discussion forums, including *Tariq al-Islam* and *al-Asr*.[13] In addition to writing several lengthy books,[14] he is a regular essayist and contributor to media debates. His interviews have appeared on Al-Jazeera television and other Saudi-sponsored channels, with comments on current affairs, especially during the Arab uprisings. Despite moving to Qatar, al-Ahmari continued to be engaged with the mobilisation in Saudi Arabia, especially in the light of the petitions presented to the leadership by Saudi intellectuals, activists, and religious scholars after the uprisings, as discussed in the first chapter. He not only signed the petition

'Towards Rights and Institutions' but was also involved in consultations with other activists in the process of drafting the petition. Al-Ahmari rejects private advice (*nasiha*), the long-cherished Salafi method of reaching out to leaders, and promotes open discussion about reform in order to ensure that ordinary people are aware of the important demands put forward in several reformist petitions. He goes as far as justifying demonstrations and anchoring this form of mobilisation in the Islamic tradition. He states that collective action was part of the Islamic tradition in its early days as people came together as a group to voice their opinions.[15]

After giving up his Saudi nationality to take up Qatari citizenship and visiting Saudi Arabia with a Qatari passport in 2013, al-Ahmari once again became the centre of controversy.[16] He announced his change of nationality on Twitter, and justified it as a reflection of his desire to work in a country that honours him as an intellectual.[17] He later appeared on several television shows to explain the decision. Al-Ahmari considers that his new citizenship does not negate his *hawiyya* (identity), as he remains anchored in an Arabian context. He was critical of the absence of real citizenship in Arab countries, and distinguished between *muwatana* (citizenship) and *musakana* (residence). In an interview on Al-Jazeera television[18] he launched an attack on Arab rulers who allow people to live on the land without granting them real citizenship with political rights. He accused Arab leaders of depriving people of real rights and allowing them only to reside within the boundaries of their own countries—a kind of *musakana*.

His critics came from both the liberal and Salafi camps. The former considered his choice of Qatari nationality as an act of ingratitude to his original homeland, while traditional Salafis used the nationality issue to undermine his previous intellectual positions and critiques of their political views. Given the tense relations between Saudi Arabia and Qatar after the former denounced Qatar and accused it of providing a safe haven for dissident Islamists in 2013, al-Ahmari's presence in Qatar became suspicious from the Saudi point of view.[19] His residence in Qatar was taken as proof of the Qatari welcome for dissident Islamists determined to undermine the national security of Gulf states, including Saudi Arabia. Many liberals consider al-Ahmari's advocacy for democracy as camouflage for radical Islamist ideas and convictions. Other liberal critics appreciated his frankness and courage, and regarded him as a global personality who may have been constrained by the local Saudi context.[20]

Al-Ahmari represents an example of a politically engaged writer who does not shy away from drawing on what Salafis regard as alien concepts and un-

DEMOCRACY AGAINST THE ISLAMISATION OF REPRESSION

Islamic values. Salafis' main concern is with his political views, especially those that glorify freedom, democracy, and the right of people to choose their rulers. For many Salafis al-Ahmari is a veteran activist of the 1990 Islamic Awakening who abandoned the defence of Islam against religious innovations and contamination of the pure creed with foreign ideas and practices and instead engaged with the opening up of debates on the Islamic tradition to foreign and dangerous ideas. His alleged subversive influence stems from his willingness to engage with foreign political concepts. Salafis consider his advocacy for democratic government as an alternative to existing political repression to be a deviation from ideas and axiomatic beliefs about authenticity and righteous Islamic government. Like those of the intellectuals discussed in the previous chapters, al-Ahmari's writings invoke foreign history and discourses to fuse his own Islamic interpretations with new dimensions. This remains objectionable in traditional Salafi circles, which insist on maintaining purity in interpreting Islamic texts. Al-Ahmari is not particularly concerned with matters specifically related to worship or creed, but is more inclined to engage with reinterpreting political theological positions in order to pursue the project of the just state among contemporary Muslims. Equally, unlike the Salafis, al-Ahmari is not engaged in denouncing other sects in Islam, for example the Shia, or engaging in intellectual battles with the liberals, especially when the government imposes these positions on intellectuals to promote its own agenda of fragmenting the political field and undermining the development of mutual understanding and common ground.

Al-Ahmari's non-partisan intellectual approach reflects a serious commitment to the kind of freedom and pluralism in Muslim society that Salafi dogma struggles to eradicate. He recalls how the early twentieth-century expansion of Wahhabiyya in Abha led to compulsion, as people were forced to wear their headgear in specific ways that were inconvenient in an agricultural society, or forcing men to cut their hair, both of which clashed with local Asiri culture. He sees no benefit in forcing people to adopt a single way of being Muslim and having to reflect this in their appearance. He argues that there is no Islamic justification for insisting on homogeneity, which was imposed on the various cultural groups by the Wahhabis. This compulsion is also manifested in the drive to eradicate cultural differences in the interpretation of the Islamic tradition. He argues that 'We can be inspired by the Mutazilites [medieval rationalists] for their prioritisation of reason and rationality. We can appreciate the Sufis for their spirituality and we can benefit from the Salafi methodology.'[21]

Al-Ahmari identifies attachments to dogmatic *ulama* as an obstacle to maintaining pluralism in the world of Sunni Islam. He interprets this as a function of people's love for an example or a 'hero' to emulate, which helps the *ulama* retain their hold over tradition. But he senses that the youth today are more independent and willing to engage with multiple interpretations and understandings of Islam in more critical ways that challenge the authority of the *ulama*. He argues that *al-tayar al-tanwiri* (the enlightenment trend) is more inclined to reject scholarly dogma in favour of a rational interpretation of religious texts. Thanks to new social media and the debate that they generate, the youth are rejecting the authority of established sheikhs, although some of those scholars may have many followers. He cites the example of Muhammad al-Oraifi, a populist Salafi sheikh who has more than 8 million followers on Twitter; but when he was arrested in 2013, nobody engaged in real mobilisation to push for his immediate release. His followers, and their campaign for his freedom, were confined to the virtual world. Al-Ahmari argues that such populist scholars have limited popularity among the intellectuals, especially those who reject the authority of dogmatic religious scholars. Even the masses are gradually dissociating themselves from dogmatic religious scholars who have supported tyranny and provided the religious umbrella under which it flourished.

Al-Ahmari rejects Saudi claims that the country represents true Islam. He says:

> Neither the Taliban of Afghanistan nor the Salafis of Saudi Arabia constitute the only model of Muslim society where religious intolerance is dominant. We should consider the Abbasid era where Jewish *wazir*s prospered and poets and thinkers such as al-Jahiz and Abu Nuwas were tolerated. Muslim society developed only with religious tolerance and freedom of thought. The atmosphere of coexistence and tolerance is part of the Islamic past and should be the condition today.[22]

Al-Ahmari's longing for a more tolerant bygone Islamic era does not prevent him from adopting a critical approach when analysing Islamic political history. His constant reference to how Muslims abandoned the natural spirit of consultation, which led to sultanic hereditary rule, is fully articulated in his book on democracy.

As a dissident intellectual who has travelled both literally and metaphorically far from his roots in western Saudi Arabia, al-Ahmari reflects a certain Islamic cosmopolitanism that is flourishing under the experience of residence in multiple locations and exposure to diverse intellectual trends. His education and experience of living in the United States encouraged him to develop an awareness of world history while nurturing a rational appreciation of his own Islamic tradition. Unlike those Islamists who shared his cosmopolitan experiences and ended up rejecting the 'corrupted and immoral West', such as Sayid Qutb, al-Ahmari was more inclined towards *taqarub*, bridging a political and intellectual divide that has been blown out of proportion by many Islamists of his generation. His predicament as an intellectual who is rejected in the dominant Saudi Salafi milieu has enabled him to benefit from finding a niche in neighbouring Qatar, from where he can reach out to a wider Muslim audience than that in Saudi Arabia, thanks to Qatar's pan-Arab media empire. His case draws attention to the limitations of the Saudi intellectual context, which remains polarised under religious and political control. While his new home in Qatar is hardly a haven for democratic practices, it has provided him with the resources and institutional support to develop his own ideas. Al-Ahmari has not engaged in debating Qatari domestic affairs, perhaps to avoid clashing with its leadership and to take advantage of its sympathetic attitude to Islamists like him.

The Salafi Wave

Al-Ahmari is convinced that the Arab world in general, and Saudi Arabia in particular, is currently suffering the impact of a Salafi/Wahhabi wave, which has had a detrimental impact on contemporary societies. He assesses the eighteenth-century Wahhabi movement, and acknowledges that it made contributions towards reviving religious observance. But he believes that it cannot now be a platform for renovating religious ideas, creating new intellectual debates, or contributing to a political renaissance. Salafis, according to al-Ahmari, 'do not offer any solutions to contemporary problems. They encourage historical enmities between Muslims on the basis of sectarian differences. Salafis offer constant criticism, tarnishing people's reputation. Salafiyya is like an angry teacher who adores insulting his students, especially those who are creative because they undermine his dogma and rigidity.'[23] What is more detrimental in the Salafi tradition and practice is blindly following the authority of the *ulama*, who have become the final source of knowledge and emulation. Al-Ahmari accuses Salafis of being obsessed with following a personal religious authority to the detriment of applying their own judgement and reason. They have become similar to Sufis who follow the leader of the *tariqa* (path). In his analysis of Salafis he uses the term *tasawwuf al-salafiyya* (the Sufication of Salafis). This is ironic given the historical Salafi denunciation of the Sufi tradition. He denounces *wisaya* (intellectual patronage) of religious scholars, and considers it a reason for backwardness. His critical analysis of the Salafi *ulama* and their monopoly over Islamic knowledge reflects the frustration of the Islamist intellectual, who combines his religious knowledge with analytical and interpretive approaches acquired outside the traditional study circles of these scholars.

According to al-Ahmari the Salafi wave has made Muslims more concerned with the length of their beards and shirts than with political rights, justice, and consultative government. The symbolism of religious appearances that is so cherished among the Salafis as a marker of religious observance and authentic identity is in fact a deviation from the fundamental concerns of justice and freedom from compulsion. Moreover, Salafis encourage enmity between the majority of Muslims and those they dub *quboriyyin* (grave worshippers, a pejorative term used by Salafis to refer to Muslims who visit graves, for example that of the Prophet, his relatives in Mecca and Madina, and other saints buried around the Muslim world, a practice common among both Shia and non-Salafi Sunni Muslims) and the Shia, according to al-Ahmari. He is critical of the Salafi education that young people receive in schools and institutes, which focuses primarily on matters such as God's names and attributes while ignoring topics such as social justice and tyranny.[24]

Al-Ahmari is critical of the diverse Saudi Islamist scene, which is still saturated with Salafi dogma—even among those Islamists who try to move away from its intellectual and religious domination. He distinguishes between the *mufakir* (thinker) and *muthaqaf* (intellectual). The first creates ideas, while the latter circulates them. In Saudi Arabia Islamist intellectuals tend to reproduce old ideas simply because they fear being ostracised if they innovate and challenge the current Salafi dogma. There is an urgent need for *ijtihad*, according to al-Ahmari. The domination of Salafi thought leads to 'phobia against *aql*, reason. But reason is the condition for being Muslim.'[25] What a country like Saudi Arabia needs is *tanwir*, defined as the end of monopoly by one religious school or interpretation, the end of controlling reason, and the end of rejecting other people's thought.[26] The only counter-current to the Salafi domination is freedom, which can only flourish in a democratic system of government, according to al-Ahmari. This conclusion has prompted him to write a detailed defence of democracy, demonstrating that it is a global heritage, and does not contradict Islam despite the claims of Salafi critics.

DEMOCRACY AGAINST THE ISLAMISATION OF REPRESSION

Democracy: Beyond Institutions and Constitutions

Openly advocating democracy is bound to lead to a clash with traditional Salafis, who prioritise reforming the personal conduct of Muslims, including the ruler, and the purification of their creed. Al-Ahmari's preoccupation with dissociating Islam from the current practices of political repression is a project anchored in reinterpreting early Islamic governance, especially the former years of the Prophet Muhammad and his companions. In this respect he remains faithful to the Salafi methodology that upholds the early Islamic polity and the righteous ancestors as a model of governance to inspire contemporary Muslims. However, al-Ahmari considers the rudimentary 'democracy' of the first caliphate as far from complete and perfect. In fact, he thinks it was the beginning of a process that was later on derailed and resulted in the perpetuation of tyranny. His critical assessment of this experience angered his Salafi critics, as they remain intolerant of revisionist historical analysis and prefer glorifying the past.

Al-Ahmari does not call for a revival of the governing practices of the early Muslim state, which he considers underdeveloped, while conceding the spirit and values of that government to be inspirational. He endorses new governing practices that draw on democratic means such as elections, representation, and freedom. In his promotion of democracy he does not stop at endorsing its institutions and constitutions, but goes further in identifying its spirit as a human natural system.

Al-Ahmari celebrated American democracy when Barack Obama was elected president in 2008, considering this as proof that the democratic spirit had triumphed over racial discrimination and exclusion.[27] He argues that democracy won over *wathaniyya* (paganism), as it allowed the representation of minorities regardless of their race.[28] For al-Ahmari, 'The West is distinguished by its imagination. It nurtures creativity rather than dwelling on the past. It always searches for those people who can innovate, which allows them to find solutions to big problems.'[29]

Al-Ahmari's overenthusiasm for the election of a black president was unsurprisingly the subject of Salafi attacks, as he was accused of uncritical glorification of the West and its politics, while ignoring the injustices inflicted by the West on Muslims. One of his most outspoken Salafi critics was Sheikh Nasir al-Omar, mentioned earlier. Al-Omar accused al-Ahmari of being obsessed with Obama's victory.[30] Al-Ahmari's celebration of Obama's election was considered proof of his enchantment with the West and his uncritical appreciation of its politics. But al-Ahmari separates his appreciation of democracy in

147

the West from his denunciation of Western foreign policies, arguing that the latter should not blind Muslims from appreciating the merits of democratic government or be used as an excuse to denounce good domestic governance in the West.

Democracy for al-Ahmari is not necessarily a Western liberal invention, but is rather the original 'natural system'. In his most detailed genealogy of the evolution of democracy and defence of its spirit and practices,[31] he argues that the original state of man is to live in a democratic context, citing examples from ancient Greece and Mesopotamia, Native Americans, Papua New Guinea, and pre-Islamic Arabian tribes. He seems to glorify and romanticise the original political state of such pre-modern societies in order to dissociate democratic government from its contemporary Western context while acknowledging that it is in the West that its spirit found the mechanisms and the institutional tools that ensure its full development and longevity. The spirit of democracy becomes *fitra*, a natural state of being, as early societies were inclined to live under the ethos of equality and sharing.[32] It is the interests of the community that generate the impulse for democracy, as people's interests are undermined by the tyranny of the few. Feudal and repressive governments become a deviation from the natural communal interest of societies. According to al-Ahmari, in their pre-modern existence humans struggled to maintain the common good as a result of sharing resources and decisions.

Does the democratic spirit manifest itself in the early Islamic polity that emerged in Madina after the death of the Prophet Muhammad in 632 CE? Like other Islamist intellectuals who are keen on bringing early Islamic practices into the debate on democracy, al-Ahmari goes back to the first Muslim caliph, Abu Bakr (r. 632–4 CE), who was 'elected' as leader of the community after the death of the Prophet.[33] He argues that the companions' choice of Abu Bakr as proof of the democratic spirit of the first Muslim political community, and that this first election in Islamic history proved that there is no hereditary rule in Islam. This interpretation of that historical moment after the death of the Prophet is generally glorified in Islamist discourse in ways that demonstrate the 'democratic' impulse among the early companions of the Prophet, but is strongly contested by other Muslims, especially the Shia. Al-Ahmari says that with the caliph Muawiyya, the founder of the Damascus-based Umayyad dynasty (661–744 CE), the spirit of democracy was undermined in Islamic history, as hereditary rule became the norm. With Muawiyya, the beginning of *inhiraf*, the derailing of the spirit of democracy, was established in Muslim society. Al-Ahmari laments that the democratic spirit of early Islamic governance gave way to *al-mulk al-adud* (monarchical tyranny). It is this that resulted in the abandoning of democratic impulses in favour of repression and the rule of unelected individuals. After this history of *inhiraf*, the basic and first need among Muslims is political freedom. This can only be achieved under a democratic government.

Like the anthropological examples of 'democratic' practices in pre-modern societies cited by al-Ahmari, the short-lived Islamic experiment in Madina proves that choosing a government by consultation renders democracy a natural system that non-Western societies equally endorsed. Al-Ahmari claims that democracy is therefore a practice that societies everywhere aspire to rather than merely a Western invention associated with the various European historical models.

By associating the spirit of democratic practices with multiple societies across the world, al-Ahmari seems to want to reclaim for the Arab world the concept and its history, which he believes does not reflect any specific ethnicity, nationality, or (Western) thinking. In his opinion the spirit of democracy is part of world heritage, historically located in multiple sites around the world at different historical moments, from the natural world of tribes to more organised agrarian communities, in addition to Madina, where the first Islamic state emerged. But democracy is always an evolving process, both in spirit and practice, and al-Ahmari acknowledges that the West may have had a better record in developing its tools. This explains why it has remained an alien concept and a despised term in other societies that have abandoned the natural democratic spirit. Today people associate the European word 'democracy' with one specific tradition, but this does not mean that it is the heritage of Europeans to the exclusion of others who had known forms of democratic politics. Al-Ahmari's historical analysis and eager enthusiasm to find the democratic spirit around the ancient world encourages his readers, and especially some Salafi Islamists, to abandon their rejection of democracy as a Western term unrelated to both the history and tradition of Muslims.

As democracy is the natural state of man, it cannot contradict his desire to live in an equitable and organised society. It is above all not a religion, but rather a system of governance whose main objective is to regulate people's interests and give them a voice in organising their affairs. Al-Ahmari recognises that democracy is not without criticism. He mentions a list of philosophical and political arguments against democracy, but concludes that it is 'the right to elect, criticise, and remove a leader', and that it remains the best available alternative to tyranny. Those who reject democracy undermine the early Islamic experience of choosing a leader and subvert the normative spirit of Islam. Here al-Ahmari has in mind the Salafi rejectionists who argue that democracy is a Western import.

Despite the fact that democracy is the natural system, its enemies are numerous. Al-Ahmari lists those who have dominated the rejectionist trend among Muslims and others. Amongst them are those autocrats whose rule can only be maintained by excluding the rest of society. Around the autocrats he identifies a circle of beneficiaries whose livelihood and prosperity depend on their subservience to a single political power. Opponents of democracy 'are scared of novel ideas and language and refuse to debate them', thus inhibiting the endorsement of alternative equitable and representative government. While al-Ahmari discusses those who reject democracy in general terms, his references and descriptions clearly correspond to identifiable groups in Saudi society.

He admits that he is not blindly passionate about foreign words such as democracy, but one must engage with their meaning in a globalised world. By its nature, democracy is a product of debate and controversy, both of which threaten those enshrined in creedal rigidity. He refers to critics of *ijtihad*, reasoning that it opens the possibility for revisionist arguments and outcomes, and says that only those who are apprehensive about rationality reject democracy. He invokes *al-aql* (reason) to convince his readers that democratic government is a necessity dictated by the common interests of humans.

The benefits of democracy require an understanding of what it allows people to avoid. Only in democracy does the mythologised autocrat cease to inspire the people. Democracy negates the cult of personality that is often associated with autocrats. Al-Ahmari dedicates considerable attention to the negative consequences of accepting a mythologised unelected super-leader who presents himself to the people as the ultimate guarantor of their well-being, security, and interest. In democracy an autocrat cannot rule without accountability as his policies are constantly scrutinised and subjected to evaluation by responsible citizenry in the context of established representative institutions. Democratic government cannot simply ignore the public opinion on which it is dependent and which performs the role of checking and aborting misguided policies that do not benefit the common good.

For al-Ahmari, democracy encourages the emergence of new social elites. In a democratic government the regeneration of elites ensures the avoidance of stagnation, which inhibits the development of creativity, new thinking, and initiatives. Whilst democracy is concerned with the common good, it makes important contributions to the well-being of the person. Once it is endorsed as a political practice, democracy ensures not only the triumph of public interest (*al-maslaha al-ama*), but also the development of ethical and responsible citizenry, resulting in the personal integrity of the individual. At the heart of the democratic ethos is the equality of people, which must be celebrated as an alternative to entrenched hierarchies that draw on blood ties, lineage, and race. Democracy is therefore a precondition for meritocracy and an alternative to the predominance of privileges based on primordial identities.

Al-Ahmari contributes to the ongoing old debate about the nature of Islamic government and whether it is civil (*madani*) or religious (*dini*).[34] This debate emerges out of Islamists' call for a return of the Islamic state, which is objectionable to secular forces in the Muslim world. He invokes the words of Egyptian Muslim reformer and modernist Muhammad Abduh (1848–1905) as he confirmed that 'the Islamic political system is civil and should be chosen by the people'.[35] Al-Ahmari rejects the idea that an Islamic state is a theocracy. He refers to the Prophetic state, in which the Prophet Muhammad was not a prince, a president, a king, or a caliph, but simply a prophet whose practices are to be emulated. The Prophet was *qudwa*, an example to inspire rather than replicate, in Muslim societies. He was instructed to practise *shura* (consultation) with all members of the community, including women. Al-Ahmari cites this as proof that the Prophet himself enlisted the opinion of the wider community in decision making. If consultation was a characteristic of the Prophetic tradition, how did Muslims come to accept that ordinary rulers may govern without it? He laments how contemporary Muslim religious scholars ignore the Prophetic *qudwa* and instead rely on practices that developed under the umbrella of late sultanic caliphates. Their passion and glorification of this history prompted them to avoid a rational assessment of the shortcomings of hereditary rule and the exclusion of people from political decisions, leading them to overlook the example of early consultation and glorify instead the autocratic rule of successive Islamic caliphs and sultans.

As al-Ahmari is aware of the 'fear' of democracy among some Muslims, he tries to respond to its critics. One of the major objectionable aspects of democracy is that it allows 'the people to become the source of legislation, thus undermining the sacred source of the law in Muslim society'.[36] He resorts to Sheikh Yusif al-Qaradawi's dismissal of this fear as he argues that a Muslim society that believes in God and the Prophet is unlikely to seek legislation that contradicts Islam. In order to prevent the adoption of non-Islamic laws, an article in a country's constitution must state that Islam is the religion of the state and that no legislation should contradict its *thawabit* (non-negotiable principles). He adds that the sovereignty of God (*hakimiyya*) should not contradict or even inhibit the sovereignty of the people to determine how they run their worldly affairs. In exercising their right to determine their own worldly affairs, people practise *ijtihad* (reasoning) within a multi-layered Islamic tradition that allows diverse interpretations. Democracy in a Muslim society does not lead to voting on the *thawabit* (fixed principles such as prayers, fasting etc.), but on those areas of Islamic affairs that are subject to multiple interpretations. People in a democracy are not going to be asked to vote on whether prayer should be abolished, but their vote is often related to issues that touch the functioning of their lives in this world, known as *al-masalih al-mursala* (extended interests). These include matters related to the welfare of society (hospitals, transport, and health, etc.), choosing rulers and government, the decision to go to war, and emergency laws. In these matters there is ample scope for people to exercise their judgement through the ballot box in a democratic system.

Those Islamists who reject democracy on the basis of its Western origins are misguided by fear of the West, argues al-Ahmari. He thinks that this fear is rooted in the long history of imperialism and colonialism, which led to a rejection of Western ideas. But there is nothing in the Islamic tradition that prohibits Muslims from borrowing 'good' ideas and innovations from non-Muslims. Again, he cites the example of how the Prophet was inspired by the Persians, who had developed the practice of shielding themselves in trenches during war. The Prophet applied the same strategy in the Battle of the Trenches, although it was not the way that Muslims had until then conducted war. Al-Ahmari is critical of the Pakistani Islamist Abu Alaa Mawdudi (1903–79), who exaggerated the threat of Western ideas and concepts, even if they are good for governance. Fear of Western ideas has become an obsession among some Muslims as a result of such rigid views, and should be subjected to rational thinking, argues al-Ahmari. He insists that 'it is natural for civilisations to benefit from an exchange of ideas, practices and talents. This is a human requirement for progress.'[37]

There is also the controversial 'majority rule' that democracy promises, which many who reject it cite as unacceptable in a Muslim context. Al-Ahmari cites a Prophetic tradition that two opinions are better than one, thus privileging those decisions made by a majority. The Prophet assured his audiences that the *umma* must be trusted, and that its consensus will always produce the right answer.[38] Moreover, in a Muslim society one should not fear the decision of the majority unless its commitment to Islam and its spirit is in doubt.

Voting on an issue is a peaceful way to deal with differences in opinions and visions. Al-Ahmari seems to think that the majority will not deviate from Islamic teachings or vote against them if given the opportunity. This opinion is contrasted with the Salafi position, which remains suspicious of the masses (*al-awam*). Instead, Salafis insist on the role of *ahl al-hal wa al-aqd*, an ambiguous elite consisting of religious scholars and others who are distinguished by their knowledge. They are expected to give advice to rulers that is informative (*mualima*) rather than compulsory (*mulzima*). Consultation, in al-Ahmari's analysis, is meaningless if it is entirely dependent on the good will of the ruler. He can simply ignore the opinions that the *ulama* or others suggest to him.[39] In al-Ahmari's opinion, elections go beyond the limited circle of the knowledgeable few to give the majority an opportunity to be involved in formulating policy that has an impact on people's lives. There is no danger in involving this majority in decision making, as it represents the consensus of the *umma*, *ijma al-umma*.[40] Instead of promoting an elitist view that undermines and patronises the masses, al-Ahmari injects positive appreciation of their potential and ability to help alter their passivity and fear under tyranny. He celebrates a deep natural desire for justice and dignity against the tyranny of political elites and religious scholars, and concludes that for human nature to reach its full potential, it needs to live in a democratic system that allows it to flourish economically, scientifically, and ethically, encouraging the masses to develop into responsible citizenry.

Al-Ahmari's enthusiasm for democracy reached a high level with the Arab uprisings. He saw in the events that swept the Arab world in January 2011 an opportunity for the fulfilment of his writings on democracy. In his assessment of the uprisings, al-Ahmari notes, 'These are extraordinary events. We have not seen them for centuries. Above all, they are a quest for spiritual freedom.'[41]

In 'The season of fear from the people', al-Ahmari glorifies the 'millions who have been described as silent and fearful'.[42] With the Arab uprisings, the majority reasserted itself as *al-shab*, the people, a critical mass that coalesced in a unity unseen in previous decades. The uprisings shifted the focus to the people who are now free to express themselves, in the magical statement 'al-Shab yurid' (the people want). The so-called masses asserted their will to be free when they temporarily came together at a revolutionary moment, abandoning their class, ethnic, and religious differences. With this shift, politics became the public concern of the people in their diversity rather than the minority that had maintained its monopoly over resources and decisions. Authoritarian rulers consulted minorities of subservient experts, *ulama*, and intellectuals while sending into exile independent thinkers, to deprive societies of benefiting from their intellectual debates. Yet the masses rose against exclusion, corruption, and prisons. Al-Ahmari cites the exile of intellectuals and activists as the outcome of the politics of fear that had been practised in countries such as Egypt and Tunisia. Perhaps his focus on the exile of other Arab intellectuals stems from his own experience in his home country. Despite his attempt to find a niche in Saudi Arabia for his modernist ideas and reinterpretations of the Islamic heritage, he had faced strong opposition from the dominant Salafi tradition.

Like many observers of the unfolding of events in the Arab uprising countries, al-Ahmari was dismayed by how authoritarian rule reasserted itself, especially in Egypt after the July 2013 coup, thanks to what became known as the counter-revolution, orchestrated by regional forces such as Saudi Arabia and other Gulf countries. In various articles and online commentaries he denounced the intervention of Saudi Arabia to thwart the transition towards democracy, interpreting this as a reflection of a fear of the people that gripped ruling elites across the Arab world. He claims that the revolutions were hijacked, but that eventually, with increased awareness, this 'Great Arab Revolution' will succeed, as long as it continues to be peaceful in its practices and demands. The transition towards democracy is inevitable in the long term, according to al-Ahmari. He admits 'that a new front had already been formed to thwart the outcomes of the revolutions. This front lacks cohesion but it is now strong because it has the one objective of destroying the prospect of democracy. These are the enemies of freedom.'[43] He rejects predictions that a perpetual revolution will be the outcome of the Arab uprisings.[44]

Yet al-Ahmari remains optimistic, and hopeful that the conditions of tyranny have already been shaken, thus allowing the emergence of personalities like Alija Izetbegovic, who became president of Bosnia and Herzegovina in 1990. Having written a book appraising the philosophical, spiritual, and freedom-loving qualities of Izetbegovic,[45] al-Ahmari asserts:

> I have hope that we will one day have an Arab Izetbegovic. The picture that we have about our society as closed, dogmatic, and intolerant is distorted. Opposition to the West should be replaced by a human approach that appreciates what the West can offer. This was the project of the Muslim free thinker, Izetbegovic.[46]

Beyond Classifications

Is al-Ahmari a critical Islamist who exposes the shortcomings of the various dominant Saudi Islamist trends? Is he simply an interlocutor of the Islamic heritage, writing against the dominant Salafi tradition in his own country? Has he abandoned Islamism altogether in favour of a reformist agenda that is critical of both secular liberalism and religiously based resistance to democracy? Is he an advocate of a nativist democracy that undermines the enchantment with its Eurocentric historical origins? In al-Ahmari's words, he is 'a Muslim before the divisions'.[47] The interpretative, political, and historical divisions that he tries to rise above relate to classifications that have dominated the way Islamists represent themselves and are represented by others.

Al-Ahmari's contribution to the debate on democracy is not meant to deliver the final philosophical and political assessment of an old concept that is still debated in the West and elsewhere. Rather, it supports a system of government that is hotly debated, with both advocates and opponents finding themselves locked in a battle about the future of Saudi Arabia. For many contributors to this debate, democracy means not only the end of religious observance, but—more importantly—the end of the privileges enjoyed by those who had lived off the claim that they are the guardians of the spirit of the nation and its religious purity. For others, democracy is the beginning of citizenship and the road to dismantling claims about Saudi *khususiyya* (exceptionalism). The prospect of democracy emerging in Saudi Arabia makes it part of world history and global human civilisation. Al-Ahmari rejects being labelled as Islamist or liberal–Islamist because he rejects classifications that fix thinkers in slippery categories. He also longs for his Islamic tradition to be integrated into debates about politics and government. For him, democracy is a process whose spirit unfolded in multiple locations. His early Islamic heritage witnessed a fleeting moment of aspects of the democratic spirit, but it was buried in successive waves of despotism before it could reach the maturity that other parts of the world developed. By tackling the religious roots of this despotism, i.e. the Islamisation of repression, al-Ahmari, like other intellectuals in this book, contributes towards both the rehabilitation of the Islamic tradition and the inclusion of his own country in world history. Above all, he demonstrates his willingness to engage in the debate about a controversial concept that has proved to be dangerous in the Saudi context.

CONCLUSION

ISLAMIST MODERNISM BEYOND RADICAL AND MODERATE DIVIDES

The narrative about Saudi Islamists and other similar groups and movements remains grounded in the classification of their ideologies and strategies, often related to security concerns. In Western scholarship on Islamism, those who adopt violence are considered radical; others who preach reforming their regimes are considered moderate; those who draw on international discourse about democracy and rights are labelled neo-reformists, post-Islamists, or Islamo-liberals. Yet from the perspective of the Saudi regime, Islamist supporters of civil society are radical and deserve long prison sentences. An Islamist who writes about the future of the country in the context of warning against succession struggles among the princes is also a radical who is subjected to interrogation and imprisonment. An activist who promotes peaceful jihad (demonstrations, civil disobedience, etc.) as an alternative to violence is equally a radical, who is, ironically, put in a high-security prison rather than the famously comfortable Jihadi rehabilitation centres designed by the Interior Ministry to de-radicalise Jihadis. Similarly, a religious scholar who considers revolution as the inevitable outcome of decades of repression is immediately labelled a radical preacher and a revolutionary zealot in disguise. Radicalism and moderation are slippery labels in the Saudi context, as both can only be clearly defined in relation to specific historical contexts. They are often particularly blurred and confounded under conditions of repression.

In order to fix Islamists in our historical imagination, we search for labels to name their projects, as if these projects are constants rather than fluid processes embedded in the social and political realities of their country. We often forget that they change, mutate, and develop in reaction to specific challenges and opportunities. They evolve in multiple directions. Some visions, such as the ones discussed in this book, are stifled by repression that may lead advocates to persevere—even in prison—or abandon the project altogether, leaving it to be picked up by others. We also cannot rule out that some activists and ideologues may drift into 'radicalism' following disappointment with peaceful mobilisation. If we consider Islamism in all its variants as a historical process that manifests itself at different times and multiple places, we are bound to move beyond rigid classifications as we have theorised them in the social sciences. Key to understanding this Islamism, including the work of those discussed in this book, is to go beyond searching for labels that resonate with an outside audience but have little relevance or significance in their native context. In order to situate the authors in an analytical framework, I invoke a mutation that has become relevant and common in their work and that of others like them. It stems from a constant search for a way out of serious political repression, exclusion, and restrictions on freedoms. The Islamists (*ulama*, intellectuals, and activists) investigated in this book do not enjoy extensive and protected freedom to contribute to the public debate about politics and the future of Saudi Arabia. When they write, they react to a local context that has its own challenges. They do not have in mind Western audiences or global intellectual communities who may or may not appreciate their discourse. Their thought mutates in interaction with this local context, in which political and religious authorities impose serious restrictions on, and even criminalise, their intellectual productions and activism.

The *ulama*, religious thinkers, and activists discussed here are anchored in divine politics, but they subject it to reinterpretations that seek freedom from repression. I have used the term modernism to capture their work not only because several amongst them identify with it, but also because that is how their opponents describe them. Modernism is not always appreciated and encouraged in a country like Saudi Arabia. But it seems to be the English word that corresponds most closely to several Arabic terms (Tanwiri, Asrani, and Aqlanis) invoked when discussing them and their work. Their modernism has two objectives. First, they reinterpret and rethink Islamic texts in ways that allow a modern political project that insists on political representation, political rights, and aspires towards democratic government. Second, the project calls for modern political institutions such as an elected national assembly and a free civil society. Several amongst them are disenchanted with existing institutions such as the Committee for Commanding Right and Prohibiting Wrong in its existing form as a government body. They return to the old

CONCLUSION

Islamic concept of *hisba*, and fuse it with a wider meaning to make it akin to a civil society that is capable of protecting personal and communal rights against the state. Jihad is equally reinterpreted as struggle by words and actions that are peaceful, while keeping military struggle as a defence against outside threats. These innovations are a function of intellectual efforts to revisit foundational texts and offer modern meanings that respond to urgent present needs. The modernism is Islamic, as it does not search for authoritative texts and inspiration from outside this tradition although it engages with other traditions in an appreciative and critical way. It remains anchored in a reconsidered and reinterpreted divine politics, in which the boundaries between the religious and secular are blurred. It does not seek to reject religion but it aspires towards its liberation from state control and manipulation. All writers discussed here worry about political repression being justified under the pretext of applying sharia. In fact, this should take place as a matter of choice rather than force, as many amongst the modernists argue. All the writers invoke the *umma*, not simply as a glorified transnational body or slogan to mobilise other Muslims, but as people who have civil and political rights within the modern territory of the nation-state. In this modernist project the *umma* is not a nostalgia or an overarching umbrella for Muslim hegemony, it is a real entity that is deprived of basic rights. Its sovereignty is a prerequisite for these rights.

However, readers must be warned that it would be counterproductive to impose Western meanings of modernism on this group of writers. Neither are readers encouraged to assign to them labels that are meaningless in the Saudi context, such as 'democratic Muslims', 'liberal Muslims', 'civil Muslims', or 'moderate Muslims'. The authors discussed in this book are Muslims trying to break away from traditional interpretations associated with a dominant religious Salafi trend that has constrained their ability to offer alternative interpretations. They engage with Islamic texts, but also show willingness to incorporate knowledge from other intellectual traditions. They are interlocutors of the history and intellectual heritage of the West, learning lessons and rejecting others. They are critical voices of both their own Salafi tradition and Western heritage. As such, they are not driven by utter rejection of what appears to be Western concepts such as democracy, civil society, and elections. In fact, they all show an appreciation and a longing for such concepts to develop roots in their own country. Even a traditional religious scholar such as Salman al-Awdah warns against the rejectionists who articulate their resistance to democracy on the basis of its image as a Western import, a position common among the dominant Saudi Salafi tradition. Muhammad al-Ahmari goes as far as reclaiming the concept of democracy as a spirit in world heritage.

The modernism of this small sample of writers is deeply rooted in the Islamic tradition rather than simply a response to outside intellectual trends. When these writers borrow from others in, for example, North Africa or the West, they simply seek to support their own interpretations of Islamic texts. When they call for democratic government and anchor this call in new interpretations of foundational Islamic texts, they bring Islam into the debate about politics and society. For all of them Islam can be relevant to political liberation despite being used as a justification for oppression and greater restrictions on civil and political rights. They are all dismayed at how a religious tradition is controlled and manipulated by political authorities in order to legitimise the criminalisation of non-violent mobilisation strategies.

The mutation of divine politics and the crystallisation of a modernist trend among a group of Saudi Islamists is a function of several factors. First is the realisation among a generation of older Islamists that reform is urgently needed, especially after the Arab uprisings and the descent of the whole region into violence. Veteran Islamists such as al-Awdah, al-Hamid, and al-Ahmari saw opportunities in these uprisings to end decades-old dictatorships in their secular and religious forms. The euphoria that accompanied the first uprisings in Tunisia and Egypt gave them hope and consolidated their faith in the power of the masses to engage in peaceful protest to bring down authoritarian regimes. They all celebrated peaceful protest and appreciated their potential against the violence and terrorism that other fringe Islamists practised against both states and people. In both Egypt in the 1990s and Saudi Arabia after 9/11 terrorism in the name of God killed many people, and was counterproductive as it strengthened the very regimes that Jihadis wanted to overthrow. The repression that followed and the detention of thousands of people without fair trials led to an impasse that the modernists felt impelled to examine. Their solution was simple but difficult to implement, as regimes resisted any opening of the political system and continued to use terrorism as a pretext to limit people's freedom and rights.

Second is the rise of a new generation of Islamist thinkers and activists who are disappointed with grand Islamist slogans invoking the sharia, the Islamic state, and the purification of Islam from unorthodox practices and alleged enemies. Saudi modernists launched detailed critiques of dominant Islamist trends such as the Salafis, the Islamic Awakening, and others who invoked divine politics. This new generation distanced itself from these slogans and

CONCLUSION

offered nuanced critical readings of contemporary conditions that require urgent reinterpretation of foundational texts. They also reflected on the success and failure of organised Islamism and questioned the merit of religious educational initiatives to Islamise societies under repression or to impose sharia when people do not enjoy free will. Their commentaries are new in the Saudi context that takes for granted so many ideas and practices and refuses to debate controversial intellectual positions. This new generation does not seem to be constrained by Salafi dogma and is willing to challenge its heritage from within.

This new generation benefits from the proliferation of new means of communication. From Facebook to Twitter, ideas travel fast, gathering momentum in a context that restricts controversial views and opinions. While new communication technology offers new opportunities to reach wider audiences, it has proved to be dangerous in the Saudi context. Virtual forums did not escape the attention of the authorities, and many activists and intellectuals were targeted following critical opinions voiced there. Vague new anti-terrorism laws criminalised opinions that allegedly tarnish the reputation of the king and kingdom, create a rift between rulers and ruled, and encourage people to engage in dissent. Under these circumstances, modernists and others struggled to express themselves in ways that do not lead to arrest and long trials in courts where judges are loyal Salafis. The new generation of modernists was dismayed by the harsh prison sentences, torture in prisons, and the judiciary's subservience to the government. Consequently, the independence of the judiciary and the separation of powers became central in their thinking about reform. In their opinion, reform can only be achieved when religion is freed from government control.

The modernists discussed in this book differ from dissident Salafis in many ways. They do not seek to return Saudi Arabia to the old Saudi–Wahhabi alliance or resist the recent superficial liberal initiatives that the Saudi government introduced following 9/11. They are not concerned with returning to a populist conservatism, like dissident Salafis who see the current state as having deviated from the original message of the eighteenth century founder of Wahhabiyya, Muhammad ibn Abd al-Wahhab. They simply seek the opening of the religious and political field to a debate that would allow reinterpretations of the religious texts to reach wider publics. Therefore, the modernists look ahead to new modes of politics rather than back to the imagined puritanical past of the first Saudi–Wahhabi state of the eighteenth century. There are those amongst them who reject this past and criticise its texts in an attempt to offer solutions to the repression that was perpetuated under its authority. In their own way, the modernists contribute to decentralising Wahhabiyya as a worldview based on literal interpretations of foundational texts. As such, they were predestined to clash with advocates of Wahhabi interpretations, some of whom play an important role in denouncing their views and criminalising their actions.

As the post-uprising Arab region appears to be descending into sectarian violence and terrorism, especially in Syria, Iraq, and Libya, the modernist project may be sidelined, and even marginalised, in the public sphere. It is also possible that the modernist ideas discussed in this book and their advocates can be derailed with some intellectuals, *ulama*, and activists drifting into the current wave of sectarianism that has gripped the Arab world. There is also the possibility that some ideas about democracy, civil society, and human rights will resist this derailment. In both cases, we will witness yet another mutation of Islamism, a progression and regression, depending on the specific historical moment in which its advocates live. The rise of groups such as the Islamic State in the Levant and the ongoing terrorism crisis is bound to be a short-lived experience, regardless of how many years such violent groups dominate the conflicts in the region. The critical thinking of the modernists may not at the moment help contain terrorism; but in the long term it may be a relevant paradigm in countries such as Saudi Arabia, where divine politics is an evolving project. The modernists engage with divine politics in ways that are reinterpretive and pragmatic. Their concern is with keeping Islam relevant to the future of the country, but the main features of this future are dependent on which Islamic narrative becomes the dominant paradigm. In Saudi Arabia the regime patronises and privileges loyal Salafi interpretations that legitimise it, and criminalises its opponents.

Modernism seeks to go beyond Saudi Salafi positions by engaging with Islam in ways that push for real political reform. However, as this book has shown, modernism and modernists remain dangerous projects; their advocates are perhaps more threatening to the Saudi regime in the long term than Jihadi violence. The regime can count on society's support when it claims that it is fighting terrorists; but when it imprisons peaceful modernist Islamists it faces serious challenges, as it cannot justify forever its repression against them.

I have traced the history of a collection of ideas and the biographies and activism of a number of intellectuals and activists who became prominent in Saudi Arabia rather than the genesis of a coherent and well-established social movement with its own famous ideologues and activists. To clearly draw the contours of a social movement gathering momentum around a number of

CONCLUSION

ideologues and activists is perhaps premature in the Saudi context. However, there is a lot of scope for the modernist ideas to flourish and even there is ample evidence that among the modernists there is a core of activists and intellectuals who are willing to sacrifice their own personal freedom in the pursuit of their political agenda. The struggle of HASM founders and followers attests to the perseverance of a minority trying to break the political stagnation of the country.

The focus on this Islamist modernist project reveals it as a relevant trend that offers the prospect of real political reform. Neither the Saudi leadership nor the Salafi constituency has produced a reform agenda that is worth considering for the future of the country. King Abdullah's post-9/11 reforms remained limited to the social sphere and cosmetic changes that overlooked serious questions relating to political representation, civil society, and constitutionalism. King Abdullah died in 2015, leaving behind the carefully constructed image of a reformist king. But during his reign several reformists, including many discussed in this book, lingered in prison. King Salman, who replaced Abdullah in January 2015, has yet to articulate an interest in freeing these prisoners or offering a political reform agenda. Instead, he chose to inaugurate his rule by launching an ambiguous and aggressive foreign policy, the first casualty being Yemen, a country torn apart by internal power struggles, made worst by Saudi military intervention and other regional powers.

It is, however, too early to reflect on King Salman's policies with regard to political reform. At the moment, the regime remains an absolute monarchy that refuses power sharing and representation of the constituency. Hard-line Salafis criticise the regime's minor 'liberalisation' without offering an agenda for reform. There are also so-called liberal voices in Saudi Arabia, but their liberalism has no political dimension or agenda. Their main concern is with religiously sanctioned restrictions on personal freedom and women. Like Salafis, many liberals are suspicious of the Islamist modernists discussed in this book, and see their reinterpretations as a camouflage for radical divine politics.

I hope this book has shown that reform within an Islamic framework can be a viable, albeit difficult, agenda in a country that is yet to experience full mobilisation in the pursuit of equitable and representative government.

NOTES

INTRODUCTION: DIVINE POLITICS IN A PROFANE WORLD

1. Muhammad Qasim Zaman, *Islamic Modernism and the Sharia in Pakistan*, Yale Law School Occasional Papers, March 2014.
2. For a revisionist analysis of the Wahhabi movement and the first Saudi state see Khalid al-Dakhil, *al-Wahabiyya bayn al shirk wa tasadu al qabila*, Beirut: Arab Network for Research and Publishing, 2013.
3. Steffen Hertog, 'The cost of counter-revolution in the GCC', 2011, available at http://mideastafrica.foreignpolicy.com/posts/2011/05/31/the_costs_of_counter_revolution_in_the_gcc; Karen Young, *The Emerging Interventionists of the GCC*, Middle East Centre Paper Series 2, London School of Economics and Political Science, 2013. See also 'Saudi and UAE ready $20 bn boost for Egypt's El-Sisi', *The Telegraph*, 1 June 2014, available at http://www.telegraph.co.uk/finance/newsbysector/banksandfinance/10868522/Saudi-and-UAE-ready-20bn-boost-for-Egypts-El-Sisi.html.
4. Other Arabic names include Asranis (contemporaries), and Aqlanis (rationalists). They are terms often used to refer to those intellectuals who promote modernist arguments in reinterpreting political theology.
5. John Bowen, *A New Anthropology of Islam*, Cambridge: Cambridge University Press, 2012, p. 181.
6. Asef Bayat (ed.), *Post-Islamism: The Changing Faces of Political Islam*, Oxford: Oxford University Press, 2013, p. 4.
7. Richard Martin & Abbas Barzegar (eds), *Islamism: Contested Perspectives on Political Islam*, Stanford: Stanford University Press, 2010, p. 2.
8. Donald Emmerson, 'Inclusive Islamism: the Utility of Diversity'. In Martin and Barzegar (eds) *Islamism*, p. 17–32.
9. Roxanne Euben and Muhammad Qasim Zaman (eds), *Princeton Readings in Islamist Thought: Texts and Contexts from al-Banna to Bin Laden*, Princeton and Oxford: Princeton University Press, 2009, p. 4.

10. Fawaz Gerges, *The Far Enemy: Why Jihad Went Global*, Cambridge: Cambridge University Press, 2005.
11. Gilles Kepel, *Jihad: The Trail of Political Islam*, London: I. B. Tauris, 2003.
12. Salwa Ismail, *Political Life in Cairo's New Quarters: Encountering the Everyday State*, Minnesota: Minnesota University Press, 2006.
13. Francois Burgat, *Face to Face with Political Islam*, London: I. B. Tauris, 2003.
14. Olivier Roy, *Holy Ignorance: When Religion and Culture Part Ways*, London: Hurst & Co., 2010.
15. Mahmood Mamdani, 'Good Muslim, bad Muslim: a political perspective on culture and terrorism', *American Anthropologist*, 104, 3 (2002), pp. 766–75.
16. See Bruce Lawrence, *Defenders of God: the Fundamentalist Revolt against the Modern Age*, South Carolina: University of South Carolina Press, 2006 and Charles Taylor, *A Secular Age*, Cambridge Massachusetts: Harvard University Press, 2006.
17. John Gray, *Black Mass: Apocalyptic Religion and the Death of Utopia*, London: Penguin, 2007. Gil Anidjar, Gianni Vattimo, and even Benedetto Croce have made very similar observations.
18. See Mamoun Fandy, *Saudi Arabia and the Politics of Dissent*, New York: St Martin's Press, 1999; Stephane Lacroix, *Awakening Islam: Religious Dissent in Contemporary Saudi Arabia*, Cambridge, Mass.: Harvard University Press, 2011; and Thomas Hegghammer, *Jihad in Saudi Arabia: Violence and Pan-Islamism since 1979*, Cambridge: Cambridge University Press, 2010.
19. Stephane Lacroix, 'Between Islamists and liberals: Saudi Arabia's new Islamo-liberal reformists', *Middle East Journal*, 58, 3 (2004), pp. 345–64.
20. See Leonard Binder, *Islamic Liberalism: A Critique of Development Ideologies*, Chicago: University of Chicago Press, 1988; Charles Kurzman (ed.), *Liberal Islam: A Source Book*, Oxford: Oxford University Press, 1998; and Charles Kurzman (ed.), *Modernist Islam: A Source Book*, Oxford: Oxford University Press, 2002.
21. Joseph Massad, *Islam in Liberalism*. Chicago: Chicago University Press, 2015.
22. Talal Asad, *The Idea of an Anthropology of Islam*, Washington, DC: Center for Contemporary Arab Studies, Georgetown University, 1986, p. 14.
23. Ibid., pp. 14–15.
24. Fawaz Gerges, *America and Political Islam: Clash of Cultures or Clash of Interests?*, Cambridge: Cambridge University Press, 1999.
25. The resurrection of the caliphate does not feature as an agenda among all Islamists. Only Hizb al-Tahrir and to a lesser extent al-Qaida have made the slogan central to their political programme. On Hizb al-Tahrir see Reza Pankhurst, *The Inevitable Caliphate? A History of the Struggle for Global Islamic Union, 1924 to the Present*, London: Hurst & Co., 2013. In 2014 the Islamic State of Iraq and Syria (ISIS), a radical global Jihadi movement, declared the establishment of a caliphate over the territories it controlled in both countries. For further details on the contemporary resurrection of the caliphate see Madawi Al-Rasheed, Carool Kersten, and

Marat Shterin (eds), *Demystifying the Caliphate: Historical Memory and Contemporary Contexts*, London: Hurst & Co., 2012.

26. Madawi Al-Rasheed, 'Saudi Arabia: the challenge of the US invasion of Iraq', in Rick Fawn and Raymond Hinnebusch (eds), *The Iraq War: Causes and Consequences*, London: Lynne Rienner, 2006, pp. 153–62.
27. Salman al-Awdah denounced the Islamist opposition abroad, namely the Movement for Islamic Reform in Arabia, led by London-based Saad al-Faqih. Other Islamists who had worked with Saad al-Faqih, such as Muhsin al-Awaji, were also critical of exiled Islamists and called on them to reconcile with the regime and return to Saudi Arabia. For further details see Madawi Al-Rasheed, *Contesting the Saudi State: Islamic Voices from a New Generation*, Cambridge: Cambridge University Press, 2007, pp. 59–101.
28. The debates that dominated the Saudi public sphere after 9/11 on gender and radicalisation are discussed in Madawi Al-Rasheed, *A Most Masculine State: Gender, Religion and Politics in Saudi Arabia*, Cambridge: Cambridge University Press, 2013, pp. 134–74.
29. Madawi Al-Rasheed, 'Sectarianism as counter-revolution: Saudi responses to the Arab Spring', *Studies in Ethnicity and Nationalism*, 11, 3 (2011), pp. 513–26; Madawi Al-Rasheed, 'No Saudi Spring: anatomy of a failed revolution', *Boston Review*, March/April 2012, pp. 33–9.
30. Toby Matthiesen, 'A "Saudi Spring"?: the Shi'a movement in the Eastern Province 2011–2012', *Middle East Journal*, 66, 4 (2012), pp. 628–59.
31. Stephane Lacroix, 'Comparing the Arab revolts: is Saudi Arabia immune?' *Journal of Democracy*, 22, 4 (2011), pp. 48–59.
32. Lacroix, 'Between Islamists and liberals'.
33. Stephane Lacroix, *Saudi Islamists and the Arab Spring*, Kuwait Programme on Development, Governance and Globalisation in the Gulf States, LSE Reports, no. 36, May 2014.
34. Stephane Lacroix, 'Saudi Arabia and the limits of post-Islamism', in Bayat (ed.), *Post-Islamism*, pp. 277–97.
35. Asef Bayat, 'The coming of a post-Islamist society', *Critique: Critical Middle East Studies*, 9 (1996), pp. 43–52; see also Bayat (ed.), *Post-Islamism*, pp. 7–32.
36. The Arab Network for Research and Publishing, available at http://arabiyanetwork.com/index.php.
37. Madawi Al-Rasheed, 'Saudi officials shut down display at book fair', 13 March 2014, available at http://www.al-monitor.com/pulse/originals/2014/03/saudi-book-display-shut-down.html.
38. Madawi Al-Rasheed, *A Most Masculine State: Gender, Politics, and Religion in Saudi Arabia*, Cambridge: Cambridge University Press, 2013.

1. PETITIONS AND PROTEST ON THE EVE OF THE ARAB UPRISINGS

1. The *sahwa* included diverse groups such as the radical messianic movement known as al-Salafiyya al-Muhtasiba, whose leader, Juhaiyman al-Otaibi, occupied the Grand Mosque in Mecca in 1979, and Hizb al-Tahrir, led by Muhammad al-Masari, in addition to Tablighi preaching groups and Muslim Brotherhood followers. The most prolific trend was, however, called the Sururis, a reference to Syrian scholar Muhammad Surur Zaiyn al-Abdin, who combined a Muslim Brotherhood orientation with a Salafi focus. He became influential in Saudi Arabia after settling there to teach in various educational institutes. On the various Sahwi trends see Madawi Al-Rasheed, *Contesting the Saudi State: Islamic Voices from a New Generation*, Cambridge: Cambridge University Press, 2007; Stephane Lacroix, *Awakening Islam: Religious Dissent in Contemporary Saudi Arabia*, Cambridge, Mass.: Harvard University Press, 2011; Thomas Hegghammer, *Jihad in Saudi Arabia: Violence and Pan-Islamism since 1979*, Cambridge: Cambridge University Press, 2010; and Abd al-Aziz al-Khodr, *al-Soudiyya sirat dawla wa mujtama*, Beirut: Arab Network for Research and Publishing, 2010.
2. Madawi Al-Rasheed, 'Saudi Arabia: the challenge of the American invasion of Iraq', in R. Fawn and R. Hinnebusch (eds), *The Iraq War: Causes and Consequences*, London: Lynne Rienner, 2006, pp. 153–62.
3. On the disengagement of Islamists after 9/11 see Pascal Menoret, 'Leaving Islamic activism behind: ambiguous disengagement in Saudi Arabia', in Joel Beinin and Frédéric Vairel (eds), *Social Movements, Mobilization, and Contestations in the Middle East and North Africa*, Stanford: Stanford University Press, 2011, pp. 43–60.
4. For example, Nasir al-Huzaymi, who was drawn to the 1979 movement of Juhaiyman al-Otaibi, wrote an autobiography exposing details of his engagement with radicalism. See Nasir al-Huzaiymi, *Ayam ma Juhayman*, 2nd edn, Beirut: al-Shabaka al-Arabiyya lil Abhath wa al-Nashr, 2011.
5. On Islamist calls for reform in the 1990s see Mansoor Jassem Alshamsi, *Islam and Political Reform in Saudi Arabia: The Quest for Political Change and Reform*, London: Routledge, 2011.
6. I have discussed this phase of activism in Al-Rasheed, *Contesting the Saudi State*, p. 230.
7. Joseph Kechichian, *Legal and Political Reform in Saudi Arabia*, London: Routledge, 2013, p. 159.
8. For English translations of the petitions see ibid., pp. 256, 262, 274, 275, 283.
9. Stephane Lacroix, 'Saudi Arabia and the limits of Islamism', in Asef Bayat (ed.), *Post-Islamism: The Changing Faces of Political Islam*, Oxford: Oxford University Press, 2013, pp. 277–97 and 'Between Islamists and liberals: Saudi Arabia's new Islamo-liberal reformists', *Middle East Journal*, 58, 3 (2004), pp. 345–64.
10. Lacroix, 'Between Islamists and liberals'.

11. In 1996 Asef Bayat among others introduced the concept of post-Islamism; for his latest revision see Bayat (ed.) *Post-Islamism.*
12. The petition and the names of signatories are available at http://www.saudireform.com/?p=petintion, accessed 20 April 2011.
13. Communication with Ahmad Adnan, April 2011.
14. The petition is available at http://dawlaty.com/services.html, accessed 20 April 2011.
15. Shabab Saudi, available at http://shababsaudi.wordpress.com/.
16. The petition is available at http://www.islamlight.net/index.php/index.php?option=content&task=view&id=21468&Itemid=33.
17. The petition is available at http://www.almokhtsar.com/node/171572.
18. Saudi media denounced the petition and described it as an-Ikhwan document, a Muslim brotherhood initiative. See http://www.alarabiya.net/ar/saudi-today/2013/07/11/بيان-إخوان-السعودية.html.
19. The party established its own web pages at http://www.islamcommaparty.org. It also started its own Twitter account, offering updates on its programme and news (@islamicommapart). See also Reuters, 'Saudi Arabia—political party formed', 10 February 2011, available at http://www.nytimes.com/2011/02/11/world/middleeast/11briefs-Saudi.html.
20. Several human rights organisations reported the arrest of the founding members. See Amnesty International, 'Saudi Arabia: men detained for founding political party', 23 February 2011, available at http://www.amnesty.org/en/library/asset/MDE23/002/2011/en/ffeaafc0-fbf7-43c4-a1a6-1b18d99b2cdd/mde230022011en.html.
21. See http://www.islamcommaparty.org/particle/436.
22. On the restoration of the caliphate in the Muslim imagination see Madawi Al-Rasheed, Carool Kersten, and Marat Shterin (eds), *Demystifying the Caliphate: Historical Memory and Contemporary Contexts*, London: Hurst & Co., 2012, pp. 1–30.
23. Hakim al-Mutairi writes critical assessments of the official Saudi Salafi tradition, especially its ban on political mobilisation and rigid interpretation of this as rebellion against rulers. For more details on his political theology see Al-Rasheed, *Contesting the Saudi State*, pp. 45–54.
24. Reza Pankhurst, *The Inevitable Caliphate? A History of the Struggle for Global Islamic Union, 1924 to the Present*, London: Hurst & Co., 2013, pp. 93–129.
25. See http://www.ommah.org.
26. Islamic Umma Party, 24 February 2011, available at http://islamcommaparty.org/statement/432.
27. In 2009, for example, activists Khalid al-Umayr and Muhammad al-Utaibi issued a statement calling for demonstrations in support of Gaza. They were arrested.
28. The Saudi Day of Rage was advertised on many web pages, several of which the

Saudi authorities blocked. Local activists quickly set up alternative Facebook pages. See, for example, http://www.facebook.com/Saudis.Revolution, accessed on 21 April 2011.

29. On Shia demonstrations and activism since 2011 see Toby Matthiesen, *Sectarian Gulf: Bahrain, Saudi Arabia, and the Arab Spring that Wasn't*, Stanford: Stanford University Press, 2013 and 'A "Saudi Spring?": the Shi'a protest movement in the Eastern Province 2011–2012', *Middle East Journal*, 66, 4 (2012), pp. 628–59. On the Shia movement in Saudi Arabia see Badr al-Ibrahim and Muhammad al-Sadiq, *al-Hirak al-shii fi al-saoudiyya*, Beirut: Arab Network for Research and Publishing, 2013.

30. On the protests in Bahrain see Toby Jones and Cortni Kerr, 'A Revolution Paused in Bahrain', *MERIP* Report, 23 February 2011.

31. Ethan Bronner and Michael Slackmann, 'Saudi troops enter Bahrain to help put down unrest', *New York Times*, 14 March 2011, available at http://www.nytimes.com/2011/03/15/world/middleeast/15bahrain.html.

32. A reliable source on the early signs of the Day of Rage on 10 March 2011 in Qatif is 'Saudi Arabia prepares for protest', available at http://www.bbc.co.uk/news/world-middle-east-12708487.

33. Between 11 March and 27 March Saudi authorities arrested more than 160 activists in various cities. See Human Rights Watch, 'Saudi Arabia: arrests for peaceful protest on the rise', 27 March 2011, available at http://www.hrw.org/en/news/2011/03/27/saudi-arabia-arrests-peaceful-protest-rise.

34. 'Saudi Arabia show of force stifles Day of Rage', BBC, 11 March 2011, available at http://news.bbc.co.uk/1/hi/programmes/newsnight/9422550.stm. After this report Lloyd-Roberts was asked to leave the country.

35. Details of women's mobilisation are discussed in Madawi Al-Rasheed, *A Most Masculine State: Gender, Politics and Religion in Saudi Arabia*, Cambridge: Cambridge University Press, 2013, pp. 286–92.

36. Local Saudi newspapers began to report on the regular protests. See http://www.alyaum.com/News/art/11147.html and http://www.alwatan.com.sa/Local/News_Detail.aspx?ArticleID=53402&CategoryID=5

37. Al-Rasheed, *A Most Masculine State*.

38. Madawi Al-Rasheed, 'Saudi duality on women', *Al-Monitor*, 30 September 2013, available at http://www.al-monitor.com/pulse/originals/2013/09/saudi-women-drive-viral-video-cleric.html.

39. For full details of official Saudi religious scholars' position on the obligation to obey rulers see Al-Rasheed, *Contesting the Saudi State*, pp. 22–58. On the Mufti's tour see al-yaum 10 May 2011, available at http://www.alyaum.com/News/art/11310.html?print.

40. The best discussion of the ability of authoritarian regimes to use the digital war against their opponents is discussed in Evgeny Morozov, *The Net Delusion: How*

Not to Liberate the World, London: Allen Lane, 2011. Morozov does not totally dismiss the internet and the freedom of information it allows, but he tempers enthusiasm for digital communication in the absence of real structural conditions for democracy.
41. Jason Benham, 'Saudi king orders more handouts, security boost', Reuters, 18 March 2011, available at http://www.reuters.com/article/2011/03/18/us-saudi-king-idUSTRE72H2UQ20110318.
42. 'Demonstrations are forbidden', *Al-Riyadh* newspaper, 7 March 2011.
43. Madawi Al-Rasheed, 'Sectarianism as counter revolution: Saudi responses to the Arab Spring', *Studies in Ethnicity and Nationalism*, 11, 3 (2011), pp. 513–26.

2. CIVIL SOCIETY IN AN AUTHORITARIAN STATE

1. On civil society in Saudi Arabia see Raed Abdulaziz Alhargan, 'Saudi Arabia: civil rights and local actors', *Middle East Policy*, 19, 1 (2012), pp. 126–39; Caroline Montagu, 'Civil society and the voluntary sector in Saudi Arabia', *Middle East Journal*, 64, 1 (2010), pp. 67–83; Mariwan Kanie, 'Civil society in Saudi Arabia: different forms, one language', in Roel Meijer and Paul Aarts (eds), *Saudi Arabia Between Conservatism, Accommodation and Reform*, The Hague: Netherlands Institute for International Relations, 2012, pp. 33–56; Toby Matthiesen, 'Diwaniyas, intellectual salons and the limits of civil society', Middle East Institute blog, 2009, posted at http://www.mei.edu/content/diwaniyyas-intellectual-salons-and-limits-civil-society?print; and Sultan Sooouad Al-Qasimi, 'The civil society movement in the Arab Gulf states', *The Huff Post*, 28 January 2013. The government forum known as the Saudi National Dialogue Forum is considered a kind of civil society in Mark Thompson, *Saudi Arabia and the Path to Political Change: National Dialogue and Civil Society*, London: I. B. Tauris, 2014.
2. ACPRA (HASM) website http://www.acpraorg.org/index.php.
3. Official human rights organisations include the National Society of Human Rights (founded 2004) and the Human Rights Commission (founded 2005). Both organisations work with the government. Reformers claim that their activities are undermined as a result of official patronage. Many other independent organisations appeared in Saudi Arabia. These include Human Rights Monitor and the Human Rights First Society. However, HASM remains the best known as a result of its overt confrontations with the regime, elaborate human rights discourse, and activism.
4. Amélie Le Renard, *Femmes et espaces publics en Arabie Saoudite*, Paris: Dalloz, 2011.
5. The case of HASM activists was publicised in a report by Amnesty International. See 'Muzzling dissent: Saudi Arabia's effort to choke civil society', London, 9 October 2014, available at http://www.amnesty.org/en/news/muzzling-dissent-saudi-arabia-s-efforts-choke-civil-society-2014-10-09.

6. Personal conversation with the author, 2013.
7. Al-Araby al-Jadid, 'Iman al-qahtani tamdah al-saoudiyya,' (Iman al-Qahtani praises Saudi Arabia), 14 February 2015, at http://www.alaraby.co.uk/medianews/2015/2/14/ http://www.alaraby.co.uk/medianews/2015/2/14/-إيمان-القحطاني تمدح-السعودية-سبحان-مغير-الأحوال, accessed on 1 June 2015
8. Madawi Al-Rasheed, 'Saudi internal dilemmas and regional responses to the Arab uprisings', in Fawaz Gerges (ed.), *The New Middle East: Protest and Revolution in the Arab World*, Cambridge: Cambridge University Press, 2014, pp. 353–79.
9. Robert Worth, 'Saudi's lonely, costly bid for Sunni–Shiite equality', *New York Times*, 14 March 2014.
10. Carnegie Endowment for International Peace, *Arab Political Systems: baseline Information and Reform-Saudi Arabia*, available at carnegieendowment.org/files/saudi_arabia_aps.doc.
11. The HASM founding statement is at http://www.acpraorg.org/index.php.
12. Madawi Al-Rasheed, *Contesting the Saudi State: Islamic Voices from a New Generation*, Cambridge: Cambridge University Press, 2007, pp. 223–30.
13. Al-Hamid's books and statements are in documented on his blog 'Abu Bilal': see http://abubelal1951.blogspot.co.uk.
14. Amnesty International, 'Document—UA 199/93—Saudi Arabia: fear of torture/ill-treatment: Dr Abdullah Al-Hamed, Dr Muhammad 'Abdullah Al-Mas'ari', 18 June 1993, available at https://www.amnesty.org/en/library/asset/MDE23/005/1993/en/23e9bacb-ecc7–11dd-85fd-99a1fce0c9ec/mde230051993en.html. On the CDLR see Mamoun Fandy, *Saudi Arabia and the Politics of Dissent*, New York: St Martin's Press, 1999 and Al-Rasheed, *Contesting the Saudi State*.
15. Trials of Saudi reformers, 10 March 2003, available at http://www.aljazeera.net/news/pages/03f446c6-a4ed-4514-a5c9–316f4e018c63.
16. Munif al-Sufuqi and Huda al-Saleh, 'Trial of three Saudis', 2 December 2004, available at http://www.aawsat.com/details.asp?issueno=9165&article=268828#.UvQmnPl_vGw.
17. Yahya al-Amir and Turki al-Suhail, 'Nine years in prison for al-Damini and al-Falih', 16 May 2005, available at http://www.alriyadh.com/article64858.html.
18. 'The King pardons prisoners', 9 August 2005, available at http://www.aawsat.com/details.asp?section=1&article=316741&issueno=9751#.UvQq9vl_vGw.
19. Amnesty International, 'Free Dr Abdullah al-Hamid', 19 March 2008, available at http://www.amnesty.org/en/node/4250.
20. CDHRAP, 30 August 2008, available at http://cdhrap.net/archive/ar/post.php?3024.
21. 'Blogger: User Profile: Abubelal1951', accessed 4 February 2014, available at https://www.blogger.com/profile/00823743862313846215.
22. Muhammad al-Shuyukh, 'Saudi Islamists', 27 March 2013, available at http://middle-east-online.com/?id=152016.
23. ACPRA, 1 February 2010, available at http://acpra-hr.org/news_view_13.html.

24. AlKarama, 'Saudi Arabia: release on bail of Mr Suleiman Al-Rashoudi', 24 June 2011, available at http://en.alkarama.org/index.php?option=com_content&view=article&id=764:saudi-arabia-release-on-bail-of-mr-suleiman-al-rashoudi-&catid=33:communiqu&Itemid=179.
25. Adalaksa.org, 'Suleyman Saleh al-Reshoudi', 3 March 2011, available at http://www.adalaksa.org/content/suleyman-saleh-al-reshoudi.
26. AlKarama, 'Saudi Arabia: senior human rights lawyer arrested for saying right to assembly is legitimate', 17 December 2012, available at http://en.alkarama.org/index.php?option=com_content&view=article&id=1026:saudi-arabia-senior-human-rights-lawyer-arrested-for-saying-right-to-assembly-is-legitimate&catid=33:communiqu&Itemid=179.
27. AlKarama, 'Saudi Arabia: release on bail of Mr Suleiman Al-Rashoudi'.
28. Amnesty International, 23 November 2011, available at http://www.amnesty.org/ar/news/saudi-arabia-lengthy-sentences-reformists-worrying-development-2011-11-23.
29. Amnesty International, 'Reform activists in Saudi Arabia must receive fair appeal hearings', 25 January 2012, available at http://www.amnesty.org/en/news/reform-activists-saudi-arabia-must-receive-fair-appeal-hearings-2012-01-25.
30. AlKarama, 'Saudi Arabia: senior human rights lawyer arrested for saying right to assembly is legitimate'.
31. Human Rights Watch, 13 February 2013, available at http://www.hrw.org/ar/news/2013/02/12/15.
32. ACPRA, 15 February 2013, available at http://www.acpra-hr.co/news_view_215.html.
33. Amnesty International, 'Saudi Arabia ramps up clampdown on human rights activists', 18 June 2012, available at http://www.amnesty.org/en/news/saudi-arabia-ramps-clampdown-human-rights-activists-2012-06-18.
34. Thomas Lippman, 'Saudi professor faces charges after fighting for free speech', 29 June 2012, available at http://www.al-monitor.com/pulse/originals/2012/al-monitor/mohammad-al-qahtani-pushes-the-l.html#.
35. Alicia Wittmeyer, 'The FP top 100 global thinkers', 26 November 2012, available at http://www.foreignpolicy.com/articles/2012/11/26/the_fp_100_global_thinkers.
36. Matruk al-Faleh, 'El-Eqtissadyah-Interview-18–12–2006', 21 February 2007, available at http://faculty.ksu.edu.sa/Alfaleh/Pages/El-eqtissadyah-Interview-18-12-2006.aspx.
37. Al Jazeera, 'Saudi hunger strike over detentions', 6 November 2008, available at http://www.aljazeera.com/news/middleeast/2008/11/2008116153455440898.html.
38. ACPRA, http://www.acpra-hr.org/news.php?action=view&id=125.
39. Amnesty International, 'Saudi Arabia ramps up clampdown on human rights activists'.

40. AlKarama, 'Saudi Arabia: prominent human rights defender risks 5 years of prison for cooperating with the UN', 29 June 2012, available at http://en.alkarama.org/index.php?option=com_content&view=article&id=961:saudi-arabia-prominent-human-rights-defender-risks-5-years-of-prison-for-cooperating-with-the-un&catid=33:communiqu&Itemid=179.
41. USCIRF, 'Saudi Arabia: release Mohammad Fahad Al-Qahtani and Abdullah Bin Hamad', 14 March 2013, available at http://www.uscirf.gov/news-room/press-releases/3952-3142013-saudi-arabia-release-mohammad-fahad-al-qahtani-and-abdullah-bin-hamad.html.
42. Abdullah al-Hamid, 'Abu Bilal' blog at http://abubelal1951.blogspot.co.uk.
43. Ibid.
44. Document sent to author.
45. These trials attracted the attention of many bloggers, who followed the details and wrote assessments of their fairness. See Nora Abdulkarim, 'Trial of Saudi civil rights activists', 2 September 2012, available at http://ana3rabeya.wordpress.com/2012/09/02/activiststrial/.

3. ON REVOLUTION

1. Mamoun Fandy, *Saudi Arabia and the Politics of Dissent*, New York: St Martin's Press, 1999; Madawi Al-Rasheed, *Contesting the Saudi State: Islamic Voices from a New Generation*, Cambridge: Cambridge University Press, 2007; Stephane Lacroix, *Awakening Islam: Religious Dissent in Contemporary Saudi Arabia*, Cambridge, Mass.: Harvard University Press, 2011.
2. Fandy, *Saudi Arabia*, p. 89; Turki al-Dakhil, *Salman al-Awdah: min al-sijn ila al-tanwir*, Beirut: Madarik, 2011, p. 45.
3. Al-Awdah's supporters documented their reaction to his imprisonment in a video when they marched in Buraiydah in his support. However, they were not able to put enough pressure on the interior minister at the time, Prince Nayif, to release him and other well-known Islamists. The Movement for Islamic Reform in Arabia (MIRA) circulated the video of his arrest and supported his cause throughout his time in prison. This changed as al-Awdah began to denounce the exiled Islamist opposition in London after 9/11. On al-Awdah's 1990 intellectual contribution to the Islamic awakening see Mansoor Jassem Alshamsi, *Islam and Political Reform in Saudi Arabia: The Quest for Political Change and Reform*, London: Routledge, 2011, p. 106.
4. Al-Rasheed, *Contesting the Saudi State*, pp. 59–101.
5. The Saudi press continues to claim that al-Awdah supported the Afghan jihad and once reported that he sought help from the authorities after his son left a note stating his intention to go to Iraq to fight against American occupation. Al-Awdah took *al-Watan* newspaper, which circulated these rumours, to court for false representation, and won. In 2013, when he issued a statement in support of political

prisoners, the Saudi press restarted a campaign against him. This is not surprising, as the press is owned by members of the regime and endorsed its instruction to target Islamists in articles and commentaries.

6. Al-Dakhil, *Salman al-Awdah*.
7. The television programme was suspended allegedly under pressure from the regime as al-Awdah expressed his support for the Egyptian revolution, which the regime denounced.
8. Al-Dakhil, *Salman al-Awdah*, p. 84.
9. The first episode of Hajar al-zawiyya was aired on 5 October 2005 and the topic was the meaning of jihad, two years after the occupation of Iraq by American forces. Al-Awdah was one of twenty-six Saudi *ulama* who signed a petition explaining the legitimacy of jihad against foreign occupation. He announced later that he was against Saudi youth joining jihad in Iraq, which seems in accord with his previous position on jihad in Afghanistan in the 1980s. He argued that military jihad against occupation in Iraq is legitimate and has a limited purpose, namely ending occupation. As such it should not be expanded into indiscriminate killing of both Muslims and others on the basis of their attitudes to this occupation, an obvious denunciation of the civil war that raged in Iraq until 2007. For further details on the many topics that al-Awdah discussed in his MBC Hajar al-zawiyya programme see al-Dakhil, *Salman al-Awdah*, p. 98.
10. Al-Dakhil, *Salman al-Awdah*.
11. Saudi Mufti Abd al-Aziz al-Sheikh continues to denounce Facebook and Twitter and to accuse those using them of telling lies.
12. Salman al-Awdah, *Asilat al-thawra*, Beirut: Markaz Inma lil-Buhuth wa al-Dirasat, 2012.
13. Ibid., p. 35.
14. Ibid., pp. 41–5.
15. Ibid., p. 48.
16. Ibid., p. 172.
17. Ibid., p. 207.
18. Salman al-Awdah's Twitter handle is @salman_alodah.
19. Hazem Sagiyyeh, *Nawasib wa rawafidh*, Beirut: Saqi, 2009, p. 159.
20. BBC, 'Saudi Arabian Mosque Hit by Bomb', 29 May 2015, at http://www.bbc.co.uk/news/world-middle-east-32929928 accesses on 1 June 2015.
21. Madawi Al-Rasheed, *A Most Masculine State: Gender, Politics and Religion in Saudi Arabia*, Cambridge: Cambridge University Press, 2013.
22. The statement is posted on @salman_alodah. It went viral on Twitter to the extent of creating an overload. All citations here draw on his Twitter statements. The letter was later published on his website, Islam Today.
23. Salman al-Awdah, @salman_alodah.
24. Ibid.

25. For detailed account of this criticism see Al-Rasheed, *Contesting the Saudi State*.
26. Salman al-Awdah, @salman_alodah and on Facebook https://www.facebook. com/DrSalmanAlOadah.
27. Ibid.
28. Tariq al-Humaid, 'Salman al-Awdah: khitab mafdoh', *al-Sharq al-Awsat*, 17 March 2013.
29. Salman al-Dowsari, 'Thawrat Salman al-Awdah', *al-Iqtisadiyya*, 17 March 2013.
30. For analysis of Saudi Islamist reactions to the Egyptian coup see Madawi Al-Rasheed, 'Egypt coup and Saudi Islamists', *Mideast Foreign Policy*, 19 August 2013, available at http://mideast.foreignpolicy.com/posts/2013/08/19/egypts_coup_and_the_saudi_opposition.
31. @salman_alodah.
32. Ibid.
33. See Chapter 2.
34. Al-Awdah *Asilat al-thawra*, p. 11.

4. BETWEEN FORCE AND CHOICE: DEBATING SHARIA IN A SALAFI CONTEXT

1. http://altagreer.com.
2. Biographical information on al-Maliki is taken from conversations with him: interview with the author, 4 October 2013.
3. Al-Maliki is active on Twitter. See @iAbuhesham.
4. The history of this trend in Saudi Arabia is discussed in Abd al-Aziz al-Khodr, *al-Saoudiyya sirat dawla wa mujtama*, Beirut: Arab Network for Research and Publishing, 2010, pp. 565–642 and Khalid al-Mushawah, *al-Tayarat al-diniyya fi al-saoudiyya*, Riyadh: Markaz al-Din wa al-Siyasat, 2012, pp. 123–8.
5. Those who denounce the Tanwiri tend are numerous. They include Nasir al-Saif, Ibrahim al-Sakran, and Walid al-Huwayrini. See Walid al-Huwayrini, *Asr al-islamiyin al-judud*, n.p.: Dar Alam al-Kutub, 2013, available at goodreads.com and Abd al-Wahab al-Ghadhif, *al-Tanwir al-Islami fi al-mashhad al-Saoudi*, n.p.: Markaz Tasil, 2013, available at goodreads.com.
6. Quoted in Nasir al-Saif, 'al-Tanwiriyun al-saoudiyoun bayn al-wahm wa al-haqiqa', Saaid al-Fawaid, available at http://saaid.net/arabic/693.htmat.
7. Interview with the author, 4 October 2013.
8. Ibid.
9. Ibid.
10. Ibid.
11. The association is discussed in Chapter 2.
12. Abdullah al-Maliki, 'Siyadat al-umma qabl tatbiq al-sharia', 11 November 2011, available at www.almqaal.com. Other articles by al-Maliki are posted on http://www.almqaal.com/?author=18.

NOTES pp. [101–117]

13. Abdullah al-Maliki, *Siyadat al-umma qabl tatbiq al-sharia*, Beirut: Arab Network for Research and Publishing, 2012.
14. Ibid., p. 94.
15. Ibid., p. 113.
16. Ibid., p. 120.
17. Ibid., p. 132.
18. Ibid., p. 136.
19. Gudrun Kramer, 'Islamist notions of democracy', Middle East Research and Information Project, volume 23, 1993, available at http://www.merip.org/mer/mer183/islamist-notions-democracy.
20. Abdullah al-Maliki, 'Limatha fashilat tajrubat al-ikhwan fi al-hukm', 13 July 2013, available at www.almqaal.com.
21. Ibid.
22. Salman al-Awdah's patronage of the first forum is announced on Islam Today, available at http://www.islamtoday.net/salman/artshow-78-131114.
23. Abdullah al-Rashid, 'Inqisamat al-islamiyyin fi al-saoudiyya', 27 May 2012, available at ww.majalla.com. Statements by Mustafa al-Hasan are on his blog page, available at http://rowaqalhasan.com/?tag=.
24. Kristin Smith Diwan, 'Youthful Saudi reformers only safe in the twittersphere', *Atlantic Council*, 20 December 2013.
25. Statement by thirty-six Saudi *ulama* against the Youth Rising Forum, available at http://www.burnews.com/news-action-show-id-35939.htm.
26. *al-Majalla*, 27 May 2012, available at ww.majalla.com.
27. Ibid.
28. Ibid.
29. Ibid.
30. Gulf Centre for Human Rights, 'Kuwait: Youth Rising Forum prevented from holding its third annual forum', 23 March 2013, available at http://gc4hr.org/news/view/102.
31. *al-Watan*, 22 March 2012, available at http://kuwait.tt/articledetails.aspx?Id=181261.
32. Al-Maliki, *Siyadat al-umma*, p. 9.

5. DECONSTRUCTING THE RELIGIOUS ROOTS OF AUTHORITARIANISM

1. Global Voices, 'Saudi Arabia: Free Saudi Scholar Dr Muhammed Alabdulkareem', 11 December 2010, available at http://globalvoicesonline.org/2010/12/11/saudi-arabia-calls-to-release-saudi-scholar-dr-mohammed-abdulkareem/.
2. Muhammad al-Abd al-Karim, 'Azmat al-sira' al-siyasi bayn al-ajniha al-hakima fi al-saoudiyya', December 2010, available at http://freealabdulkreem.wordpress.com/category/مقالات-الدكتور-محمد-العبدالكريم/.

177

3. Muhammad al-Abd al-Karim, 'La lil-muwatana bil ma'na al-soudi', December 2010, available at http://freealabdulkreem.wordpress.com/category/مقالات-الدكتور-مح/مد-العبدالكريم.
4. Ibid.
5. See https://www.facebook.com/pages/ 154624781246102/-د-محمد-العبدالكريم-فضيلة-الشيخ.
6. Muhammad al-Abd al-Karim, *Sahwat al-tawhid: dirasa fi azmat al-khitab al-siyasi al-islami*, Beirut: Arab Network for Research and Publishing, 2012, p. 12.
7. Ibid., p. 16.
8. Roel Meijer (ed.), *Global Salafism, Islam's New Religious Movement*, London: Hurst & Co., 2009. For a nuanced argument about the multiple religious trends that have coexisted and competed in Saudi Arabia since the 1960s see Michael Farquhar, 'Expanding the Wahhabi Mission: Saudi Arabia, the Islamic University of Medina and the Transnational Religious Economy', Ph.D. thesis, London School of Economics and Political Science, 2014.
9. Stephane Lacroix, *Awakening Islam: Religious Dissent in Contemporary Saudi Arabia*, Cambridge, Mass.: Harvard University Press, 2011, pp. 38–73.
10. Ibid.
11. Abd al-Nabi al-Hari, 'Muhawalat tasil lil-dimouqratiyya fi biya salafiyya', available at al-www.almqaal.com.
12. Al-Abd al-Karim, *Sahwat al-tawhid*.
13. Ibid., p. 28.
14. Ibid., pp. 90–1.
15. On al-Albani see Stephane Lacroix, 'Between revolution and apoliticism: Nasir al-Din al-Albani and his impact on the shaping of contemporary Salafism', in Meijer (ed.), *Global Salafism*, pp. 58–80.
16. Al-Abd al-Karim, *Sahwat al-tawhid*, pp. 101–2.
17. On the Sururis see Madawi Al-Rasheed, *Contesting the Saudi State: Islamic Voices from a New Generation*, Cambridge: Cambridge University Press, 2007; Lacroix, *Awakening Islam*; and Abd al-Aziz Al-Khodr, *al-Soudiyya sirat dawla wa mujtama*, Beirut: Arab Network for Research and Publishing, 2010.
18. Al-Abd al-Karim, *Sahwat al-tawhid*, p. 104.
19. On the 2011 protest and the position of the Islamists see Madawi Al-Rasheed, 'No Saudi Spring: anatomy of a failed revolution', *Boston Review*, March/April 2012, pp. 33–9. See also Stephane Lacroix, 'Comparing the Arab revolts: is Saudi Arabia immune?', *Journal of Democracy*, 22, 4 (2011), pp. 48–59.
20. Al-Abd al-Karim, *Sahwat al-tawhid*, p. 133.
21. On the 1990 Movement for Legitimate Rights in Saudi Arabia see Mamoun Fandy, *Saudi Arabia and the Politics of Dissent*, New York: St Martin's Press, 1999; Al-Rasheed, *Contesting the Saudi State*; and Lacroix, *Awakening Islam*.
22. Al-Abd al-Karim, *Sahwat al-tawhid*, p. 166.

23. Ibid., p. 37.
24. Muhammad al-Abd al-Karim, *Tafkik al-istibdad*, Beirut: Arab Network for Research and Publishing, 2013.
25. Ibid., p. 22.
26. Ibid., p. 28.
27. Ibid., p. 33.
28. Sura al-nisa 59, calling upon Muslims to obey God, the Prophet, and those who rule.
29. Al-Abd al-Karim, *Tafkik al istibdad*, p. 76.
30. Ibid., p. 102.
31. Ibid., p. 106.
32. Ibid., p. 107.
33. Ibid., p. 108.
34. Amnesty International, Country Report Saudi Arabia 2013, available at http://www.amnesty.org/en/region/saudi-arabia/report-2013.
35. Al-Abd al-Karim, *Tafkik al-istibdad*, p. 120.
36. Ibid., p. 122.
37. Madawi Al-Rasheed, 'Preachers of hate as loyal subjects', *New York Times* Room for Debate, 11 March 2011, available at https://www.nytimes.com/roomfordebate/2011/03/14/how-stable-is-saudi-arabia/preachers-of-hate-as-loyal-subjects.
38. Al-Abd al-Karim, *Tafkik al-istibdad*, p. 134.
39. Muhammad al-Abd al-Karim, *al-Ihtisab al-madani*, Beirut: Arab Network for Research and Publishing, 2011.
40. Ibid., pp. 20–1.

6. DEMOCRACY AGAINST THE ISLAMISATION OF REPRESSION

1. As Muhammad al-Ahmari openly calls for democracy, he is often referred to as a neo-reformist. See Saud al-Sarhan, 'The neo-reformists: a new democratic Islamic discourse', Middle East Institute, 1 October 2009, available at http://www.mei.edu/content/neo-reformists-new-democratic-islamic-discourse; Stephane Lacroix, *Saudi Islamists and the Arab Spring*, Kuwait Programme on Development, Governance and Globalisation in the Gulf States, LSE Reports, no. 36, May 2014; Rashid Bou Tayib, 'Fi al-haja ila al-dimouqratiyya wa naqdaha', 2014, available at http://ar.qantara.de/content/rwy-mhmd-lhmry-lmfhwm-ldymqrty-fy-lhj-l-ldymqrty-wnqdh-lmfkr-lswdy-mhmd-lhmry-nmwdhjan.
2. Muhammad al-Ahmari's biographical details are constructed out of information he provided during interviews on 18 May 2014, in addition to several televised interviews and articles. A series of interviews with al-Ahmari appeared in print in Ahmad

Fal al-Din, *Mutarahat fi al-fikr wa al-din wa al-siyasa*, Beirut: Dar Al-Khuloud, 2014.

3. Madawi Al-Rasheed, *A History of Saudi Arabia*, 2nd edn., Cambridge: Cambridge University Press, 2010, pp. 158–81.
4. Chris Heffelfinger, *Radical Islam in America: Salafism's Journey from Arabia to the West*, Washington DC: Potomac Books, 2011.
5. Interview with the author, 18 May 2014.
6. Saud al-Hashemi and sixteen other activists were accused of forming a secret organisation, attempting to seize power, incitement against the king, financing terrorism, and money laundering. See Amnesty International, 'Saudi Arabia: lengthy sentences for reformists a worrying development', 23 November 2011, available at https://www.amnesty.org/en/news/saudi-arabia-lengthy-sentences-reformists-worrying-development-2011-11-23.
7. Interview with the author, 18 May 2014.
8. Interview with the author, 18 May 2014.
9. Muhammad al-Ahmari, 'The trick of creedal analysis', 4 August 2006, available at http://www.alasr.ws.
10. Ali Al-Amim, 'Al-Ahmari ... khidat al-tahlil al-aqadi wa al-susuriyya', *al-Sharq al-Awsat*, 18 March 2012.
11. Interview with the author, 18 May 2014.
12. Fal al-Din, *Mutarahat*, p. 4.
13. *Tariq al Islam* at http://ar.islamway.net and *al-Asr* at http://www.alasr.ws.
14. Muhammad al-Ahmari, *Malamih al-mustaqbal*, Riyadh: Obaikan, 2005; *Nabt al-Ardh wa ibn al-sama: al-huriyya wa al-fan ind Izetbiogovic*, Riyadh: Obaikan, 2010; *al-Dimoqratiyya al juthur wa ishkaliyat al-tatbiq*, Beirut: Arab Network for Research and Publishing, 2012; *Muthakarat Qari'*, Beirut: Dar al-Kholoud, 2014. Short articles, conferences, and debates are posted on al-Ahmari's web at http://alahmari.org.
15. Muhammad al-Ahmari, 'Mashruiyat al-muthaharat', available at http://ar.islamway.net.
16. Muhammad al-Ahmari's interview after he gave up his Saudi nationality is available at http://sabq.org/5jcfde.
17. Muhammad al-Ahmari on Twitter: @alahmarim.
18. Fi al-Omq, Al-Jazeera television, available at http://www.youtube.com/watch?v=37iQ7ygFhEU.
19. Hasan al-Hasan, 'Making Qatar an offer it can't refuse', *Foreign Policy*, 22 April, 2014, available at http://www.foreignpolicy.com/articles/2014/04/22/making_qatar_an_offer_it_cant_refuse_saudi_arabia_gulf_diplomacy.
20. Ali al-Mousa, 'Law tanazalt an jinsiyati', 6, February 2012, available at http://www.alwatan.com.sa/Articles/Detail.aspx?ArticleId=9427.
21. Interview with the author, 18 May 2014.

22. Interview with the author, 18 May 2014.
23. Fal al-Din, *Mutarahat*, p. 65.
24. Ibid., p. 21.
25. Ibid., p. 100.
26. Ibid., p. 148.
27. Al-Sarhan, 'The neo-reformists'.
28. Muhammad al-Ahmari, 'Intisar al-dimouqratiyya ala al-wathaniyya fi al-intikhabat al-amrikiyya', available at http://www.alasr.ws.
29. Fal al-Din, *Mutarahat*, p. 74.
30. Al-Sarhan, 'The neo-reformists'.
31. Al-Ahmari, *al-Dimoqratiyya*.
32. Ibid., pp. 22–3.
33. Ibid., p. 33.
34. Ibid., p. 99.
35. Ibid.
36. Ibid., p. 219.
37. Ibid., p. 230.
38. Ibid., p. 158.
39. Ibid., p. 227.
40. Ibid., p. 251.
41. Fal al-Din, *Mutarahat*, p. 149.
42. Muhammad al-Ahmari, 'The season of fear from the people', 14 July 2011, available at http://alahmari.org.
43. Fal al-Din, *Mutarahat*, p. 150.
44. Ibid., p. 127.
45. Al-Ahmari, *Nabt al-Ardh*.
46. Interview with the author, 18 May 2014.
47. Interview with the author, 18 May 2014.

BIBLIOGRAPHY

al-Abd al-Karim, Muhammad, *al-Ihtisab al-madani* [Civil commanding right and forbidding wrong], Beirut: Arab Network for Research and Publishing, 2011.

────── *Sahwat al-tawhid: dirasa fi azmat al-khitab al-siyasi al-islami* [Monotheistic awakening: study of the crisis of Islamic political discourse], Beirut: Arab Network for Research and Publishing, 2012.

────── *Tafkik al-istibdad* [Deconstructing oppression], Beirut: Arab Network for Research and Publishing, 2013.

al-Ahmari, Muhammad, *al-Dimoqratiyya al juthur wa ishkaliyat al-tatbiq* [Democracy: the roots and problematics of application], Beirut: Arab Network for Research and Publishing, 2012.

────── *Malamih al-mustaqbal* [Aspects of the future], Riyadh: Obaikan, 2005.

────── *Muthakarat Qari'* [A reader's memoir], Beirut: Dar al-Kholoud, 2014.

────── *Nabt al-Ardh wa ibn al-sama: al-huriyya wa al-fan ind Izetbigovic* [Growth of the earth and the son of the sky: freedom and art for Izetbegovic], Riyadh: Obaikan, 2010.

Alhargan, Raed Abdulaziz, 'Saudi Arabia: civil rights and local actors', *Middle East Policy*, 19, 1 (2012), pp. 126–39.

Alshamsi, Mansoor Jassem, *Islam and Political Reform in Saudi Arabia: The Quest for Political Change and Reform*, London: Routledge, 2011.

Amnesty International, *Saudi Arabia's ACPRA: How the Kingdom Silences its Human Rights Activists*, London: Amnesty International, 2014.

Asad, Talal, *The Idea of an Anthropology of Islam*, Washington, DC: Center for Contemporary Arab Studies, Georgetown University, 1986.

al-Awdah, Salman, *Asilat al-thawra* [Questions of the revolution], Beirut: Markaz Inma lil-Buhuth wa al-Dirasat, 2012.

Bayat, Asef, 'The coming of a post-Islamist society', *Critique: Critical Middle East Studies*, 9 (1996), pp. 43–52.

Bayat, Asef (ed.), *Post-Islamism: The Changing Faces of Political Islam*, Oxford: Oxford University Press, 2013.

BIBLIOGRAPHY

Binder, Leonard, *Islamic Liberalism: A Critique of Development Ideologies*, Chicago: University of Chicago Press, 1988.

Bowen, John, *A New Anthropology of Islam*, Cambridge: Cambridge University Press, 2012.

Burgat, Francois, *Face to Face with Political Islam*, London: I. B. Tauris, 2003.

al-Dakhil, Khalid, *al-Wahabiyya bayn al shirk wa tasadu al qabila* [Wahhabiyya between blasphemy and the collapse of tribalism], Beirut: Arab Network for Research and Publishing, 2013.

al-Dakhil, Turki, *Salman al-Awdah: min al-sijn ila al-tanwir* [Salman al-Awdah: from prison to enlightenment], Beirut: Madarik, 2011.

Donald Emmerson, 'Inclusive Islamism: the Utility of Diversity'. In Richard Martin and Abbas Barzegar (eds.) *Islamism: Contested Perspectives on Political Islam*, Stanford: Stanford University Press, 2010, p. 17–32.

Euben, Roxanne and Muhammad Qasim Zaman (eds.), *Princeton Readings in Islamist Thought: Texts and Contexts from al-Banna to Bin Laden*, Princeton and Oxford: Princeton University Press, 2009.

Fal al-Din, Ahmad, *Mutarahat fi al-fikr wa al-din wa al-siyasa* [Disputations on thought, religion, and politics], Beirut: Dar Al-Khuloud, 2014.

Fandy, Mamoun, *Saudi Arabia and the Politics of Dissent*, New York: St Martin's Press, 1999.

Farquhar, Michael, 'Expanding the Wahhabi Mission: Saudi Arabia, the Islamic University of Medina and the Transnational Religious Economy', Ph.D. thesis, London School of Economics and Political Science, 2014.

Gerges, Fawaz, *America and Political Islam: Clash of Cultures or Clash of Interests?* Cambridge: Cambridge University Press, 1999.

—*The Far Enemy: Why Jihad Went Global*, Cambridge: Cambridge University Press, 2005.

al-Ghadhif, Abd al-Wahab, *al-Tanwir al-Islami fi al-mashhad al-Saoudi* [Enlightenment in the Saudi context], n.p.: Markaz Tasil, 2013, available at goodreads.com.

Gray, John, *Black Mass: Apocalyptic Religion and the Death of Utopia*, London: Penguin, 2007.

Haykel, Bernard et al. (eds.), *Saudi Arabia in Transition: Insights on Social, Political, Economic and Religious change*, Cambridge: Cambridge University Press, 2015.

Heffelfinger, Chris, *Radical Islam in America: Salafism's Journey from Arabia to the West*, Washington, DC: Potomac Books, 2011.

Hegghammer, Thomas, *Jihad in Saudi Arabia: Violence and Pan-Islamism since 1979*, Cambridge: Cambridge University Press, 2010.

al-Huwayrini, Walid, *Asr al-islamiyin al-judud* [The age of new Islamists], n.p.: Dar Alam al-Kutub, 2013, available at goodreads.com.

al-Huzaiymi, Nasir, *Ayam ma Juhayman* [Days with Juhayman], 2nd edn., Beirut: al-Shabaka al-Arabiyya lil Abhath wa al-Nashr, 2011.

BIBLIOGRAPHY

al-Ibrahim, Badr and Muhammad al-Sadiq, *al-Hirak al-shii fi al-saoudiyya* [The Shia mobilisation in Saudi Arabia], Beirut: Arab Network for Research and Publishing, 2013.

Ismail, Salwa, *Political Life in Cairo's New Quarters: Encountering the Everyday State*, Minneapolis: Minnesota University Press, 2006.

Kanie, Mariwan, 'Civil society in Saudi Arabia: different forms, one language', in Roel Meijer and Paul Aarts (eds.), *Saudi Arabia Between Conservatism, Accommodation and Reform*, The Hague: Netherlands Institute for International Relations, 2012, pp. 33–56.

Kechichian, Joseph, *Legal and Political Reforms in Saudi Arabia*, London: Routledge, 2013.

Kepel, Gilles, *Jihad: The Trail of Political Islam*, London: I. B. Tauris, 2003.

al-Khodr, Abd al-Aziz, *al-Soudiyya sirat dawla wa mujtama* [Saudi Arabia: the trajectory of state and society], Beirut: Arab Network for Research and Publishing, 2010.

Kurzman, Charles (ed.), *Liberal Islam: A Source Book*, Oxford: Oxford University Press, 1998.

Kurzman, Charles (ed.), *Modernist Islam: A Source Book*, Oxford: Oxford University Press, 2002.

Lacroix, Stephane, *Awakening Islam: Religious Dissent in Contemporary Saudi Arabia*, Cambridge, Mass.: Harvard University Press, 2011.

——— 'Between Islamists and liberals: Saudi Arabia's new Islamo-liberal reformists', *Middle East Journal*, 58, 3 (2004), pp. 345–64.

——— 'Between revolution and apoliticism: Nasir al-Din al-Albani and his impact on the shaping of contemporary Salafism', in Meijer (ed.), *Global Salafism*, pp. 58–80.

——— 'Comparing the Arab revolts: is Saudi Arabia immune?', *Journal of Democracy*, 22, 4 (2011), pp. 48–59.

——— 'Saudi Arabia and the limits of post-Islamism', in Bayat (ed.), *Post-Islamism*, pp. 277–97.

——— *Saudi Islamists and the Arab Spring*, Kuwait Programme on Development, Governance and Globalisation in the Gulf States, LSE Reports, no. 36, May 2014.

Lawrance, Bruce, *Defenders of God: the Fundamentalist Revolt against the Modern Age*, South Carolina: South Carolina University Press, 2006.

Le Renard, Amélie, *Femmes et espaces publics en Arabie Saoudite*, Paris: Dalloz, 2011.

al-Maliki, Abdullah, *Siyadat al-umma qabl tatbiq al-sharia* [Sovereignty of the *umma* before application of sharia], Beirut: Arab Network for Research and Publishing, 2012.

Mamdani, Mahmood, 'Good Muslim, bad Muslim: a political perspective on culture and terrorism', *American Anthropologist*, 104, 3 (2002), pp. 766–75.

Martin, Richard & Barzegar, Abbas (eds.), *Islamism: Contested Perspectives on Political Islam*, Stanford: Stanford University Press, 2010.

Massad, Joseph, *Islam in Liberalism*, Chicago: University of Chicago Press, 2015.

BIBLIOGRAPHY

Matthiesen, Toby, *The Other Saudis: Shiism, Dissent and Sectarianism*, Cambridge: Cambridge University Press, 2015.

―― 'A "Saudi Spring"?: the Shi'a movement in the Eastern Province 2011–2012', *Middle East Journal*, 66, 4 (2012), pp. 628–59.

―― *Sectarian Gulf: Bahrain, Saudi Arabia, and the Arab Spring that Wasn't*, Stanford: Stanford University Press, 2013.

Meijer, Roel (ed.), *Global Salafism, Islam's New Religious Movement*, London: Hurst & Co., 2009.

Menoret, Pascal, 'Leaving Islamic activism behind: ambiguous disengagement in Saudi Arabia', in Joel Beinin and Frédéric Vairel (eds.), *Social Movements, Mobilization, and Contestations in the Middle East and North Africa*, Stanford: Stanford University Press, 2011, pp. 43–60.

Montagu, Caroline, 'Civil society and the voluntary sector in Saudi Arabia', *Middle East Journal*, 64, 1 (2010), pp. 67–83.

Morozov, Evgeny, *The Net Delusion: How Not to Liberate the World*, London: Allen Lane, 2011.

al-Mushawah, Khalid, *al-Tayarat al-diniyya fi al-saoudiyya* [Religious movements in Saudi Arabia], Riyadh: Markaz al-Din wa al-Siyasat, 2012.

Pankhurst, Reza, *The Inevitable Caliphate? A History of the Struggle for Global Islamic Union, 1924 to the Present*, London: Hurst & Co., 2013.

Rahman, Fazlur, 'Islamic modernism: its scope, method and alternatives', *International Journal of Middle Eastern Studies*, 1 (1970), pp. 317–33.

Al-Rasheed, Madawi, *Contesting the Saudi State: Islamic Voices from a New Generation*, Cambridge: Cambridge University Press, 2007.

―― *A History of Saudi Arabia*, 2nd edn., Cambridge: Cambridge University Press, 2010.

―― *A Most Masculine State: Gender, Religion and Politics in Saudi Arabia*, Cambridge: Cambridge University Press, 2013.

―― 'No Saudi Spring: anatomy of a failed revolution', *Boston Review*, March/April 2012, pp. 33–9.

―― 'Saudi Arabia: the challenge of the US invasion of Iraq', in Rick Fawn and Raymond Hinnebusch (eds.), *The Iraq War: Causes and Consequences*, London: Lynne Rienner, 2006, pp. 153–62.

―― 'Saudi internal dilemmas and regional responses to the Arab uprisings', in Fawaz Gerges (ed.), *The New Middle East: Protest and Revolution in the Arab World*, Cambridge: Cambridge University Press, 2014, pp. 353–79.

―― 'Sectarianism as counter revolution: Saudi responses to the Arab Spring', *Studies in Ethnicity and Nationalism*, 11, 3 (2011), pp. 513–26.

Al-Rasheed, Madawi, Carool Kersten, and Marat Shterin (eds.), *Demystifying the Caliphate: Historical Memory and Contemporary Contexts*, London: Hurst & Co., 2012.

BIBLIOGRAPHY

Roy, Olivier, *Holy Ignorance: When Religion and Culture Part Ways*, London: Hurst & Co., 2010.

Sagiyyeh, Hazem, *Nawasib wa rawafidh* [Sunnis and Shia], Beirut: Saqi, 2009.

Thompson, Mark, *Saudi Arabia and the Path to Political Change: National Dialogue and Civil Society*, London: I. B. Tauris, 2014.

Taylor, Charles, *A Secular Age*, Cambridge, Massachusetts: Harvard University Press, 2006.

Young, Karen, *The Emerging Interventionists of the GCC*, Middle East Centre Paper Series 2, London School of Economics and Political Science, 2013.

Zaman, Muhammad Qasim, *Islamic Modernism and the Sharia in Pakistan*, Yale Law School Occasional Papers, March 2014.

Newspaper articles

Al-Amim, Ali, 'Al-Ahmari ... khidat al-tahlil al-aqadi wa al-susuriyya' [The trick of creedal analysis and the Sururis], *al-Sharq al-Awsat*, 18 March 2012.

Bronner, Ethan and Michael Slackmann, 'Saudi troops enter Bahrain to help put down unrest', *New York Times*, 14 March 2011, available at http://www.nytimes.com/2011/03/15/world/middleeast/15bahrain.html.

'Demonstrations are forbidden', *Al-Riyadh* newspaper, 7 March 2011.

al-Dowsari, Salman, 'Thawrat Salman al-Awdah' [The revolution of Salman al-Awdah], *al-Iqtisadiyya*, 17 March 2013.

al-Humaid, Tariq, 'Salman al-Awdah: khitab mafdoh' [Salman al-Awdah: scandalous discourse], *al-Sharq al-Awsat*, 17 March 2013.

Smith Diwan, Kristin, 'Youthful Saudi reformers only safe in the twittersphere', *Atlantic Council*, 20 December 2013.

Worth, Robert, 'Saudi's lonely, costly bid for Sunni–Shiite equality', *New York Times*, 14 March 2014.

Web-based articles

al-Abd al-Karim, Muhammad, 'Azmat al-sira' al-siyasi bayn al-ajniha al-hakima fi al-saoudiyya' [The crisis of political struggle among the Saudi royal family], December 2010, available at http://freealabdulkreem.wordpress.com/category/مقالات-الدكتور-محمد-العبدالكريم/.

—— 'La lil-muwatana bil ma'na al-soudi' [No to citizenship in its Saudi meaning], December 2010, available at http://freealabdulkreem.wordpress.com/category/مقالات-الدكتور-محمد-العبدالكريم/.

Abdulkarim, Nora, 'Trial of Saudi civil rights activists', 2 September 2012, available at http://ana3rabeya.wordpress.com/2012/09/02/activiststrial/.

Adalaksa.org, 'Suleyman Saleh al-Reshoudi', 3 March 2011, available at http://www.adalaksa.org/content/suleyman-saleh-al-reshoudi.

al-Ahmari, Muhammad, 'Intisar al-dimouqratiyya ala al-wathaniyya fi al-intikhabat al-amrikiyya' [The triumph of democracy over paganism in the American elections], available at http://www.alasr.ws.

BIBLIOGRAPHY

———— 'Mashruiyat al-muthaharat' [The legitimacy of protests and demonstrations], available at http://ar.islamway.net.

———— 'The season of fear from the people', 14 July 2011, available at http://alahmari.org.

al-Ahmari, Muhammad, 'The trick of creedal analysis', 4 August 2006, available at http://www.alasr.ws.

al-Amir, Yahya and Turki al-Suhail, 'Nine years in prison for al-Damini and al-Falih', 16 May 2005, available at http://www.alriyadh.com/article64858.html.

Amnesty International, Country Report Saudi Arabia 2013, available at http://www.amnesty.org/en/region/saudi-arabia/report-2013.

———— 'Document—UA 199/93—Saudi Arabia: fear of torture/ill-treatment: Dr Abdullah Al-Hamed, Dr Muhammad 'Abdullah Al-Mas'ari', 18 June 1993, availableathttps://www.amnesty.org/en/library/asset/MDE23/005/1993/en/23e9bacb-ecc7-11dd-85fd-99a1fce0c9ec/mde230051993en.html.

———— 'Free Dr Abdullah al-Hamid', 19 March 2008, available at http://www.amnesty.org/en/node/4250.

———— 'Reform activists in Saudi Arabia must receive fair appeal hearings', 25 January 2012, available at http://www.amnesty.org/en/news/reform-activists-saudi-arabia-must-receive-fair-appeal-hearings-2012-01-25.

———— 'Muzzling dissent: Saudi Arabia's effort to choke civil society', London, 9 October 2014, available at http://www.amnesty.org/en/news/muzzling-dissent-saudi-arabia-s-efforts-choke-civil-society-2014-10-09.

———— 'Saudi Arabia: lengthy sentences for reformists a worrying development', 23 November 2011, available at https://www.amnesty.org/en/news/saudi-arabia-lengthy-sentences-reformists-worrying-development-2011-11-23.

———— 'Saudi Arabia: men detained for founding political party', 23 February 2011, available at http://www.amnesty.org/en/library/asset/MDE23/002/2011/en/ffeaafc0-fbf7-43c4-a1a6-1b18d99b2cdd/mde23002201len.html.

———— 'Saudi Arabia ramps up clampdown on human rights activists', 18 June 2012, availableathttp://www.amnesty.org/en/news/saudi-arabia-ramps-clampdown-human-rights-activists-2012-06-18.

Benham, Jason, 'Saudi king orders more handouts, security boost', Reuters, 18 March 2011, available at http://www.reuters.com/article/2011/03/18/us-saudi-king-idUSTRE72H2UQ20110318.

Bou Tayib, Rashid, 'Fi al-haja ila al-dimouqratiyya wa naqdaha' [On the need for democracy and its critique], 2014, available at http://ar.qantara.de/content/rwy-mhmd-lhmry-lmfhwm-ldymqrty-fy-lhj-l-ldymqrty-wnqdh-lmfkr-lswdy-mhmd-lhmry-nmwdhjan.

Carnegie Endowment for International Peace, *Arab Political Systems: baseline Information and Reform-Saudi Arabia*, available at carnegieendowment.org/files/saudi_arabia_aps.doc.

BIBLIOGRAPHY

al-Faleh, Matruk, 'El-Eqtissadyah-Interview-18–12–2006', 21 February 2007, available at http://faculty.ksu.edu.sa/Alfaleh/Pages/El-eqtissadyah-Interview-18–12–2006.aspx.

Fi al-Omq [In depth], Al-Jazeera television, available at http://www.youtube.com/watch?v=37iQ7ygFhEU.

Global Voices, 'Saudi Arabia: Free Saudi Scholar Dr Muhammed Alabdulkareem', 11 December 2010, available at http://globalvoicesonline.org/2010/12/11/saudi-arabia-calls-to-release-saudi-scholar-dr-mohammed-abdulkareem/.

Gulf Centre for Human Rights, 'Kuwait: Youth Rising Forum prevented from holding its third annual forum', 23 March 2013, available at http://gc4hr.org/news/view/102.

al-Hamid, Abdullah, 'Blogger: user profile: Abubelal1951', accessed 4 February 2014, available at https://www.blogger.com/profile/00823743862313846215.

al-Hari, Abd al-Nabi, 'Muhawalat tasil lil-dimouqratiyya fi biya salafiyya' [An attempt to explain democracy in a Salafi context], available at al-www.almqaal.com.

al-Hasan, Hasan, 'Making Qatar an offer it can't refuse', *Foreign Policy*, 22 April, 2014, available at http://www.foreignpolity.com/articles/2014/04/22/making_qatar_an_offer_it_cant_refuse_saudi_arabia_gulf_diplomacy.

Hertog, Steffen, 'The cost of counter-revolution in the GCC', 2011, available at http:// mideastafrica. foreignpolicy.com/posts/2011/05/31/the_costs_counter_revolution_in_the_gcc.

Human Rights Watch, 'Saudi Arabia: arrests for peaceful protest on the rise', 27 March 2011, available at http://www.hrw.org/en/news/2011/03/27/saudi-arabia-arrests-peaceful-protest-rise.

Al Jazeera, 'Saudi hunger strike over detentions', 6 November 2008, available at http://www.aljazeera.com/news/middleeast/2008/11/2008116153455440898.html.

Jones, Toby and Cortni Kerr, 'A Revolution Paused in Bahrain', *MERIP* Report, 23 February 2011, available at http://www.merip.org/mero/mero022311?ip_login_no_cache=ca0c16ed820c507e1069b7f09b47f97e.

AlKarama, 'Saudi Arabia: prominent human rights defender risks 5 years of prison for cooperating with the UN', 29 June 2012, available at http://en.alkarama.org/index. php?option=com_content&view=article&id=961:saudi-arabia-prominent-human-rights-defender-risks-5-years-of-prison-for-cooperating-with-the-un&catid=33:co mmuniqu&Itemid=179.

AlKarama, 'Saudi Arabia: release on bail of Mr Suleiman Al-Rashoudi', 24 June 2011, available at http://en.alkarama.org/index.php?option=com_content&view=artic le&id=764:saudi-arabia-release-on-bail-of-mr-suleiman-al-rashoudi-&catid= 33:communiqu&Itemid=179.

AlKarama, 'Saudi Arabia: senior human rights lawyer arrested for saying right to assembly is legitimate', 17 December 2012, available at http://en.alkarama.org/index.php?option=com_content&view=article&id=1026:saudi-arabia-senior-

BIBLIOGRAPHY

human-rights-lawyer-arrested-for-saying-right-to-assembly-is-legitimate&catid=3 3:communiqu&Itemid=179.

'The king pardons prisoners', 9 August 2005, available at http://www.aawsat.com/details.asp?section=1&article=316741&issueno=9751#.UvQq9vl_vGw.

Kramer, Gudrun, 'Islamist notions of democracy', Middle East Research and Information Project, volume 23, 1993, available at http://www.merip.org/mer/mer183/islamist-notions-democracy.

Lippman, Thomas, 'Saudi professor faces charges after fighting for free speech', 29 June 2012, available at http://www.al-monitor.com/pulse/originals/2012/al-monitor/mohammad-al-qahtani-pushes-the-l.html#.

al-Maliki, Abdullah, 'Limatha fashilat tajrubat al-ikhwan fi al-hukm' [Why the Ikhwan failed in government], 13 July 2013, available at www.almqaal.com.

—— 'Siyadat al-umma qabl tatbiq al-sharia' [The sovereignty of the *umma* is before the application of sharia], 11 November 2011, available at www.almqaal.com.

Matthiesen, Toby, 'Diwaniyas, intellectual salons and the limits of civil society', Middle East Institute blog, 2009, available at http://www.mei.edu/content/diwaniyyas-intellectual-salons-and-limits-civil-society?print.

al-Mousa, Ali, 'Law tanazalt an jinsiyati' [Even though I renounced my nationality], 6, February 2012, available at http://www.alwatan.com.sa/Articles/Detail.aspx?ArticleId=9427.

Al-Qasimi, Sultan Soouad, 'The civil society movement in the Arab Gulf states', *The HuffPost*, 28 January 2013, available at http://www.huffingtonpost.com/sultan-soooud-alqassemi/.

Al-Rasheed, Madawi, 'Egypt coup and Saudi Islamists', *Mideast Foreign Policy*, 19 August 2013, available at http://mideast.foreignpolicy.com/posts/2013/08/19/egypts_coup_and_the_saudi_opposition.

—— 'Preachers of hate as loyal subjects', *New York Times* Room for Debate, 11 March 2011, available at https://www.nytimes.com/roomfordebate/2011/03/14/how-stable-is-saudi-arabia/preachers-of-hate-as-loyal-subjects.

—— 'Saudi duality on women', *Al-Monitor*, 30 September 2013, available at http://www.al-monitor.com/pulse/originals/2013/09/saudi-women-drive-viral-video-cleric.html.

—— 'Saudi officials shut down display at book fair', 13 March 2014, available at http://www.al-monitor.com/pulse/originals/2014/03/saudi-book-display-shut-down.html.

al-Rashid, Abdullah, 'Inqisamat al-islamiyyin fi al-saoudiyya' [The Islamist divisions in Saudi Arabia], 27 May 2012, available at ww.majalla.com.

al-Saif, Nasir, 'al-Tanwiriyun al-saoudiyoun bayn alwahm wa al-haqiqa' [Saudi Tanwiris between fantasy and reality], Saaid al-Fawaid, available at http://saaid.net/arabic/693.htmat.

al-Sarhan, Saud, 'The neo-reformists: a new democratic Islamic discourse', Middle East

BIBLIOGRAPHY

Institute, 1 October 2009, available at http://www.mei.edu/content/neo-reformists-new-democratic-islamic-discourse.

'Saudi Arabia prepares for protest', available at http://www.bbc.co.uk/news/world-middle-east-12708487.

'Saudi Arabia show of force stifles Day of Rage', BBC, 11 March 2011, available at http://news.bbc.co.uk/1/hi/programmes/newsnight/9422550.stm.

'Saudi and UAE ready $20 bn boost for Egypt's El-Sisi', *The Telegraph*, 1 June 2014, available at http://www.telegraph.co.uk/finance/newsbysector/banksandfinance/10868522/Saudi-and-UAE-ready-20bn-boost-for-Egypts-El-Sisi.html.

al-Shuyukh, Muhammad, 'Saudi Islamists', 27 March 2013, available at http://middle-east-online.com/?id=152016.

al-Sufuqi, Munif and Huda al-Saleh, 'Trial of three Saudis', 2 December 2004, available at http://www.aawsat.com/details.asp?issueno=9165&article=268828#.UvQmnPl_vGw.

USCIRF, 'Saudi Arabia: release Mohammad Fahad Al-Qahtani and Abdullah Bin Hamad', 14 March 2013, available at http://www.uscirf.gov/news-room/press-releases/3952-3142013-saudi-arabia-release-mohammad-fahad-al-qahtani-and-abdullah-bin-hamad.html.

Wittmeyer, Alicia, 'The FP top 100 global thinkers', 26 November 2012, available at http://www.foreignpolicy.com/articles/2012/11/26/the_fp_100_global_thinkers.

Websites

http://abubelal1951.blogspot.co.uk.
http://www.acpraorg.org/index.php.
http://acpra-hr.org/news_view_13.html.
http://www.acpra-hr.co/news_view_215.html.
http://www.acpra-hr.org/news.php?action=view&id=125.
http://alahmari.org.
http://www.alasr.ws.
http://www.aljazeera.net/news/pages/03f446c6-a4ed-4514-a5c9-316f4e018c63.
http://www.almqaal.com/?author=18.
http://altagreer.com.
http://www.alwatan.com.sa/Local/News_Detail.aspx?ArticleID=53402&CategoryID=5.
http://www.alyaum.com/News/art/11147.html.
http://www.alyaum.com/News/art/11310.html?print.
http://www.amnesty.org/ar/news/saudi-arabia-lengthy-sentences-reformists-worrying-development-2011-11-23.
http://ar.islamway.net.
http://www.burnews.com/news-action-show-id-35939.htm.
http://cdhrap.net/archive/ar/post.php?3024.
http://dawlaty.com/services.html.

BIBLIOGRAPHY

https://www.facebook.com/pages ف\ضيلة-الشـيخ-د-محمد-العبدالكر 1\5462478 1246102.
http://www.facebook.com/Saudis.Revolution.
http://www.hrw.org/ar/news/2013/02/12/15.
http://www.islamicommaparty.org: http://www.islamicommaparty.org/particle/436; http://islamicommaparty.org/statement/432.
http://www.islamlight.net/index.php/index.php?option=content&task=view&id=21468&Itemid=33.
http://www.islamtoday.net/salman/artshow-78-131114.
http://kuwait.tt/articledetails.aspx?Id=181261.
http://www.majalla.com.
http://www.nytimes.com/2011/02/11/world/middleeast/11briefs-Saudi.htm.
http://www.ommah.org.
http://rowaqalhasan.com/?tag=.
http://sabq.org/5jcfde.
http://www.saudireform.com/?p=petintion.
http://shababsaudi.wordpress.com/.
http://www.youtube.com/watch?v=37iQ7ygFhEU.

INDEX

9/11 1, 9, 31
Abbasids 121–2
Abd al-Jabiri, Muhammad 120
al-Abd al-Karim, Muhammad 8–9, 24, 29, 97, 116–36
Abd al-Latif, Abdul Aziz 107
Abd al-Salam, Rafiq 120
Abduh, Muhammad 125, 151
Abdullah, King 34, 39, 50, 87, 163
Abu Bakr 127, 148
Abu al-Kheir, Walid 4
activism and protest in Saudi Arabia 24–5, 28–9, 42–4, 45–50, 73–4, 87–9, 134: before the Arab uprisings 31–53; civil disobedience 134; civil rights organisations 24–5; digital 42–4, 48; for economic rights 47–8; as *fitna* 132; foreign workers 49; as *jihad silmi* 63, 67–9; lack of support for 46, 52, 53, 75, 125; mass demonstrations 7, 27, 28, 29; petitions 27, 28, 33–40, 53; regime response to 45–53; for release of political prisoners 7, 27, 45, 47, 58, 63, 64, 87–8, 134; in Shia regions 21–1, 45–6; small and individual protests 46–8, 50; and social media 28–9, 39, 42, 45, 50, 57, 61, 62, 88, 115–16;
ulama and 51; women and 7, 27, 42, 47, 48, 63, 87–8; youth and 37, 39, 42; Zaynabiyya processions 45; *see also* 'Day of Rage'; HASM
advice: *see nasiha*
al-Ahmad, Yusif 52, 94
al-Ahmari, Muhammad 6, 7, 24, 30, 37, 97, 137–55, 160
Alawites 21, 91
al-Albani, Muhammad Nasir al-Din 122–3
al-Amer, Tawfiq 45
al-Amim, Ali 140
Amnesty International 62, 63, 64
Aqlanis 158
Arab International Affairs Forum 141
Arab Network for Research and Publishing 25, 97
Arab uprisings 3–4, 10–11, 75–6, 79–80, 109–11: in Bahrain 21, 43–4, 52, 59, 91; in eastern Saudi Arabia 22, 43, 45; in Egypt 3, 4, 11, 21, 41, 75, 79, 80, 82, 89, 91, 95, 123, 154, 160; Islamists and 4, 21, 28; in Libya 21, 41, 80; in Oman; Salafi reaction to 123; Saudi regime and 3, 6, 41, 44, 52–3, 73, 92, 115–16, 154; and sectarian conflict

INDEX

21–2, 91; and sharia 10, 29, 82, 83, 95, 110; in Syria 21, 91; in Tunisia 3, 4, 21, 75, 79, 80, 82, 89, 91, 95, 123, 160; women in 87; in Yemen 21, 44, 45; *see also* revolution
Arkoun, Muhammad 96
Asad, Talal 14
al-Asr 97, 141
Asranis 107–8, 158
al-Awaji, Muhsin 38, 92
Awakening, Islamic: *see* Sahwa
al-Awdah, Abdullah Salman 98
al-Awdah, Salman 6, 7, 8, 12, 24, 29, 37, 64, 74, 75–94, 106, 107, 113, 119, 159, 160: *Asilat al-thawra* 79–80; social media 80, 88

al-Bana, Hasan 77
Bayat, Asef 23, 35
al-Bijadi, Muhammad 65–6
Bin Ali, Zine al-Abdine 41, 75, 79
Bin Laden, Osama 19, 78
Bodin, Jean 102
al-Buraik, Abdulrahman 106
al-Buraik, Saad 133

caliphate: Umma Party and 41
civil society 55–74, 99–100: draft legislation on 60; *hisba* and 159; Islamist reformers and 9, 23–4, 32, 53, 81, 99; Salafis and 107; separation of powers 99, 120; *see also al-dawla al-madaniyya*; HASM
Commission on International Religious Freedom (USCIRF) 65
Committee for Commanding Right and Prohibiting Wrong 9, 158; *see also hisba*
Committee for the Defence of Legitimate Rights (CDLR) 63
consultation: *see shura*
Consultative Council 132: and draft civil society law 60; women and 49, 87
Council of Higher Ulama 51, 115

al-Daish, Sultan 65
Dalil 80
al-Damini, Ali 34, 64
al-dawla al-madaniyya/dawla madaniyya 2, 12, 83, 108: separation of powers 83; *see also* civil society
'Day of Rage' 22, 42–4, 46, 50, 79, 125
de Gaulle, Charles 105
al-Dhahiyan, Suleiman 97
divine politics 4–5, 10, 22, 158, 159, 160, 162
al-Dosari, Hala 107
al-Dowsari, Salman 90
al-Dughaythir, Saud 40
Durkheim, Émile 4

Euben, Roxanne 12

Facebook 6, 18, 35, 39, 42, 47, 48, 80, 88, 113, 115, 116–17, 118, 161
al-Falih, Matruk 34, 57, 63, 64, 65, 126
Fanon, Frantz 80
al-Fawzan, Salih 129, 133
fiqh al-taa 25
fiqh taharur 127
fitna 8, 29, 132, 136: political parties as 40; and resisting injustice 132; revolution as 79
Free Youth Movement 42

Ghabra, Shafiq 107
al-Ghamdi, Ahmad 40
Grand Mosque (Mecca) 1
Gulf Cooperation Council (GCC) 43–4: Desert Shield 43

Hadith 10, 15, 40, 58, 129–30
Haif, Muhammad 108

INDEX

al-Hamid, Abdullah 7, 8, 34, 39, 57, 62, 63–4, 65, 67–8, 70, 73, 101, 112, 126, 160
al-Hamid, Isa 63
al-Harbi, Fawzan 67
al-Hasan, Mustafa 106
HASM (Jamiyyat al-Huquq al-Siyasiyya wa al-Madaniyya) 24, 25, 28–9, 55–74, 112, 163: and Arab uprisings 59; campaigns for reform 56, 58; campaigns for release of prisoners 58, 63; dissemination of literature on reform 58, 61, 62, 67, 74; dissolution of 65; foundation statement 60–2; and human rights abuses 62; imprisonment of founders 56, 58, 63, 64, 65, 66, 101; and international human rights organisations 62; overcoming Islamist–liberal divide 57–9, 73; and reform of the judicial system 60–1, 63; regime reaction to 56; rejection of authoritarian rule 63, 71, 72; and religious scholars 57; and social media 57, 61, 62, 70, 73; trials of activists and founders 57–8, 63, 65–6, 69–73, 101, 123
al-Hayat 58
hisba 9, 29, 134–5, 159: as civic duty 134, 135
Hizbollah 139
Hizb al-Tahrir 41
Hobbes, Thomas 102
al-Howaider, Wajiha 48
al-Humaid, Tariq 89–90
human rights: abuse of by Saudi regime 33, 39–40; modernists and 6, 7, 9, 33, 53; *see also* HASM
Human Rights Watch 62, 64
al-Husan, Abdulaziz 67

Ibn Abd al-Wahhab, Muhammad 2, 37, 131, 161

Ibn Baz, Abdul Aziz 51, 77, 123
Ibn Saud, Muhammad (Muhammad ibn Saud) 37
ijtihad 81, 83, 146, 150, 152
Iran: and Bahrain uprising 21–2, 44; conspiracy theories about 51, 52, 91; Islamist modernists and 85, 86, 91; post-Islamism 23; and Syria uprising 91
Islamic Assembly of North America (IANA) 138
Islamic State in the Levant 162
Islamism: and the Arab uprisings 21–2, 29, 109; classifications of 13–14, 16; diversity of 12–13; Islamism reconsidered 11–16; and Jihadism 12, 19–20; and modernism 1–4; mutations of 8–24, 30, 55, 76, 93–4, 113, 119–21, 158, 160, 162; post-9/11 16–24, 31–3, 55, 93, 96; radical 2, 20, 32, 157; 'reformed' Saudi Islamists 16–17, 18–19, 21; and terrorism 20–1, 31–3
Islamist modernist project 22–3, 28, 157–63: and Arab uprisings 29, 99; lack of support for 22; popular support for 23; and post-Islamism 23, 157
Islamist modernists, Saudi: activism and protest 7, 9, 22, 24, 142; and Arab uprisings 4, 10–11, 21–2, 28, 79–80, 90–3, 95, 99, 109–11, 122, 132, 137–8, 153–4, 160; banned or imprisoned 3, 4, 10, 22, 25, 38, 41, 77, 80, 84–5, 117, 119, 125–6, 139; and civil society 9, 23–4, 32, 53, 81, 84, 88, 99; criticism of royal family 117–18; debates with Salafi *ulama* 139; and democracy 6, 9, 10, 22, 23, 30, 32, 41, 53, 76, 81, 84, 91, 99, 101–6, 110, 113, 137–55, 158–60; disputes among 16; dissemination

195

INDEX

of ideas 24–5, 77–80, 85, 91, 96–7, 115, 142, 161; and human rights 7, 9, 22, 23, 53; on Iran 85, 86, 91; and Jihadism 1, 9; as 'liberal' 14, 35, 96, 101, 106–9, 155; and liberation theology 127–35; and non-Islamic intellectual traditions 13, 14, 29–30, 79, 80, 84, 102, 113, 119–20, 137, 147–8, 149, 152, 159, 160; and petitions for reform 27, 33–40, 100; reinterpretation of traditional concepts and texts 8–10, 12, 15, 23, 25, 29–30, 52, 63, 76, 84–5, 99, 103, 113, 116, 121–2, 127–36, 143, 158–60; rehabilitation after imprisonment 77–8; rejection of authoritarian rule 83, 98, 100–1, 115–55; travel restrictions on 3, 38, 66, 80, 90, 92, 94; trials of 10, 25, 29; and Saudi media 89–90, 93; and the Saudi regime 3, 4, 5, 10, 22, 32–3, 92–3, 139, 140–1, 143, 161, 162; scholarly analysis of 22; and sectarian minorities 85–6, 139–40; and social media 3, 10, 35, 161; on television 77–8; and theocracy 12, 83, 102, 119–20, 151; and women 85, 86–7; youth as supporters of 25–6, 85
Islam Today 80, 85, 88, 97
Izet Begovic, Alija 154

Al-Jazeera 43–4, 78, 141, 142
jihad: in Afghanistan 1, 12, 33; in Iraq 31; *jihad al-kalima* 67; peaceful jihad (*jihad silmi*) 61, 63, 67–9, 159
Jihadis: attack on the Shia 46; denounced by rehabilitated Islamists 77–8; reaction against Salafi *ulama* 123; repentance and rehabilitation of 31, 157; and sharia 123–5
Jihadism 1, 12, 17: post-9/11 17, 31, 160; and 'reformed' Islamists 18–19; terror campaign in Saudi cities 31–2
al-Juhni, Khalid 46–7
al-Jumairi, Sultan 95

Kechichian, Joseph 34
Al-Khalifa family 43–4
al-Kharashi, Sulaiman 107
al-Khodr, Abd al-Aziz 97
al-Khodr, Abd al-Karim 40
khuruj ala al-hakim 8, 133; *see also* rebellion

La Boétie, Étienne: *The Politics of Obedience: Discourse on Voluntary Servitude* 134
Lacroix, Stéphane 107
Lewis, Bernard 81
Lloyd-Roberts, Sue 46
Locke, John 102

al-Mahfuth, Muhammad 34
al-Majd television channel 80
al-Maliki, Abdullah 24, 29, 37, 94, 95–113, 119, 124
al-Maqal 95, 97, 101
Marx, Karl 80
Massad, Joseph 14
al-Mawardi, Abu al-Hasan 81, 134
Mawdudi, Abu Alaa 152
MBC 78
modernists: *see* Islamist modernists
Morsi, Muhammad 38, 41, 92, 105, 106
Movement for Legitimate Rights in Saudi Arabia 125, 126
Mubarak, Hosni 41, 42, 75, 79
mufakir islami 6, 7
al-Mufrih, Muhammad 40, 41
Muhammad 43, 58, 127, 147, 148, 151, 152
Muhammad ibn Nayif, Prince 47, 88

196

INDEX

al-Mukhtar, Saud 139
Multaqa al-Nahdha al-Shababi: *see* Youth Rising Forum
Muslim Brotherhood 11, 12, 17, 21, 38, 77, 91, 92, 95, 105–6, 121, 126
al-Mutairi, Hakim 41

al-Nahda 21, 91
al-Najjar, Ghanin 107
nasiha 8, 37, 68, 79, 130, 134, 142, 153
National Coalition 42
National Dialogue Forums 86
Nayif, Prince 33, 56
al-Nimr, Nimr 43, 45

Obaikan 138
Obama, Barack 44, 147
al-Omar, Hamad 67
al-Omar, Nasir 37, 52, 106, 139, 141, 147
Omelil, Ali 120
Omm Saud 139
al-Oraifi, Muhammad 38, 52, 92, 94, 144

petitions for reform 28, 33–40, 42, 53, 100, 126, 141–2: and constitutional reform 34, 36, 39, 42, 53, 126; about Egypt 38; online 35, 37; and regional autonomy 36; and rights 36; Riyadh Spring (2004) 34; Salafi 37–8, 53, 141; and social media 35; women and 27; youth and 37, 39
Popper, Karl 80
post-Islamism 23, 35

al-Qahtani, Iman 57–8
al-Qahtani, Muhammad, 57, 65, 69, 101
al-Qaida 19, 78
al-Qaida in the Arabian Peninsula 19, 31

al-Qaradawi, Yusif 151
Qashgari, Hamza 58, 59
al-Qasim, Abdulaziz 97, 126
Qasim Zaman, Muhammad
al-Qudaimi, Nawaf 25, 97
Quran: and freedom 103; HASM and 58; *huddud* 83; and justice 130; in petitions 38; reinterpretations of 10; replaced by interpretation 81; as Saudi constitution 4, 99–100, 126; as tool of repression 129; traditional interpretation of 15; Umma Party and 40
Qutb, Sayid 77, 145

Raysouni, Ahmad 120
rebellion 8, 133: civil disobedience 132–3, 134; Jihadis and 17, 123, 125; justification of 18, 32, 130, 132; peaceful protest and 133; replaced by reform 17; Salafis and 76, 102, 133–4; *see also* revolution
reformers 32–40, 126–7: Salafi criticism of 123; trials of 57, 69–73, 101
religious scholars: *see ulama*
revolution 75–94: collective action and 82; fusion of Western and Islamic thinking on 80, 84, 119–20; and democracy 81; justification of 8, 10–11, 29, 59, 74, 79–80, 130, 157; peaceful 75, 79, 82, 130–1; Salafi tradition and 8, 29
Rousseau, Jean-Jacques 102
al-Rushoudi, Suleiman 4, 7, 37, 57, 64–5, 70, 71, 101

Saddam Hussein 90, 138
al-Sadlan, Salih 133
al-Safar, Hasan 86
al-Saghir, Abd al-Majid 120
Sahwa 77, 112, 140, 143
al-sahwa al-islamiyya (concept of Islamic awakening) 16, 91

197

INDEX

al-Sahwa al-Islamiyya (Islamist groups) 31, 32: failure to support reformers 35
al-Said, Abdullah 67
al-Saif, Tawfiq 34, 107
Salafis 8, 9–10, 15, 17, 122–7, 145–54: and Arab uprisings 123; and authoritarianism 127–8; and communication technology 18, 100; critique of 122–7; Jihadi reaction to 123; as judges 123, 128, 161; lack of popular support for 144; and obedience to rulers 6, 8, 25, 51, 76, 111, 119, 123, 128–33, 134; and petitions 37–8, 141; and 'reformed' Islamists 19; and reformers 34, 35, 101, 142–3; resistance to democracy 138, 143, 147, 149–50, 153; and revolution 29, 74, 75–94; as Saudi religious establishment 17–18, 19–21; and Tanwiris 5–6, 9–10, 97–8; and the Shia 91, 139, 146; and Sufis 145–6; *ulama al-salatin* 19; and Umma Party 40–2; youth and 144; *see also ulama*; Wahhabiyya
Salih, Ali Abdullah 41, 43
Salman, King 163
Al-Saud family 2, 8: criticised 116–18
Saudi Association for Civil and Political Rights (ACPRA): *see* HASM
al-Shammari, Mikhlif 58
sharia 95–6, 109–11, 123–5: and Arab uprisings 10, 29, 95, 110; and democracy 101–6, 110–11; distanced from human rights abuses 60; *huddud* 83; Jihadis and 123–4, 125; post-revolution 82–3, 95, 104, 110; and repressive government 128, 134, 159, 161; Saudi regime and 4, 5, 11, 111; as source of law 4, 40, 83, 102
al-Sharif, Manal 48
al-Sharq al-Awsat 89, 140

al-Shayib, Jafar 34
al-Sheikh, Mufti Abd al-Aziz 49–50, 78
Shia 9, 91: and Bahrain uprising 21, 43–4; conspiracy theories about 51–2, 59, 91; HASM and 59; Islamist modernists and 85–6; Jihadi attacks on 46, 86; protests in Eastern Province 21–2, 43, 45–6, 91; Salafis and 91, 139–40, 146
shura 6, 8, 81–2, 98–9, 103–4, 113, 126, 131–2, 137, 144, 151, 153
al-Sisi, General Abdul Fatah 92
social contract 82: Magna Carta 82, 84; oath of allegiance as 103
Sufis 9, 145–6
Sururis 17, 124, 126, 140
Surur Zaiyn al-Abdin, Muhammad 77

al-Tagreer 96, 97
Tanwiris 5–6, 7–8, 9, 13, 97–8, 158
Tariq al-Islam 141
al-Tayar al-Tanwiri 34, 97, 144
al-Tayib, Muhammad Said 34, 39
thawra 8
al-Thaydi, Mishari 108
de Tocqueville, Alexis 80
Twitter 6, 10, 18, 25–6, 27, 61, 80, 97, 161: censorship of 116; and demonstrations 47, 88; and digital activism 42, 113; and petitions 35, 39; and trials of HASM founders 25, 29, 70–1, 72; youth and 39, 42, 109

ulama 2, 3, 6, 7, 18–20, 144: co-opted by the state 98, 111, 117, 123; justification of repression 134; monopolisation of religious knowledge 145–6, 153; rewarded by regime 51; *ulama al-fadhaiyat* 20; *ulama munafiqin* 19–20; *ulama al-salatin* 19; *see also* Salafis
Umayyads 121, 148
umma 16, 33, 86, 159: consensus of

198

INDEX

153; consultation of 82, 103–4, 131–2; and oath of obedience 131; and resisting injustice 131; sovereignty of 29, 76, 85, 99, 101–6, 108, 110, 111–12, 152, 159
Umma Party 40–2: and caliphate 41; foundation statement 40–1; online presence 41
al-Uthaymin, Muhammad 51, 77, 123

al-Wadani, Muhammad 46
Wahhabiyya 2, 38, 145, 161–2: compulsory implementation of 143; as model for the state 38; neo-Wahhabis 52; and obedience to rulers 52; *see also* Salafis
wali al-amr 8

wasatiyya 17
women 27–8, 48–9, 86–8, 94, 141: and Consultative Council 49, 87; driving protests 48; gender debates 87; Islamist 27; Islamist modernists and 86–7; liberal 27; in protest action 7, 27, 42, 47, 48, 87–8
al-Wuhaibi, Abd al-Aziz 40

Youth Rising Forum (Multaqa al-Nahdha al-Shababi) 106–9: cancellation of 108, 112; criticism of 108; Salafi criticism of 106–8; transnational nature of 109, 112–13
YouTube 40, 46, 47, 48, 52, 61, 80

Zaman, Muhammad Qasim 1, 12